COMMON
CALLINGS
AND
ORDINARY
VIRTUES

COMMON CALLINGS AND ORDINARY VIRTUES

Christian Ethics *for* Everyday Life

BRENT WATERS

Baker Academic
a division of Baker Publishing Group
Grand Rapids, Michigan

© 2022 by Brent Waters

Published by Baker Academic
a division of Baker Publishing Group
PO Box 6287, Grand Rapids, MI 49516-6287
www.bakeracademic.com

Printed in the United States of America

Library of Congress Cataloging-in-Publication Data
Names: Waters, Brent, author.
Title: Common callings and ordinary virtues : Christian ethics for everyday life / Brent Waters.
Description: Grand Rapids, Michigan : Baker Academic, a division of Baker Publishing Group,
    [2022] | Includes bibliographical references and index.
Identifiers: LCCN 2021043088 | ISBN 9780801099427 (paperback) | ISBN 9781540964595
    (casebound) | ISBN 9781493432578 (ebook) | ISBN 9781493432585 (pdf)
Subjects: LCSH: Christian ethics. | Conduct of life. | Vocation—Christianity.
Classification: LCC BJ1251 .W38 2022 | DDC 241—dc23
LC record available at https://lccn.loc.gov/2021043088

Baker Publishing Group publications use paper produced from sustainable forestry practices and post-consumer waste whenever possible.

22   23   24   25   26   27   28   7   6   5   4   3   2   1

For
Diana and Erin

Contents

Preface

The purpose of this book is to examine selected theological and moral themes that are embedded in the commonplace features of everyday life. Why would I expend time and energy inquiring into the humdrum when there are presumably more lively topics on offer? Because the realm of the ordinary, a prominent aspect of the human condition that is too frequently ignored, is foundational to properly ordering the Christian life in general and the Christian moral life in particular. Specifically, everyday relationships and activities develop habits that help to form one's character, and how one goes about performing daily chores and tasks enacts a sense of moral regard for one's neighbors. The commonplace is both a school of virtue and a vocational setting for refining what is learned. Consequently, my thesis is that by attending to ordinary relationships and mundane activities, we gain a deeper appreciation of what is most important in our lives and what is required for our flourishing.

When I started this project, I thought it would be easy to write a book on everyday life. I have, after all, lived a long, ordinary life, so I have plenty of experience to draw upon. I was wrong. This has been a difficult book to write. I think there are three principal culprits to blame for this difficulty.

First, the ordinary is both ubiquitous and sparse, and therefore elusive. The ordinary is unobvious, uninteresting, and all around us—otherwise it wouldn't be, well, ordinary. In those rare moments when the ordinary catches our attention we find it to be intractably dull, mind-numbingly boring. Some ordinary events, however, are also common occurrences shared by members of a group but experienced infrequently and uniquely by individuals. Most people fall in love and suffer the loss of or estrangement from loved ones. These are commonplace events shared by countless people, yet each individual experiences them rarely and responds to them uniquely. The ordinary eludes our attempts to categorize and generalize because it consists of both the mundane and the eventful. It is untidy.

Second, my profession works against me. I was trained to be a moral theologian. I have developed critical and interpretive skills that help me focus on questions of good and evil, right and wrong, virtue and vice. Such disciplinary skills enable me to contribute to the discourse of Christian ethicists, which is presumably of some value to the academy, the church, and society. But my academic focus also means that I miss much else. I miss much not only because focusing on certain subjects necessarily makes me inattentive to others, but also because I have been shaped by the values and prejudices of my professorial guild. And those values and prejudices treat the ordinary with indifference if not contempt. How can I be bothered with such trivial concerns as shopping and chance encounters with strangers when I must solve the monumental issues of war and peace, justice, and genetic engineering? Ethics deals with big questions, larger-than-life issues. Even those rare attempts to pay attention to the quotidian often twist the mundane into something it should not and cannot be. Weeding an organic garden, for instance, is elevated to saving the planet from an ecological apocalypse. This is a vain boast because it bestows on the task a false significance that deceives, signaling a virtue where none exists. Weeding will not save the planet. It is simply a necessary, mundane act of gardening, and it is excruciatingly dull and monotonous.

Third, my cultural context is largely apathetic (and at times hostile) to the ordinary. The late-modern technoculture in which I live and work—and in which I assume most of my readers reside as well—is fixated on the extraordinary. Everything is great, grand, awesome. Everyone is the best there ever was at whatever they do. We are addicted to personal excellence and get our fixes through a variety of technological aids and self-help strategies. It is all fantasy. If everything and everyone is extraordinary then nothing and no one is. It is a fantasy that flatters and thereby deludes. Like all fantasies, it distracts us from the real: a reality that is mundane, filled with ordinary people. The real world is not extraordinary, but it is where we are called to love God and neighbor. And that love is known and expressed, given and received, most often in unexceptional ways—in the routines and patterns of daily life.

To assume that I have liberated myself from the liabilities noted above and have gone on to write an extraordinary book on the ordinary would itself be a deadly fantasy. Rather, I think (hope) that my awareness of these perceptions and distortions has enriched my understanding and appreciation of the mundane as a vital setting of moral formation and action.

So what kind of book did I end up writing? In answering, I begin by describing what the book is not, an approach that is bound to irritate my publisher. But stay with me; I soon switch to the positive.

This is *not* a formal book on or about ethics. I do not use the ordinary to develop, refine, or illuminate a tightly reasoned theory of moral vision, agency, or action. Nor do I propose any solutions to the hot issues of the day.

This is *not* a book that summarizes or utilizes ethnographic studies. Some excellent books on the ethics of everyday life have used this methodology,[1] and I have no intention or ability to duplicate or supplement these works. Instead of observing, describing, and applying the ordinary in constructing a social anthropology, I try to enucleate[2] the mundane as a formative and normative narrative of the commonplace relationships and activities that are required for human flourishing.

This *is* a book on how the ordinary helps to form one's character. Attending to commonplace relationships and activities helps develop habits that in turn contribute to the formation of character by predisposing one toward virtue rather than vice. Learning to be courteous instead of rude, for instance, is morally significant when habituated or when such habituation fails.

This *is* a book on how the ordinary helps to reinforce social bonds. Humans are social creatures. We are drawn to one another and cannot survive for very long alone and isolated. These social bonds are most often maintained by mundane acts routinely performed by nameless people we encounter daily. For example, it is primarily strangers who produce, sell, or otherwise provide the goods and services—such as food and shelter—we require to sustain ourselves. The ordinariness of most of our basic needs and wants reminds us how much we depend on each other, day in and day out.

This *is* a book that looks to the commonplace for clues about the centrality of love in the Christian moral life. "Love your neighbor" is a direct command. Obeying it, however, is neither simple nor obvious. People have a host of varying needs and issues that must be addressed in the right place, at the right time, and in a fitting manner. Fashioning elaborate social and political responses that address perennial questions of good and evil, justice and injustice, and the like certainly has its place in Christian ethics. The "big" question of the human condition must not be ignored. But neither should the "little" questions of daily life. And the responses to these questions must be fitting if they are to be both faithful and efficacious. When a person is desperately

---

1. See, e.g., Banner, *Ethics of Everyday Life*.
2. "To enucleate means to extract the kernel of a nut, the seed of a tree." Grant, *Time as History*, 13.

hungry, she needs food to eat, not a lecture on or action plan for rectifying the injustices of the food chain.

This *is* a book that looks to the commonplace for some hints about human flourishing. It is a moral duty to attend to the physical and material wellbeing of human beings. As embodied creatures, we require a wide range of goods and services. But this is not enough. Humans also need mutuality and fellowship if they are to flourish. They need a place where they belong and people with whom they belong. To use a crude analogy, the work of surviving must end in Sabbath rest. We flourish when we are at leisure. The ordinary and the mundane orient us toward this end of entering into rest.

In writing this book, I have engaged a number of intellectual conversation partners.[3] In the following chapters I drop a few prominent names, such as Saint Augustine, Saint Thomas Aquinas, Martin Luther, C. S. Lewis, Karl Barth, Hannah Arendt, John Webster, and Gilbert Meilaender. I hope I have done them justice. Two writers, however, exert the heaviest influence. Oliver O'Donovan's work provides the principal theological pillars for explicating and ascribing the implicit moral patterns and ends of everyday life. Humankind's common callings and ordinary virtues are framed by God's extraordinary acts of creation, incarnation, and resurrection. As is apparent in the following chapters, O'Donovan's account of "entering into rest" is an especially fruitful concept, vividly capturing the end or *telos* of the Christian moral life, a life—it must be added—that is not at all divorced from the foibles and commonplace experiences of loving and living with neighbors.

The philosopher and novelist Iris Murdoch is the other writer. Her notion of "unselfing" plays a central role in this book. Unselfing helps us overcome "the fat relentless ego," which is the enemy of moral excellence.[4] The unselfed person is better equipped to be attentive to the other, learning what the good of the other entails and what she or he needs or requires of us, a process that is not unlike loving one's neighbor. Per Murdoch, we attend to the other primarily in and through the muddle of commonplace relationships and activities. She refines this contention in both her philosophical treatises and her novels, but I believe that the import of unselfing is most clearly and richly revealed in Murdoch's fiction.

My hunch about Murdoch's fiction has also led me to consult a broader range of novelists. As the reader will discover, I frequently turn to them to illustrate my remarks about the moral implications of the mundane. I do so because these implications become most explicit when presented as story

---

3. "Engag[ing] . . . conversation partners" is a euphemism for plundering.
4. See Murdoch, *Sovereignty of Good*, 50–51.

rather than as precept. Disclosure: I have not studied literary criticism enough to even qualify as a rank amateur. But I am a voracious reader of fiction, and I hope my plundering of these novelists is not too far off the mark.

A final prefatory note: I set out to write a book praising the mundane because I believe that in respect to the Christian moral life the mundane is highly formative and evocative, and almost always ignored. But to lift up the mundane is to encounter a stubborn challenge. The mundane is tedious, dull, repetitive, and boring. And trying to make it the least bit exciting would rob it of its formative and evocative power. So how does one write about this? The challenge is to make the mundane interesting enough to keep the reader's attention but not so interesting that it ceases to be genuinely mundane. I hope that in the following pages I have struck a tolerable balance, providing an account of the common and ordinary that is not too dull and not too exciting, but just right.

Acknowledgments

There are many students, colleagues, and friends to whom I am indebted. I do not think they were aware that in the classroom or seminar or around the corner table at the pub they were helping me think through some key ideas for this book. It is a long list, and for fear of accidently excluding someone, I offer this general expression of gratitude. I am also grateful that my institution's former president, Lallene Rector, and current president, Javier Viera, reminded me on occasion that my vocation as a member of a theological faculty includes taking some time to read, think, and write. Many thanks to the editors and staff at Baker Academic. They are a highly competent, patient, and good-humored team who make writing a joy rather than a chore.

David Hogue read several early drafts of selected chapters. His comments and our dinner conversations were most helpful. He is both a trusted colleague and a good friend, and I count him as one of my most astute teachers.

I have dedicated this book to my wife, Diana, and to my daughter, Erin. I dedicated my first book, *Dying and Death*, to them as well. That was not the nicest topic to draw my loved ones into, but at the time I did not know whether I would ever write another book. The topic this time is far more suitable, for Diana and Erin remind me of the centrality of love that pervades life, day in and day out.

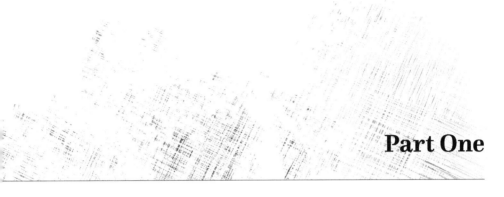

Part One

THEOLOGICAL AND MORAL THEMES

CHAPTER 1

Creation, Incarnation, and Resurrection

Recognizing the importance of the ordinary requires contrast. The ordinary can be understood only in comparison to the extraordinary. The extraordinary consists of those rare, at times unrepeatable, occasions that break the repetitious and expected. It is this rupture that sustains and gives the ordinary its significance and texture. To use a crude example, a vacation is enjoyable and renewing because it breaks the patterns of daily life. A vacation is a relatively rare occasion when we have the time to relax, to see new sights, or to play. At the end of a vacation, we also have (hopefully) renewed energy for once again undertaking the mundane tasks of daily living. But it is only because vacations are rare that they are pleasurable and refreshing. If we were always on vacation, the vacation would be a dull activity to be endured.

Discerning the theological importance of the extraordinary also requires contrast. To invoke a supreme understatement, God is *the* extraordinary reality that casts light on our ordinary lives as creatures. In God, we encounter the source of our being, and we are drawn out of ourselves into a realm that is far vaster than ourselves. In God, we face the eternal that transcends the temporal; the beginning and end of all that has been, is, and shall be. Extraordinary! And yet the commonplace and mundane activities of our daily living are not unrelated or unimportant to God. Before exploring what this relation and importance entails, we first need to visit three extraordinary acts of divine love.

Three Acts of God's Love

First, it is extraordinary that there is a creation. God did not need to create the world that you and I inhabit. God was not unfulfilled or incomplete until God created. God is *simple*, which means that God is complete simply by virtue of being God; to be God is to be without needs or desires that can be fulfilled only through subsequent acts to fill the voids.[1] Humans, however, are complex. They have many needs and desires they strive to meet through their own creative acts. There are many voids to be filled—and many, if not most, remain empty. Humans, on their own initiative, can never attain a godlike simplicity that is full and complete in itself. Consequently, borrowing from Saint Augustine, our hearts are restless.[2]

Why, then, did God create? It was, and is, an act of gratuitous love.[3] But if creation is an act of God's love, does this not challenge the concept of divine simplicity? If God is the only pure object of love, then shouldn't God's undivided attention be rightfully directed not outward but inward—that is, toward loving God? Doesn't creation imply a lack in God that God is trying to rectify? This is a good question, and to answer it we must try to be clear about what love is—or at least about how we understand it from our limited, creaturely standpoint. The "flow" of love, so to speak, is not unidirectional. Love may be said to have both inward and outward trajectories. There is love of self, and there is love of the other. It is hard to imagine a genuine love that is entirely self-contained; narcissism, after all, is a behavioral disorder.

The love I described in the preceding paragraph is admittedly the kind experienced by incomplete creatures striving to satisfy unfulfilled cravings and desires. What does this love, then, have to do with God? It is important to keep in mind that for Christians, God is not monistic but triune. When we refer to God, we mean Father, Son, and Holy Spirit. Within the Godhead, love is shared among three persons.[4] Admittedly, this love is not identical to that which humans experience, but the two are not entirely unrelated. There is giving and receiving, and there is a strong relational component—there can be no Father without the Son. But the love shared among the persons of the Trinity is a perfect love that is not directed toward correcting any deficiency. The sharing of such perfect love, however, is not necessarily perpetually cyclical or self-contained. Perhaps such love cannot resist an impulse to create

---

1. See, e.g., Augustine, *On the Holy Trinity*; Aquinas, *Summa Theologica* I.3; and Barth, *Church Dogmatics* II/1, 28–31.

2. Augustine, *Confessions* I/1.

3. See Edwards, *Dissertation on the End*; and Barth, *Church Dogmatics* III/1.

4. See Barth, *Church Dogmatics* I/1, 8–12; LaCugna, *God for Us*, chap. 8; Moltmann, *Trinity and the Kingdom*; Pannenberg, *Systematic Theology* I/5.

something other than itself for no other reason than to express itself. To use a crude analogy again, the love shared by the persons of the triune Godhead spilled over to create the world as something other than God.

Gratitude is a fitting response to this gratuitous act of love. Life is a gift to be cherished, and its giver is acknowledged and worshiped as its creator. The fact that God did not need to create but did so nonetheless should elicit a joyful astonishment, for we are created literally for no reason. And humans carry within their being the mark of this gratuitous love—namely, the image and likeness of their creator. This is not to suggest that each person carries a divine spark, implying that humans are lesser gods. Rather, the *imago Dei* serves to remind humans of the creator who created them. Existence is a gift that humans can only receive and never reciprocate in kind to its giver.

This extraordinary and gratuitous act of divine love also offends because it is utterly undeserved. No one is entitled to be created, and life is therefore an unqualified and unmerited gift of love. This insults our sensibilities, however, for we want to be loved because we are deserving; we strive to earn the love of others. This is an imperfect expression of love that tries to rectify the deficiencies and fill the voids of our being, but has no standing before God's perfect love. There is nothing we can do to merit God's love; it is simply given. This tension between the joy and offense of a gratuitous creation shapes, in part, the fabric, purposes, and importance of ordinary, everyday living as examined in subsequent chapters. It suffices at this juncture to indicate that it is in the mundane that we learn to love people who do not deserve to be loved, and in turn we learn to receive the unmerited love of others. In other words, it is in the ordinary that we often encounter grace.

The second extraordinary act of God's love is the incarnation. "The Word became flesh and made his dwelling among us" (John 1:14). God became a human being. The incarnation is a core Christian conviction, requiring elaborate doctrinal exposition. For the purpose of this book, however, noting two implications will suffice. First, the incarnation of the Word reaffirms what God has created. Creation is good, but it is fallen, no longer enjoying an untroubled relationship with its creator. The underlying cause of the fall is a failure to trust God, exhibited through willful disobedience. God forbids Adam and Eve to eat of the tree of the knowledge of good and evil, but they do so anyway (see Gen. 3). The consequences are disastrous. The easy liaison between creator and creature is broken. When God visits Eden, Eve and Adam try to hide, for they are ashamed of their nakedness, which they had never noticed before. The tranquil bond between Adam and Eve is also severed. They refuse to take responsibility for their actions and are at odds with each other. The rapport between humans and the earth is ruined. No longer is their gardening a carefree activity; it becomes painful and tedious toil. The fall exacts a heavy cost.

Presumably, God could have reacted to this disobedience by abandoning or destroying creation. Instead, God enters into covenant with these fallen, deeply flawed creatures, as attested in Scripture with the people of Israel. Within the Christian theological tradition, this covenant culminates in the incarnation. God does not choose merely to be in covenant with the human creatures God created; in Jesus, God decides to become one of them. In becoming one with us, God undoes the fall, healing the resulting brokenness of creation and its creatures. Additionally, the incarnation affirms the love that created us in the first place. It is a steadfast and unwavering love: a love that will not let us go, regardless of how unlovable we may be.

It is also a costly love. To undo the fall, God in Christ must take on the brokenness of creation and its creatures. Or, to use a theological concept that is no longer very fashionable in some circles, Christ must take on the sins of the world to redeem the world, to recreate its proper relationship with its creator. Jesus must die to accomplish this end. Regardless of which doctrinal account of atonement one employs,[5] there is no escaping the necessity of Jesus's death. There can be no Christianity without a cross, for the crucifixion is the paramount act of God's love. It is only in and through Jesus's death that creation can be emancipated from its sin and have its ruptures healed. In short, love, especially love of the other, entails suffering. It entails death.

But love does not end in death, which leads us to the third extraordinary act of God's love: Jesus is raised from the dead. If there can be no Christianity without the cross, then so too there can be none without the empty tomb. The church does not remember a dead founder but worships and serves a living savior. Good Friday has no significance or meaning without Easter. The risen Jesus is the centerpiece of the singular but tripartite culmination of the incarnation, entailing crucifixion, resurrection, and ascension.[6] The crucifixion is God's simultaneous pronouncement of *no* and *yes* to the human condition. A *no* is pronounced against disordered human desires stemming from the fall, while a *yes* is uttered in favor of reordering our desires in line with Christ's work of reconciling us with the triune God. In a related manner, the ascension moves this reordering beyond historical and temporal limitations. Together, the intertwined events of crucifixion, resurrection, and ascension create a pattern of ordering human life to which we should aspire to conform. When

---

5. See, e.g., Baillie, *God Was in Christ*, esp. chaps. 7–8; Barth, *Church Dogmatics* IV/1, 57–58; Moltmann, *Crucified God*.

6. See Waters, "Incarnation and the Christian Moral Life."

the gospel is proclaimed in ways that diminish or ignore any of these related moments, it becomes distorted and incomplete.[7] Since resurrection is the centerpiece, however, we must spend some time pondering its theological import.

What exactly was God doing in raising Jesus from the dead? The significance of the resurrection is not confined to lionizing the man Jesus. If it were, Jesus would be merely a hero whom God rewarded for living an exemplary life. Jesus, however, is not a heroic figure but the savior, the Christ in whom and through whom creation is redeemed, healed, and reconciled. The import of the empty tomb is much broader and deeper. The resurrection is the undoing of the fall. It is through the same Christ, the Word, that creation was created and is redeemed.[8] In Christ's "conquest over death" we see humankind as it is meant to be seen.[9] This proper human status cannot be accomplished or known in the world's fallen condition. Consequently, Christ's redemptive work refers to a created order because it "suggests the recovery of something given and lost"—namely, the properly ordered relationship among the creator, creation, and its creatures.[10] This, in part, is why creation cannot be whole and complete without the suitable exercise of human dominion and stewardship, and why the redemption of creation first requires the reconciling salvation of human beings.

The resurrection, then, discloses the incarnation of the Word as the prerequisite of creation's redemption. The resurrection presupposes the incarnation because, in Oliver O'Donovan's words, "through a unique presence of God to his creation, the whole created order is taken up into the fate of this particular representative man at this particular point of history, on whose one fate turns the redemption of all." Furthermore, Jesus's resurrection points toward a general resurrection when creation shall be "totally restored at the last."[11] The resurrection is God's exculpation of life and a "reversal of Adam's choice of sin and death." For in Christ all shall be made alive. The resurrection affirms the initial gift of life, meaning that God has not forsaken creation but has became incarnate. "Before God raised Jesus from the dead, the hope that we call 'gnostic', the hope for redemption *from* creation rather than for the redemption *of* creation, might have appeared to be the only possible hope." Because of Christ, humans have "not been allowed to uncreate what God created."[12]

7. See O'Donovan, *Desire of the Nations*, chap. 4.
8. See John 1:1–5. See also Webster, *Word and Church*, chap. 7.
9. See O'Donovan, *Resurrection and Moral Order*, 53–54.
10. See O'Donovan, *Resurrection and Moral Order*, 54–55.
11. O'Donovan, *Resurrection and Moral Order*, 15.
12. O'Donovan, *Resurrection and Moral Order*, 13–14 (emphasis original).

In sum, the resurrection of Jesus from the dead vindicates what God has created. The resurrection "tells us of God's vindication of his creation, and so of our created life."[13] To reiterate the affirmation of the incarnation: it is good to be a creature, and a mortal one at that. Yet, as resurrection makes clear, mortality is not the final act of what Eric Voegelin calls the "drama of being"[14]—for Jesus Christ, the resurrected and living Lord Christ, "is the vindication of creation from death, the manifestation of its wholeness."[15] The creation that God did not allow humans to uncreate echoes God's declaration on the sixth day of creation that "it was very good" (Gen. 1:31).

It needs to be emphasized, however, that God's vindication of creation is not an event confined to the past. Easter is not encased in amber. Rather, vindicating creation not only reaffirms its origin in God's love, it also launches its proper trajectory toward its end or *telos* in its final redemption in Christ. And redemption is *not* restoration. The Bible begins in a garden but ends in the new Jerusalem; a new heaven and earth await us (Rev. 21:1–5). As O'Donovan argues, "The redemption of the world, and of mankind, does not serve only to put us back in the Garden of Eden where we began"; consequently, "the outcome of the world's story cannot be a cyclical return to the beginnings, but must fulfil that purpose in the freeing of creation from its 'futility' (Rom. 8:20)."[16] The transformation of the world is neither endless repetition nor the negation of creation. "It is the historical *telos* of the origin, that which creation is intended *for*, and that which it points and strives *towards*."[17] History, then, has meaning and direction that can be understood and described within a narrative structure, one that is being drawn toward an eschatological end. It is within this narrative structure that Christians should order their lives, including the ordinary patterns of daily living.

That creation, incarnation, and resurrection are extraordinary acts of God's gratuitous love is an article of faith that Christians believe, as attested in their doctrine, tradition, and experience over the centuries. But what does this have to do with the ordinary relationships and mundane activities that dominate the daily lives of humans? Quite a bit. It is only in contrast to something truly extraordinary that the ordinary has meaning, for it provides a delineating and delimiting context for ordering human life as creaturely existence. The reality of the triune God's love that simultaneously transcends, pervades, and

13. O'Donovan, *Resurrection and Moral Order*, 13.
14. See Voegelin, *Collected Works*, 14:1:39–43.
15. O'Donovan, *Resurrection and Moral Order*, 62.
16. O'Donovan, *Resurrection and Moral Order*, 55.
17. O'Donovan, *Resurrection and Moral Order*, 55 (emphasis original).

draws us toward our destiny provides both the limits and the expectations of what it means for us to be finite and mortal creatures. We are to order our lives according to this love. Acknowledging the astonishing reality of God's love as the beginning and end of our being should, at the very least, inspire a response of gratitude, humility, and patience.

This is a hard sell in our contemporary culture. When belief in God's extraordinary love is affirmed with little conviction or effectively dismissed altogether, the ordinary loses its defining context. When the genuinely extraordinary is effectively absent, its loss is compensated for with fabricated and hyperbolic alternatives. These alternatives are futile, however, because they are based on fantasies or on attempts to confer an unwarranted hyperimportance upon the ordinary. The former is seen in the transhumanist delusion of using technology to convert humans into superior beings with unimaginable physical and cognitive capabilities, perhaps even achieving personal immortality.[18] Attitudinal efforts to transform virtually all activities or efforts, however dull or commonplace they may be, into peak experiences are examples of the latter. (Even cleaning the bathroom can be an ecstatic experience!)

The problem is that both of these alternative routes denigrate who we are and how we spend most of our time. The transhumanists effectively loathe their status as embodied creatures because of the severe constraints that embodiment places on the will. A body limits what one can do and how long one can live. Consequently, the many mundane tasks required for meeting the needs of embodied beings are resented as wasted time and effort. On the other hand, the attempt to make almost anything a potentially exuberant experience is a failed strategy from the start, for if everything becomes extraordinary, then nothing is. Without contrast, the extraordinary and ordinary lose their respective import.

But even if a proper contrast is maintained, why should the mundane attract our attention? Isn't it, well, boring? Yes, and other unattractive adjectives such as dull, tedious, monotonous, mind-numbing, and disagreeable could be added to the list, which is why the mundane should attract our notice. The mundane is formative. The routine and repetitive patterns of daily living help form who we are and who we are aspiring to become. Make no mistake: there is nothing exciting about these patterns. Washing clothes or dishes, picking up after others, mowing the lawn, and shoveling snow are all boring; and as Michael Raposa has observed, boredom is nothing to celebrate.[19] He

18. See Moore and Vita-More, *Transhumanist Reader*, for a sampling of transhumanist literature. For a critique of transhumanism, see Waters, *From Human to Posthuman*; and Waters, *This Mortal Flesh*, esp. chaps. 8–9.
19. See Raposa, *Boredom and the Religious Imagination*.

goes on to chronicle the evils boredom promotes: indifference, distraction, emptiness, and—worst of all—the sin of acedia.[20]

Yet boredom also has its benefits. For instance, it can stimulate imaginative responses. And, more importantly, boredom can teach us to wait: to wait *for* someone or something, and also to wait *on* someone, as in providing a service.[21] Waiting is an important religious practice. In being attentive to our neighbors, for example, we wait for them to disclose their wants and needs, their good. If the mundane is filled with boring activities, then their routine and repetitive performance helps to form us as waiting people. And since waiting entails both presence and anticipation, it is, broadly construed, both an incarnational and an eschatological act.

The mundane is iconic. The ordinary sometimes reveals facets of the eternal that bracket the temporal, in turn giving us some insight into what should be genuinely most important in loving God and neighbor. Through these partial glimpses, we learn something about the proper ordering of the penultimate and ultimate, so that the former is neither denigrated nor inordinately extolled and the latter is prevented from becoming a distraction or fantasy.

In pursuing this proper ordering, Roger Scruton's contrast between what he calls "scrupulous optimism" or "judicious pessimism" and a progressive optimism that creates false hope is helpful.[22] According to Scruton, "Scrupulous optimists strive to fix their hopes as best they can on the things they know and understand, on the people who are close to them, and on the small-scale local affections that are the foundations of our happiness. They know that they are vulnerable, like everyone, to the external and public events, and that they must provision against them."[23] This orientation promotes a greater love of neighbor than does the orientation of those who are dedicated to constructing a better future. Again, in Scruton's words, "Judicious pessimism teaches us not to idolize human beings, but to forgive their faults and to strive in private for their amendment. It teaches us to limit our ambitions in the public sphere, and to keep open the institutions, customs and procedures whereby mistakes are corrected and faults confessed to, rather than to aim for some new arrangement in which mistakes are never made."[24] Moreover, religion should neutralize optimism to prevent it from pursuing a false and destructive hope. Judicious pessimists "accept the world and its imperfections, not because it cannot be improved, but because many of the improvements that matter

20. Raposa, *Boredom and the Religious Imagination*, 11–35.
21. See Raposa, *Boredom and the Religious Imagination*, 168.
22. Scruton, *Uses of Pessimism*.
23. Scruton, *Uses of Pessimism*, 35.
24. Scruton, *Uses of Pessimism*, 36.

we fulfill our various callings and vocations in a good and faithful manner and thereby become good and faithful (i.e., *virtuous*) people.

Christian moral theology and philosophy have traditionally affirmed the three theological virtues of faith, hope, and love (taken from 1 Cor. 13) and the four cardinal virtues of prudence, justice, fortitude, and temperance.[33] Additionally, there are other classic virtues, such as courage and fidelity, that are compatible with and have been incorporated within traditional Christian thought and practice. Each of these virtues denotes a quality of excellence that humans should seek to practice and habituate. How do good habits become virtues? Repetitious practice: doing the same good act, with the assistance of God's grace and guidance of the Spirit, over and over again so they become part of our second nature. We become habitually faithful people, for instance, by constantly performing acts of faith. Paying attention to the requisite virtues that instantiate the good is also attending to one's soul.

Speaking of virtue, however, requires that we also say something about *vice*. Again, for the purpose of this book, a vice may be understood as actions or habitual behaviors that prevent one from being virtuous. A vice diminishes or prevents virtuous behavior most often through either excess or deficiency. The vices corresponding to the virtue of courage, for example, are rashness and cowardice. To perpetually practice or surrender to vice makes one a *vicious* person. In many respects, vice is similar to sin, as reflected in the Christian tradition's enumeration of the seven deadly sins: pride, envy, gluttony, lust, anger, greed, and sloth.

The virtues are both instrumentally and intrinsically crucial in pursuing one's callings and vocations. The virtues are instrumentally valuable because attending to the good of one's own soul also makes one more attentive to the people one is called to serve. As Gilbert Meilaender contends, "Doing what is right requires being good."[34] For example, adept ministers, physicians, and military officers promote the good of those they serve through example and conduct beyond their respective professional proficiencies. A life of virtue is also inherently good, for it requires introspection and self-transcendence. This is a fading art in late modernity, in which it is often assumed that performance is all that matters. Yet ministers, doctors, and military personnel who are judged to be excellent solely on the basis of the performance of their duties are not necessarily good human beings. Virtue forces us to constantly revisit the question, What is an excellent human being, the kind of creature God created us to be?

---

33. See Pieper, *Faith Hope Love*; and Pieper, *Four Cardinal Virtues*.
34. Meilaender, *Theory and Practice of Virtue*, 26.

As I argue in chapter 3, practicing the virtues should play an important role in the Christian life. More broadly, the virtues should also play a prominent role in human life generally, especially in respect to the professions.[35] Theoretical accounts of virtue, however, tend to focus on "larger" questions and issues of public conduct and behavior, concentrating on the suitable character of political, ecclesial, and business leaders and the like while ignoring more common virtues associated with daily life. This emphasis is understandable, since everyone suffers from vicious leadership and the ordinary virtues associated with daily living tend to be less obvious and are often ill-defined, thereby not lending themselves easily to intellectual reflection and exposition.

Giving the ordinary short shrift in discourse about the virtues is unfortunate, however, because it results in an incomplete portrayal of what it means to be an excellent human being. This is especially the case for human creatures attempting to align their lives to the vindicated order of creation—an endeavor that is quite mundane. To illustrate, marital fidelity is something more than avoiding adultery or resisting its temptation. Spouses also divide household chores, run errands, comfort each other, and are courteous. It is, at least in part, in practicing such ordinary virtues that a couple becomes habitually faithful to each other.[36]

As finite and mortal creatures, humans pursue their common callings and ordinary virtues over *time* and in particular *places*. The themes of time and place are developed more fully in chapter 4, but a few precursory remarks are in order. For Christians, time has a dual meaning. There is linear time, as in one day or year giving way to the next. There is also sacred time, which is cyclical, as exemplified in the church's liturgical calendar. Both senses of time assist us in aligning our lives with a vindicated creation and its eschatological trajectory. In brief, I argue that linear time (roughly associated with the secular and ordinary) is bracketed by cyclical time (roughly associated with the sacred and extraordinary), and in this bracketing the mundane is both formative and iconic.

Place reminds us that as embodied creatures, humans must be somewhere at any given time. This may seem obvious, but late moderns are increasingly nomadic, believing the illusion that they can be almost anywhere or nowhere at any time. Indeed, there is a growing preference for temporary and virtual spaces over enduring physical places.[37] Yet humans cannot flourish by being constantly on the move, either physically or imaginatively; they need to be in

---

35. See, e.g., Wheeler, *Minister as Moral Theologian*; Pellegrino and Thomasma, *Philosophical Basis of Medical Practice*; Fisher, *Morality and War*.

36. See, e.g., McCarthy, *Sex and Love in the Home*.

37. See Waters, *Christian Moral Theology in the Emerging Technoculture*, esp. chap. 7.

place for a time, to have a place to congregate. As noted above, humans are by nature social creatures, drawn to one another. And they need places, physical locales, where they associate with one another: a variety of locales, such as households, churches, parks, marketplaces. Moreover, these locales need to be built, maintained, and cared for (all very mundane activities) if they are to be hospitable places for human habitation and association.

To a significant extent, human *action*, especially corporate action, is organized and performed in specific places over time. A people organize and perpetuate themselves politically as a nation spanning generations in a land. A city occupies a piece of territory, lending itself to commercial and cultural enterprises. A family lives together in a house. Admittedly, places and the people associated with them change over time. Nations come and go; cities are rebuilt, and their population may change dramatically due to demographic shifts; a family disperses. Yet despite these changes, humans continue to associate and do so while in place for either relatively lengthy or relatively short periods of time.

It is in this interplay of place and time that humans find their *belonging*, at least this side of eternity. We discover, in particular places and over time, where and with whom we belong. We belong with fellow citizens, fellow workers, fellow family members. These relationships are established and sustained through largely routinized and repetitive actions that over time demonstrate a mutual trustworthiness and reliability. Again, these relationships change over time. Fellowship among citizens may grow stronger or become frayed due to changing political or economic circumstances. People change jobs. The parental relationship with young children is not the same as that with adult daughters and sons. But despite these changes, humans cannot escape the need, acknowledged or not, to belong somewhere and with some others.

This belonging is recognized and instantiated in *ritual*. At times, these rituals are highly formal. A civic event might commemorate a city's founding. Liturgy and the sacraments express faith. But, more commonly, there is a plethora of informal rituals that shape the patterns of daily life. Friends meet regularly at a favorite pub, and rituals are quickly established regarding conversation and who pays the tab. Workplace rituals help determine the formal and informal patterns of the work week. Families follow routines in preparing, sharing, and cleaning up after a meal. In short, ritual helps to order the ordinary actions that sustain our mutual belonging, because ritual is always a shared activity. Even when the principal object of a ritual is extraordinary, such as the Eucharist, it nonetheless draws attention to and affirms the mundane through sheer contrast. Through ordinary bread and wine, for instance,

Christians partake of their Lord's body and blood. It is through ritual, in part, that we affirm and act out our belonging in a vindicated creation.

Before proceeding, I wish to alert the reader that I will be frequently revisiting and developing two themes in the following chapters, especially in part 2 and part 3. I will say little about these themes at this juncture, other than to highlight a few key terms to place them on the reader's radar screen, so to speak.[38] The first theme draws on Simone Weil and Iris Murdoch's concept of "unselfing." According to Murdoch, the "fat relentless ego"[39] often diminishes or prevents human flourishing because we fail to be attentive to the good of our neighbors. Acknowledging and attending to the mundane is a good first step in putting the ego on a diet.

The second theme is play. The ordinary is a playful domain. But how can this be if, as I have claimed, it comprises monotonous, dull, tedious, downright boring activities? Because play requires rules, for without rules there can be no play, and learning and obeying rules is common and routine. Counterintuitively, tending to the mundane helps develop a capacity for playfulness, and this is an important capacity because God created humans to be, in part, playful creatures. The mundane, in brief, helps us acknowledge that life is too important to treat it with undue seriousness.

---

38. I am reflecting my advanced age by using radar imagery. Perhaps it would be more current to suggest that I am here dropping two pins on the reader's GPS app. (I am obliged to my editor, a millennial, who helped me with this wording.)

39. Murdoch, *Sovereignty of Good*, 51.

CHAPTER 2

Calling and Vocation

There is a tendency to draw a sharp distinction between calling and vocation. *Calling* often connotes a profession held in high esteem, such as ministry or medicine, while *vocation* is associated with humdrum work, such as collecting rubbish or flipping burgers. A calling is lofty while a vocation is lowly. Pursuing a calling entails years of specialized education, while a vocation may require mastering a few rudimentary skills. There are no universities or professional schools dedicated to rubbish collecting or burger flipping, and seminaries and medical schools are not usually referred to as vocational training centers.

This popular bifurcation is inaccurate and unfortunate. In the first place, the division is artificial. Any calling requires a set of vocational skills as a matter of practicality. For example, to pursue my calling as a seminary professor I had to learn a number of vocational skills required for teaching and research, but I was taught nothing about repairing cars or building furniture. There was no need for me to be taught the latter because such vocational skills are practiced by mechanics and carpenters.[1] To pursue a calling is to simultaneously take on a vocation. My calling to be a professor is also my vocation, and there is little reason to assume that the vocations of mechanics or carpenters are devoid of any sense of calling.

Secondly, the perceived split between calling and vocation is arbitrary. To contrast so-called "lofty" callings with "lowly" vocations is to assign inherent

---

1. Although there are some rare professors who are adept at repairing a car or at carpentry, these skills are not directly pertinent to their academic calling and vocation.

values to different pursuits and skills. But the value of a calling and vocation is instrumental rather than inherent, for its purpose is to serve the needs of neighbors, and these needs vary in terms of particular wants and circumstances. Although my teaching and research may serve some needs of my students and members of the church and the academy, I certainly do not serve all their needs—many are met by others pursuing their respective callings and vocations. And I have no reason to believe that my particular vocation is *always* more useful than other vocations. There are some occasions, for instance, when the most pressing need of a student is met by a mechanic rather than by my lecture.

Finally, concocting a hierarchy of callings and vocations is theologically mistaken. If there are "higher" callings as opposed to "lower" vocations, then presumably one should aspire to pursue the former—suggesting that in pursuing a high calling, one somehow becomes a better Christian. This suggestion, however, is based on the unfounded assumption that spiritual concerns are vastly superior to their material counterparts. This is a dangerous assumption to make, especially by those who follow a faith that is centered on incarnation. In the Word made flesh, the embodied status of human creatures is affirmed by God, and attending to their material wellbeing should not therefore be discounted or denigrated. Rather, vocations attending to both spiritual and material needs are complementary, not hierarchical. This complementarity is seen especially in the imagery of the church as the body of Christ (see 1 Cor. 12:12–31). The church comprises many different, interdependent parts. One part cannot say to another, "I don't need you," if the body is to be healthy (1 Cor. 12:21). Each part plays an important, functional role in maintaining the body. Consequently, a wide range of vocations is required to meet the myriad needs of embodied and ensouled brothers and sisters in Christ and, more broadly, of neighbors throughout the world. In my vocation as a professor I hope to serve some of the intellectual and spiritual needs of my neighbors, but I do this in conjunction with others who are called to build houses, flip burgers, and provide parental care.

In the remainder of this chapter, I describe a theological construal of calling and vocation (drawing heavily on the work of Martin Luther) and suggest some practical implications this construal might have for what I call "common" callings and vocations: those that are often overlooked in the patterns of everyday life. Finally, I argue that the late-modern proclivity to fixate on the self, largely in isolation from others, impedes human flourishing, and I explore how attending to these common callings and vocations promotes "unselfing" as a way of correcting this fixation.

Callings and Vocations

Much of the popular division between calling and vocation noted above is residue from previous centuries of Christian thought and practice. Early Christian teaching never condemned material reality or embodiment, since both were parts of God's good creation. Nonetheless, there was a tension between body and spirit and how they should be ordered. This tension is seen in the New Testament, especially in Saint Paul's letters, where he often describes the conflict between flesh and spirit in almost warlike terms.[2] Disputes with Gnostics and Manichaeans heightened this conflict, given their emphasis on the primacy of a good soul over an evil body. Many of the patristic writers acknowledged the superiority of the life of the spirit over that of the flesh but did not condemn the latter, given the church's core belief in resurrection. If the body is unimportant or evil, then why was the tomb empty that first Easter Sunday, and why are Christians taught to look forward to their own bodily resurrection when Christ returns?[3]

These theological convictions, however, did not diminish the necessity of controlling the body and worldly desire.[4] Consequently, some Christians adopted ascetic practices such as sexual continence, sustained periods of fasting, and wearing uncomfortable clothing—all designed to discipline the desires originating in bodily needs and cravings. More dramatically, some withdrew to the desert or wilderness to become hermits, living lives devoid of physical comforts to devote themselves to prayer and contemplation.[5] These ascetics were often lionized as spiritual exemplars who should be admired but whom few could emulate. The emerging cult of virginity also served to emphasize the preeminence of the spiritual over the physical. Saint Ambrose and Saint Jerome, for instance, urged young men and women to forsake marriage and other worldly pursuits and devote themselves to prayer, contemplation, and ministries of the church, demonstrating a single-hearted dedication to Christ.[6] In effect, a small cadre of superior Christians was emerging in the body of Christ on earth, one that wanted little to do with earthly necessities.

This spiritual superiority, however, was achieved at the expense of belittling the vast majority of church members who were involved in tending to the earthly realities of human life. Saint Augustine reacted against this denigration

---

2. See Rom. 8; 1 Cor. 15; and Gal. 5. See also Dunn, *Theology of Paul the Apostle*, chap. 2.
3. See, e.g., Augustine, *City of God* 22.
4. See Brown, *Body and Society*.
5. See Brown, *Body and Society*, part 2.
6. See Brown, *Through the Eye of a Needle*, part 2; and Waters, *Family in Christian Social and Political Thought*, chap. 1.

of ordinary or mediocre Christians.[7] He defended marriage as a good, indeed as a sacrament,[8] and he warned virgins not to look down on their married counterparts.[9] More broadly, he commended the work of spouses, parents, magistrates, and others who contributed to the common good. Although the life of the spirit is preferable, embodied life is not to be despised.

Despite Augustine's warnings, monasticism grew rapidly in the late antique period and in the early Middle Ages. Why the attraction? Monastic life was seen as a superior way of living. There were two ways of being a Christian: one was to be enmeshed within nature (involved in the affairs of marriage, family, and commerce), and the other was to be above nature (meaning one was free to focus on prayer and contemplation).[10] The latter way was preferable because it offered a more promising path to being in the world but not of it. The danger of worldly affairs was that they deflected attention from God. Consequently, monastic life offered a surer way to salvation, and hence the vow of poverty and renunciation of all worldly goods.

A cloistered life, however, could not entirely transcend natural necessities. Monks and nuns engaged in physical labor, often maintaining farms and vineyards. But these activities were devoid of any vocational significance. As Mark Tranvik notes, the "active life of work can be found within the monastery's walls, but the rationale for such activity is the support of the contemplative life."[11]

Moreover, this division between elite and conventional Christians purportedly reflected the very nature of the universe. The world was envisioned as similar to a three-story building: In the penthouse are God and the heavenly host. The tenants of the middle floor are the "religious people—monks, priests, nuns—who, by virtue of their vows, have callings or vocations. Their public declarations to lead holy lives, characterized by poverty, chastity, and obedience, put them closer to their Creator and also provide greater assurance of blessed entrance into God's kingdom at the end of their lives. On the ground floor is the vast multitude of humanity. They are the folks who keep life going—the merchants, farmers, blacksmiths, midwives, mothers, and fathers. They are said to lack vocations because their daily activities inevitably involve worldly compromise that dilutes the pure love of God."[12]

---

7. See Markus, *End of Ancient Christianity*, chap. 4; and Waters, *Family in Christian Social and Political Thought*, chap. 1.

8. See Augustine, *On the Good of Marriage*; and Augustine, *On Marriage and Concupiscence*.

9. See Augustine, *Of Holy Virginity*.

10. See Tranvik, *Martin Luther and the Called Life*, 10–12.

11. Tranvik, *Martin Luther and the Called Life*, 13.

12. Tranvik, *Martin Luther and the Called Life*, 1–2.

This is a tidy arrangement, especially if one resides in the middle level. But is it faithful to the gospel, since it implies that God is fully present only in the cloister and nowhere else in the world? Martin Luther's reply was a resounding no. Luther's principal complaint was that, in devoting themselves to the spiritual works of prayer and contemplation, monastics often thought they were earning their salvation.[13] This belief, however, is contrary to the gospel. Salvation is God's free gift of grace that cannot be earned. Consequently, works are irrelevant to one's eventual salvation. Rather, works are a response of gratitude to the unmerited gift of grace. Works, then, are performed for the glory of God and not for the fate of one's soul. In this respect, works are an obedient response of an individual's love of God. In Luther's words, "Works themselves do not justify [a person] before God, but he does the works out of spontaneous love in obedience to God and considers nothing except the approval of God, whom we would most scrupulously obey in all things."[14]

Luther grounded his understanding of the role of works in a theological understanding of creation rather than redemption.[15] Specifically, works are performed within the three mandates of creation: church, state, and household.[16] Each of these spheres of human association and action was mandated by God as a practical or concrete venue in which people served the needs of one another. In grounding works in these mandates, Luther vastly expanded the range of Christian vocation, for in virtue of their baptism, all Christians were responding to Christ's calling. This calling involved not only the love of God but also the love of neighbor. Clergy are called to preach the gospel and administer the sacraments, but magistrates, parents, and workers are also called to meet the needs of their neighbors. Vocation is a tangible manifestation of the love of God and neighbor in joyful and obedient response to Christ. "Here faith is truly active through love [Gal. 5:6], that is, it finds expression in works of the freest service, cheerfully and lovingly done, with which a man willingly serves another without hope of reward; and for himself is satisfied with the fullness and wealth of his faith."[17] In and through our vocations, we give ourselves to our neighbors and in doing so become Christ to each other.[18] Although works are not

---

13. See Luther, *Judgment of Martin Luther on Monastic Vows*.

14. Luther, *Freedom of a Christian*, 359.

15. Although the two are not unrelated.

16. Modern accounts of these mandates add a fourth of work, which Luther included within the household. See, e.g., Bonhoeffer, *Ethics*, 179–84; cf. Brunner, *Divine Imperative*, part 3.

17. Luther, *Freedom of a Christian*, 365.

18. See Luther, *Freedom of a Christian*, 367–68.

directed to God, it is nonetheless through our vocations that God's love takes form on earth.

Since works are always performed on behalf of neighbors, all vocations are relational. One cannot be a pastor without parishioners, a magistrate without citizens, a parent without a child, or an employee without an employer. Moreover, it is through these various relationships, grounded in love, that we discover the good of our neighbors, for in the day in and day out of sustaining these relationships we become (or should become) more attentive to one another's needs, more accustomed to living for others. And since needs vary widely, various vocations reflect the variety of gifts constituting Christ's church. In this respect, vocational work is also a work of the Holy Spirit.

We attend to the good of others, however, as imperfect people in a fallen world. Neighbors love and serve one another as sinners in need of grace and mutual forbearance. Vocations are not always joyous or fulfilling; they often involve tedium, disappointment, even suffering in serving the neighbor. This is why calling and vocation are closely associated with baptism.

Although more will be said about baptism in chapter 4, a few brief comments are needed at this juncture. Baptism is the "church's fundamental sacrament"[19] and the "sacrament of daily life."[20] It is fundamental because in baptism we are joined with Christ in his death and resurrection. Baptism, in turn, empowers our daily life with neighbors, because we also share Christ's ministry and suffering. To be joined with Christ and share his ministry inevitably entails suffering, for we serve the needs not only of imperfect fellow creatures but of finite and mortal ones as well. A calling and vocation is simultaneously, and ambiguously, a joy and a burden, a work of love and a work of obligation. Yet in this ambiguity we discover, counterintuitively, our freedom. As Luther puts it, "A Christian is a perfectly free lord of all, subject to none. A Christian is a perfectly dutiful servant of all, subject to all."[21] In short, it is through such dutiful freedom that Christians live out their baptism. To be made one with Christ by sharing in his death and resurrection is admittedly extraordinary. Surprisingly, this reality is made known predominantly through the shared, mundane life of ordinary saints,[22] in the lives of the common, mediocre Christians that Augustine defended long ago.

---

19. See Wingren, *Luther on Vocation*, 28–29.
20. See Tranvik, *Martin Luther and the Called Life*, 40.
21. Luther, *Freedom of a Christian*, 344.
22. See Benne, *Ordinary Saints*.

Common Callings and Vocations

To reiterate, callings and vocations are concrete expressions of neighbor love, and this love encapsulates both duty and pleasure. For Christians, loving one's neighbors is not optional; it is commanded by God (Matt. 22:37–40). Loving God cannot be separated from loving fellow human beings. This is not always an easy command to fulfill, for we may be required to love unlikable people, a circumstance that many pastors and siblings have undoubtedly encountered. Yet loving our neighbors may also be a source of delight. A neighbor is not merely an object of obligation, but also a gift. In commenting on Luther's understanding of vocation, Gustaf Wingren asserts, "There is nothing more delightful and lovable on earth than one's neighbor. Love does not think about doing works, it finds joy in people; and when something good is done for others, that does not appear to love as works but simply as gifts which flow naturally from love. Love never does something because it has to. It is permitted to act."[23]

Although love undergirds both the duty and the joy of our callings and vocations, a cautionary note must be raised. Popular notions of love are often squalid or simplistic. On the one hand, love may be debased to sexual desire. "Making love," for instance, is effectively reduced to mastering techniques of mutual gratification or self-gratification. Lovers become objects to be manipulated. On the other hand, love may be transfigured into emotional ecstasy that somehow transcends the ordinary world. The beloved becomes an idealized and unrealistic caricature, an object to be admired like a piece of art. In both of these instances, love is turned into a passion that must be continuously stoked and magnified. But such passion can neither be sustained nor can it sustain. Eventually, attempts to gratify reach a point of diminishing return, and a relationship cannot endure over time if it is based entirely on physical attraction. Eventually, the beloved refuses to be idealized any longer, and after a while the lover loses interest in the counterfeit object of devotion. Passion is not unrelated to love, but the two are not synonymous.

Christians have a readily available summary of true love in 1 Corinthians 13. The chief characteristics are familiar: love is patient and kind; it is not envious, boastful, arrogant, rude, or self-seeking. Love rejoices in the truth, and it bears, believes, hopes, and endures all things. Unfortunately, this wise insight has tended to become sentimentalized. It must be remembered that Saint Paul did not write these words for the purpose of being read at weddings. Rather, he wrote this passage for a troubled congregation whose members

23. Wingren, *Luther on Vocation*, 43.

were finding it difficult to navigate their callings and vocations as Christians, especially their daily life together as neighbors. The apostle was not enumerating lofty and unobtainable ideals but commending that which holds together the fabric of everyday life. Patience and kindness, for example, are quite ordinary—walking a crying baby late at night, giving directions to a lost stranger. Performing such simple acts, however, does not lessen their importance—what would become of crying babies without patient parents, or lost strangers without kind natives?

Additionally, individuals pursue an array of overlapping vocations because they encounter a wide range of neighbors with a variety of needs that God calls them to serve. Returning to Wingren: "Vocation means that those who are closest at hand, family and fellow-workers, are given by God: it is one's neighbor whom one is to love. Therein vocation points toward a world which is not the same for all people."[24] In and through vocations, we engage the rich, pluriform character of God's creation and the human creatures inhabiting it. But such engagement is accomplished most often through dull, unremarkable, and even onerous activities. Summarizing Luther, Wingren insists that a "Christian finds himself called to drab and lowly tasks, which seems less remarkable than monastic life, mortifications, and other distractions from our vocation. For him who heeds his vocation, sanctification is hidden in offensively ordinary tasks."[25] Indeed, he goes so far as to insist, "One does not demand that a work be 'interesting' before accepting it as a vocation."[26] We are not called to serve our neighbors because the work entailed is exhilarating but because it is needed, and through this service the Christian is liberated to follow Christ and become Christ to the one served.

Living together in a household exemplifies the unexciting yet essential work of serving the needs of neighbors. "In fact," Tranvik writes, "there is no more honorable calling than to be deeply involved in the smells, dirt, laughter, and tears of domestic life."[27] Household members share significant joys and milestones such as births, graduations, and weddings, but they also spend an inordinate amount of time doing such mundane things as brushing teeth, sleeping, eating, and doing chores.[28] Truly, "God must love the ordinary because so much of our time is spent in our homes, just tending to basic *stuff*."[29] It is in tending to this stuff that we perform, in large measure,

24. Wingren, *Luther on Vocation*, 172.
25. Wingren, *Luther on Vocation*, 73.
26. Wingren, *Luther on Vocation*, 166.
27. Tranvik, *Martin Luther and the Called Life*, 83.
28. See Tranvik, *Martin Luther and the Called Life*, 86–88.
29. Tranvik, *Martin Luther and the Called Life*, 86 (emphasis original).

our vocations as spouse, parent, and sibling in and through the commonplace patterns of everyday life.[30]

Yet attending to the basic stuff of life is formative and iconic. It is formative because in routinely and repetitively doing something it becomes habitual. Habits form who we are; we are, as the cliché reflects, creatures of habit. Usually, we do not suddenly or unexpectedly choose to be patient or kind. Rather, it is part of our character to be patient and kind people, and one's character is formed through practice over time. It is through daily and simple, and over time almost unmindful and effortless, acts of patience and kindness that we become patient and kind people.

Habituation alone, however, is not sufficient. The question is, How and in what ways are we formed? Bad habits form us badly. If one consistently succumbs to impatience or cruelty, then one becomes a habitually impatient or cruel person. As I argue in the following chapter, performing these simple acts, and performing them well, provides a foundation for more formal moral and theological virtues. Likewise, failing to perform these simple acts, or performing them badly, makes us more us susceptible to vices. As Paul intimates in 1 Corinthians 13, we become what we love,[31] or—perhaps more accurately—we become how we respond to the offer of God's love.

Our common callings and vocations are also iconic. An icon is an object that allows us to see through it and catch a glimpse of a greater reality it represents. It is, in a sense, a transportive vessel. I am suggesting that the mundane tasks related to our ordinary callings and vocations can be iconic by enabling us to catch glimpses of what constitutes a good life, or a life that is good, for human creatures created in the image and likeness of God. These insights are admittedly fleeting and ambiguous, not unlike the puzzling reflections in a mirror noted by Paul (see 1 Cor. 13:12), but they are nonetheless revelatory.

To illustrate, the novel *The Sea* by John Banville is a story about a man who must deal with his terminally ill wife and later come to terms with his loss and grief. On the day he hears the terrible news that his wife is dying, he makes the following observation: "The kettle came to the boil and switched itself off and the seething water inside it settled down grumpily. I marveled, not for the first time, at the cruel complacency of ordinary things. But no, not cruel, not complacent, only indifferent, as how could they be otherwise?"[32] This seeming indifference, however, provides an important backdrop to the story. It is in and through the mundane things that the man does in caring

---

30. See Benne, *Ordinary Saints*, chap. 7; Waters, *Family in Christian Social and Political Thought*, chaps. 5–6; and Wong, *Beginning from Man and Woman*.

31. Smith, *You Are What You Love*.

32. Banville, *The Sea*, 15.

for his wife (sometimes well and sometimes badly) and later in and through the ordinary things that he does in coming to terms with his loss and grief (again, sometimes well and sometimes badly) that he discovers that over time life takes on a revealing rhythm of its own. Again, in coming to grips with the impending reality of his wife's death, his life has become unalterably redirected. He observes, "But then, at what moment, of all our moments, is life not utterly changed, until the final, most momentous change of all?"[33] Cumulatively, these changes against the apparent indifference of the ordinary produce a profound insight in reference to his daughter, Chloe: "In her I had my first experience of the absolute otherness of other people. It is not too much to say—well, it is, but I shall say it anyway—that in Chloe the world was first manifest for me as an objective entity."[34] As a husband, parent, and widower, he learns that he is not the center of the universe.

In our common callings and vocations, through which we love and serve our neighbors, we catch a glimpse of what a good life entails. Most importantly, it requires decentering ourselves. Our neighbors do not exist to serve us but to be served as God's gifts, and this service, done out of gratitude, is really quite plain and simple. In replying to the question, "What . . . does 'daily bread' mean?" Luther offers this summary: "Everything included in the necessities and nourishment of our bodies, such as food, drink, clothing, shoes, house, farm, fields, livestock, money, property, and upright spouses, upright children, upright members of the household, upright and faithful rulers, good government, good weather, peace, health, decency, honor, good friends, faithful neighbors and the like."[35] It is in the mundane act of receiving our daily bread that we catch a glimmer of the life for which we were created and redeemed. Bread: unremarkably ordinary, extraordinarily iconic.

Emphasizing the significance of the ordinary is countercultural. Many of us live in cultures that are infatuated with the extraordinary: Every act must be thrilling or rewarding; all time spent must be productive or meaningful; all time must be quality time. Such an expectation, however, is the very denial of calling and vocation, for it places oneself rather than the other in the center of attention. Life is all about me instead of about God and neighbor. For example, when I was a university chaplain, students would sometimes talk to me about the prospect of marriage and family. When I asked them why they might want to marry and have children, their answer almost always boiled down to the notion that it would be highly rewarding and self-fulfilling. Being a spouse

33. Banville, *The Sea*, 25.
34. Banville, *The Sea*, 124–25.
35. Quoted in Tranvik, *Martin Luther and the Called Life*, 149.

and parent may, and often does, prove to be personally enriching. But sharing a home requires a lot of unrewarding and unfulfilling hard work. Moreover, becoming a spouse or parent with the primary expectation of self-gratification virtually reduces marriage and parenthood to an expedient means of fulfilling selfish desires. Whatever pleasure comes with sharing a home together is (or should be) the result of covenantal faithfulness, of pursuing one's vocations of meeting the needs of close-by and intimate neighbors.

The reader might object that all this emphasis on serving the needs of others is unrealistic and destructive. If vocation is only about giving and never about receiving, then it is merely a recipe for burnout and self-diminishment. It should be kept in mind, however, that we serve the needs of others ideally in the company of neighbors who are also attentive to and serving our needs. Healthy human relationships entail give-and-take, and it is a grace to gratefully receive the care of others when one is in need. A family devoid of reciprocity would be hellish. Moreover, appropriate self-care, both physical and spiritual, is needed in order to fulfill one's callings and vocations, in order to be a loving neighbor to others. Being attentive to the self is not synonymous with selfishness. Taking care of oneself is especially necessary for one who, for example, has suffered prolonged physical or emotional abuse. Appropriate self-care does not diminish loving and serving one's neighbors. Neighbors cannot be loved properly if one is impaired by self-loathing.

Nevertheless, talking about self-care should be nuanced in a culture that is becoming increasingly self-oriented, if not narcissistic.[36] All caring is a calculated investment of limited time, which means that effectively caring for others reduces the amount of time we have to care for ourselves. It keeps us from crossing the line from healthy and appropriate self-care into narcissistic self-indulgence. Many, if not most, of us need to hear again the scriptural teaching about losing ourselves in order to find ourselves (Matt. 10:39). Stated more prosaically, in pursuing our common callings and vocations, we often need to get over ourselves in order to love and serve other selves.

Unselfing

The admission "I am *not* the center of the universe" seems obvious. The universe is vast, and assuming that it revolves around oneself is the height of vain folly. Nonetheless, we often act as if it does. We do things calculated to inflate our sense of importance in the eyes of others, and we expect that others

---

36. See Lasch, *Culture of Narcissism.*

should serve our interests.[37] Indeed, we may treat others well only to the extent that we perceive it will somehow benefit us. At its most extreme, this selfish orientation may effectively reduce others to means of self-aggrandizement rather than other persons. Moreover, these proclivities are reinforced and exploited by late-modern cultures, especially in respect to the consumption of goods and services. Most advertising is predicated on the subtle message that you are worth every dollar you spend on yourself.

A proper self-regard is not the issue here. Morality, for instance, is implausible without some sense of personal agency or self-awareness,[38] and a properly ordered self-love is commended by Scripture (Mark 12:30–31). A neighbor cannot be loved and served by a non-self. The self, however, must transcend itself to love and serve the neighbor. Neighbor love, to use a crude analogy, does not seek to draw the other into one's orbit but is drawn outward to the other as *another self*[39]—another person to whom one is related in virtue of one's shared being with them, but who is also other than oneself. Why is this self-transcendence crucial? How can it be accomplished? How can the mundane acts and relationships associated with our common callings and ordinary virtues help us unself? This section is devoted to addressing these questions.

Iris Murdoch was acutely aware of this difficult challenge.[40] She attempts to solve the problem of the self, especially in respect to ethics, through her concept of "unselfing."[41] According to Murdoch, freedom, as a core human trait and value, does not consist in an isolated individual leaping "in and out of an impersonal logical complex"; rather, "it is a function of the progressive attempt to see a particular object clearly."[42] Love is central to the process of gaining clarity. It is in loving the world in general as an objective reality and individuals in particular as other persons that we come to see both more clearly in their own respective rights, for in doing so we "apprehend" their respective and related goodnesses that "belong to a continuous fabric of being."[43]

Following Simone Weil, we must cast a loving and just gaze upon the reality of the other to be genuinely attentive to its own good. This attentive love "can prompt a process of unselfing wherein the lover learns to see, and cherish and

---

37. See, e.g., DeYoung, *Vainglory*.

38. See Murdoch, "Against Dryness," 16–20; and Smith, *Theory of Moral Sentiments*.

39. See Meilaender, *Faith and Faithfulness*; O'Donovan, *Self, World, and Time*; Spaemann, *Persons*.

40. The remainder of this paragraph and the one following are taken, in slightly adapted form, from Waters, "Willful Control and Controlling the Will."

41. See Antonaccio, *Philosophy to Live By*; and Widdows, *Moral Vision of Iris Murdoch*.

42. Murdoch, *Sovereignty of Good*, 23.

43. Murdoch, *Sovereignty of Good*, 29.

disinterested in her son that she treats him as she would any other child; the only reason the two are somehow "related" is through a biological accident.

The mundane can help create this space by shrinking the fat relentless ego. There is nothing more unself-oriented than being focused on serving the needs of others. And also nothing more humbling: changing an infant's diaper (how can a cute baby create such foul stench?), bringing a glass of water to a sick spouse, running an errand at a most inopportune hour. These are simple acts that serve the needs of neighbors. They are also boring. There is nothing inherently good about being bored, but boredom has its value. It can stimulate imaginative responses, for instance, and more importantly, boredom can teach us to wait: to wait for someone or something, and to wait on others (as in providing a service).[55] Waiting can assist unselfing. In being attentive to others, we wait for them to disclose their wants and needs, their good. If the mundane is filled with boring activities, then their routine and repetitious performance forms us as waiting people, and since waiting entails both presence and anticipation, it is, broadly construed, both incarnational and eschatological.

The mundane, however, is also iconic. The ordinary may reveal facets of the eternal that bracket the temporal, in turn giving us a glimpse at what should be genuinely most important in loving God and neighbor. Through these partial insights, we learn something about the proper ordering of the penultimate and ultimate so that the former is neither denigrated nor lionized and the latter is prevented from becoming a distraction or fantasy. It is not in the extraordinary but in the ordinary or mundane that we learn what is most important about life. To reiterate, it is in the mind-numbing, boring, and tedious chores of taking care of ourselves and others that we catch a glimpse of what God created us to be and to become.

To illustrate, I return to Banville's novel *The Sea*. Much of the story unfolds around routine tasks, such as caring for a dying wife and finding ways to keep going after her death. It is hard and tiresome work, often accompanied by uncertainty and unease. The principal character and narrator of the story reflects, "These days I must take the world in small and carefully measured doses, it is a sort of homeopathic cure I am undergoing, though I am not certain what this cure is meant to mend. Perhaps I am learning to live amongst the living again."[56] It is also a story about waiting: waiting on others (such as an ill wife, a tempestuous daughter, old friends) and waiting for the future (when, perhaps, healing might occur and equilibrium be restored). This

55. See Raposa, *Boredom and the Religious Imagination*, 168.
56. Banville, *The Sea*, 143.

eschatological element is important, for it provides whatever shred of hope appears in this story, a hope that helps one to not remain mired in the past. Remembrance can be consoling, but it can also overwhelm. "There are moments when the past has a force so strong it seems one might be annihilated by it."[57] If we cannot wait, we cannot hope—and the mundane helps us learn how to wait and thereby how to hope.

Waiting is a vocational act, a work of love of God and neighbor. Through these works we learn something important about ourselves in relation to God and neighbor. Borrowing the words of Ellen Charry, "To know God is to know ourselves, and understanding ourselves theocentrically in terms of Genesis 1:26 is true self-knowledge for true self-love. True self-love is the healing of disordered love (i.e., sin)."[58] And only the "healed person can love well, and loving well is the basis of a flourishing life."[59] Leading a flourishing life is synonymous with being happy, and a "happy life is not sensational" because it does not "mistake excitement for happiness."[60] Moreover, a properly ordered self-love, upon which flourishing or happiness is based, cannot be constructed but only received and embraced. To know ourselves is to be, counterintuitively, unselfed. Additionally, through our vocations we come to know ourselves: a crucial knowledge, since without a vocation we cannot "restrain our natural lust for power and approval."[61]

In serving our neighbors through our common callings and vocations, and with the aid of God's grace, we begin to see and encounter our neighbors as they truly are, as fellow beings whose origin and destiny is in the eternal love that creates and redeems us. C. S. Lewis contends that, day in and day out, we help each other to wait for this destiny, and it is in this light that "we should conduct all our dealings with one another, all friendships, all loves, all play, all politics."[62] He goes on to add, "There are no *ordinary* people. You have never talked to a mere mortal."[63] It is beings heading toward an eternal destiny "whom we joke with, marry, snub, and exploit," which is why our "charity must be a real and costly love."[64] It is the mundane that shapes or misshapes us for the eschaton. "Next to the Blessed Sacrament itself, your neighbour is the holiest object presented to your senses."[65]

57. Banville, *The Sea*, 35.
58. Charry, *God and the Art of Happiness*, 157.
59. Charry, *God and the Art of Happiness*, 159.
60. Charry, *God and the Art of Happiness*, 219–20.
61. Auden, *Complete Works of W. H. Auden*, 2:181.
62. Lewis, *Weight of Glory*, 46.
63. Lewis, *Weight of Glory*, 46 (emphasis original).
64. Lewis, *Weight of Glory*, 46.
65. Lewis, *Weight of Glory*, 46.

On the day of judgment, I think we shall be surprised by what is taken into account and assessed and what is ignored. We will be stunned by what is asked and not asked, by what is condemned and what is commended. We might be dismayed if we are not asked whom we voted for in the extraordinary presidential election of 2020 or what we accomplished after being given tenure. You might be astonished at being praised for washing the dishes that evening when it was your wife's turn but she was exhausted and needed to rest. We were created by love for eternity, and our preparation for this destiny entails the routine, the repetitious, and the habitual. The mundane is pretty good at that.

It is important to note that not every conceivable act is related to callings and vocations. I doubt, for instance, that anyone is called to a career of committing fraud or to vocational thievery. Rather, these acts represent failures or distortions that should be corrected or, better yet, avoided in the first place. The sole criterion of a calling and vocation, common or otherwise, is its orientation toward serving the neighbor. Frauds and thieves serve no one but themselves at the expense of their neighbors.

Additionally, there is the important matter of discerning one's callings and vocations, about which I have said nothing and will say very little in what follows. Robert Benne offers some helpful guidelines for vocational discernment involving one's faith and about assessment of personal strengths, weaknesses, and skills, as well as realistic possibilities.[66] I am reluctant, however, to comment on Benne's guidelines or to develop any general ones of my own. The reason for my reluctance is that I believe discerning one's callings is a unique and personal process, more art than technique. In my own case, for example, my vocational discernment has involved a series of fitting responses—such as marriage, parenthood, and teaching—to what God is requiring and enabling me to do and to be.[67] Along the way I have made many mistakes and taken many wrong turns that needed correction, but I do not know whether such muddled discernment is applicable to anyone else, especially since (as my wife is fond of reminding me) I am rather odd. I do believe, however, that there are universal guidelines for loving God and neighbor, and loving them well. That leads us to the next chapter, on virtue.

66. See Benne, *Ordinary Saints*, part 2.
67. My approach to vocational discernment has been most deeply informed by Gustafson, *Ethics from a Theocentric Perspective*, vol. 2, chap. 9; and Niebuhr, *Responsible Self*, chap. 1.

CHAPTER 3

Virtue and Vice

The word *virtue* carries many different meanings. In the popular mind, for instance, it is often associated with overly scrupulous behavior, or may even be limited to sexual continence or purity. Certain professions may equate virtues with codes of conduct. Virtue, however, refers most generally to a characteristic or quality of excellence, thereby encompassing an expansive and variegated range of theoretical and practical concerns. There are, for example, moral virtues, but there are also intellectual, theological, and civic virtues. Truth telling, for instance, is a virtue exemplifying all of these realms: a virtuous person, scholar, Christian, and citizen tells the truth. In brief, the virtues exemplify and inculcate behavior that promotes human flourishing.

Vice is the antonym of virtue. Again, there is a popular perception that often limits vice to a narrow set of disreputable acts or crimes. Vice, however, involves failing to practice a virtue or practicing its corruption. Vice may stem from ignorance, personal weakness, or willful disregard for or loathing of excellence. Rather than telling the truth, for example, I might utter a falsehood because I think it is true, or I might fear the consequences of telling a difficult truth, or I might want to harm a competitor. Lying, as opposed to truth telling, is a vicious act that can be committed for a variety of reasons.[1] In brief, the vices exemplify and inculcate behavior that diminishes human flourishing.

Virtuous or vicious conduct is not mere performance, acts designed to curry favor or promote one's self-interests at the expense of others. It is not only

---

1. See Augustine, *On Lying*; and Griffiths, *Lying*.

a matter of doing but also of being. Virtue grows out of one's inherent love of goods: the love of God and neighbor, for instance. We tell neighbors the truth not only because God commands it but also out of love for neighbors who deserve to be told truths rather than lies. To lie is not only to disobey God but also to hold the neighbor in contempt.[2] Virtuous or vicious conduct grows out of and reflects the kind of person one is or is aspiring to become. Virtue and vice inevitably entail the question of one's character, of what one ultimately loves and devotes one's life to.

The remainder of this chapter is divided into three sections. In the first section I examine virtue. Given the limited scope of this chapter, I do not offer an extensive summary of various theories of virtue but concentrate on selected aspects that are most germane to this book. I repeat this process in the following section on vice. In the third section I apply these descriptions of virtue and vice to the question of character. In particular, I concentrate on how a virtuous life is related to everyday life.

Virtue

For the ancients, virtue denoted a state of excellence. But how do we know that something is excellent? This determination is made in respect to purpose and function. Things are created to achieve a purpose that may also be described as its end or *telos*. This purpose, however, cannot be arbitrary or frivolous, but must be aimed at a good end. Its function is assessed by its ability to achieve this good end. A hammer, for example, is excellent if it is proficient at driving a nail to achieve the good of constructing a sturdy table.

What is true for inanimate objects is even more true for human beings. An excellent person strives to achieve the end of the good life. What exactly is this good life that we should endeavor to attain? Aristotle devoted a great deal of time answering this question. In the *Nicomachean Ethics*, he begins his inquiry by noting that every choice and action aims at some good, and these choices and actions are directed toward varying ends. The end of medicine, for example, is health, while the end of commerce is wealth. Most of our choices and actions are aimed at subordinate ends, such as health and wealth. The more pressing question for Aristotle is, What is the chief end toward which individuals should aim if they want to be excellent human beings? His succinct answer is *happiness*. By this he does not mean banal cheerfulness or pleasant sensations or sentiments. Happiness is an inherent good—the highest good.

---

2. That said, a case can be made for the occasional fib that spares the neighbor unnecessary distress or suffering. See, e.g., Bonhoeffer, *Ethics*, 326–34.

The truly happy person is one who desires and knows this good and aligns one's life accordingly.

Aristotle admits that we may differ over what this happiness means and entails, but we may discover it through politics, our common life in the *polis*. Why politics? Because the highest good is self-sufficient, and for the ancients the city is the only form of human association that is self-sufficient. Consequently, all other forms of human action fall under its purview. Such self-sufficiency, however, does not imply solitude, because humans are born to be citizens. It must be stressed that this highest good is not a human artifact or invention but is a given; we become happy by conforming to the nature of being human. For Aristotle, this given human nature to which we should conform in order to be happy is a divine gift, for "if there is any gift of the gods to men, it is reasonable that happiness should be god-given, and most surely god-given of all human things inasmuch as it is the best."[3] Happiness, then, is an activity of the soul that accords with virtue, and in politics, the highest form of human association, the chief virtue is justice. In short, politics is the most important part of one's life; our material and spiritual wellbeing comes to us as citizens.

Knowing and achieving this happiness requires two kinds of virtue: intellectual and moral. To be happy, we must know what this good is, and we acquire this knowledge through study, reason, and contemplation. One cannot be happy by remaining ignorant. But knowledge is not enough, for happiness also requires action. We cannot think our way into being happy. For example, we do not become just and courageous people by thinking about justice and courage. Rather, we become just and courageous people by doing just and courageous deeds. Action is tied directly to the moral virtues that are formed through habituation. Ordering the soul, then, is not only an intellectual activity; it is also directing the passions or affections toward justice as the state of happiness. In this respect, virtue is a condition of character that enables us to make choices that make us good; hence, it is "evident that it is impossible to be practically wise without being good."[4]

Additionally, Aristotle notes that a life of virtue, moral excellence, cannot be separated from pleasure and pain, because humans are driven by passions that often overrule reason. He contends that "if the virtues are concerned with actions and passions, and every passion and every action is accompanied by pleasure and pain, for this reason also virtue will be concerned with pleasures and pains."[5] Presumably virtue is pleasurable since it leads to happiness,

3. See Aristotle, *Nicomachean Ethics* 1.9.
4. See Aristotle, *Nicomachean Ethics* 6.12.
5. See Aristotle, *Nicomachean Ethics* 2.3.

whereas vice is painful because it prevents us from being happy. This is why punishment is an effective teacher of virtue and deterrent to vice. Aristotle admits, however, that although true, this scheme is not so clear-cut. Doing what is best is difficult rather than easy. A virtuous life inevitably entails pain and suffering. This suffering often stems from a conflict between self-interest and what may be characterized as the common good. "Do men love, then, the good, or what is good for them? These sometimes clash."[6] This is why the brave warrior is justly praised, because it is more difficult to endure the personal sacrifice and dangers of the battlefield than to merely abstain from self-indulgent pleasures.

The virtues, then, are also a means of controlling, even overcoming, the passions in pursuing a life of moral excellence. Through the power of reason and the will, we make choices. Neither the virtues nor the vices are passions. We are not praised or blamed for our passions, but for our virtues and vices. We do not choose our passions, but we choose our virtues and vices. It is in our power to be either virtuous or vicious, and Aristotle was confident that humans possess an inherent ability to prefer the former over the latter.

Saint Augustine did not share this confidence. On his view, humans cannot simply choose to be good because their reason and wills are corrupted by sin. Whatever virtue we might obtain is a gift of divine grace and the leading of the Holy Spirit. To assume that individuals possess sufficient reason and willpower to construct themselves through habituation is to imply a latent Pelagianism. But despite this skepticism of innate human potential,[7] Augustine agrees that happiness is the end toward which we should strive. He sees this striving, however, occurring not in the justice of the *polis* but in the church—prefiguring eternal fellowship with the triune God.[8] Yet even with the rise of this quite different understanding, Aristotle was not banished from subsequent Christian thinking on the virtues.

Saint Thomas Aquinas incorporated an Aristotelian understanding of virtue within a more expansive theological framework. Rather than maintaining the division between intellectual and moral virtues, he divided them into theological[9] and cardinal[10] virtues. The three theological virtues are faith, hope, and love (also referred to as charity or, in Latin, *caritas*). These virtues are supernatural in origin, surpassing the constraints of human nature, and

---

6. See Aristotle, *Nicomachean Ethics* 8.2.
7. See Herdt, *Putting On Virtue*, chap. 2.
8. See Augustine, *On the Morals of the Catholic Church*.
9. See Aquinas, *Summa Theologica* II-II.1–46.
10. See Aquinas, *Summa Theologica* II-II.47–170. (My focus here is on II-II.49–66.)

are therefore distinct from natural intellectual and moral virtues. In short, these virtues can only be received as gifts of the Spirit.

In contrast, the four cardinal virtues—prudence, justice, temperance, and fortitude—include both intellectual and moral virtues. These virtues are inherent in human beings and can be developed through practice and habituation. Prudence is the primary virtue, followed by justice, temperance, and fortitude. These four help keep the passions in check. As Thomas succinctly puts it, "any virtue that causes good in reason's act of consideration, may be called prudence; every virtue that causes the good of right and due in operation, be called justice; every virtue that curbs and represses the passions, be called temperance; and every virtue that strengthens the mind against any passions whatever, be called fortitude."[11]

Thomas, however, offers an important caveat. Although humans possess natural aptitudes that can lead to virtue, these are, at best, inchoate. These propensities can be developed through human actions directed by reason, but divine grace is also required to achieve habituation. Moreover, the cardinal virtues, in addition to their theological counterparts, can be infused by God, although they are not given to everyone. Consequently, through a combination of human effort and God's grace, people can be made virtuous through habituation.

We may turn to Josef Pieper to put some flesh on the Thomistic skeleton described in the preceding paragraphs.[12] At its most basic, faith entails believing in "someone" or "something" that is objective and not merely a projection of the believer.[13] Faith, then, presupposes revelation; the someone or something must disclose itself. Faith involves reason but is not confined to intellectual assent. Faith encompasses one's entire being. We believe only if we want to, because belief is based not on demonstrable truth but on love. "We believe, not because we see, perceive, deduce something true, but because we desire something good."[14] Moreover, placing one's faith in God is directing one's desire and attention toward something both true and real. Belief is not limited to participating in the mere *knowledge* of God; it is, more fully, a participation in the divine reality. We place our faith in that which we attend to. The antonym of belief is not unbelief but inattention.

According to Pieper, hope is the bridge between faith and love.[15] It is the virtue that sustains the life of pilgrimage in which Christians are in the world

---

11. Aquinas, *Summa Theologica* I-II.61.3.
12. Cf. Porter, *Perfection of Desire.*
13. See Pieper, *Faith Hope Love,* 29.
14. Pieper, *Faith Hope Love,* 36.
15. See Pieper, *Faith Hope Love,* 89.

but not of it. To live in hope is to wait patiently but expectantly for one's destiny of fellowship with God. As a virtue, hope reorients humans toward the fulfillment of their true nature as God's creatures, a fulfillment that has its source in the reality of grace in human existence and is directed toward "supernatural happiness in God."[16] Hope, however, is an opaque, even fragile virtue because it is aimed at an unknown future. Christians may be tempted to fall into despair because their hope seems unfulfilled. This temptation should be steadfastly resisted, for despair is the denial of redemption; hence the vital necessity of habituating the virtue of faith.

Love is, to a great extent, an act of will indicating approval. We love others because we approve them, and conversely, we wish to be approved and loved by others. Love, then, is manifestly a relational virtue, for it cannot be practiced or habituated in seclusion. "Above all, the ability to love, in which our own existence achieves its highest intensification, presupposes the experience of being loved by someone else."[17] But there is nothing sentimental about the virtue of love. Love does not require sparing the beloved from suffering or exuding a superficial kindness. One should not, for instance, easily overlook the beloved's preference for convenience over the good. Another example Pieper uses to portray a realistic love is forgiveness.[18] Excusing and forgiving are not synonymous. Forgiving must preserve the dignity of the one forgiven, so if a person does not want to be forgiven, he or she should not be forced to be so. The virtue of love is, in large part, the practice of creating the distance and space that allows the other to be other while maintaining bonds of mutual approval.

We turn now to the cardinal virtues. Prudence is the premier virtue from which the other three—justice, fortitude, and temperance—are derived. Prudence entails making the right choice of action for the right reasons. And to be right requires that one be oriented to the good, for "whatever is good must first have been prudent."[19] The Ten Commandments exemplify the centrality of prudence, for every sin is opposed to prudence. All sin, in short, is imprudent action. Although prudence is the prototype of the good, it is also in keeping with what is real. Doing the good presupposes that our knowledge corresponds with reality. Only then can prudent choices be made. Additionally, prudence presupposes the theological virtues of faith, hope, and charity. One cannot be prudent if one is faithless, hopeless, or loveless.

Prudence is especially concerned with the practical relationship between ways and means. Prudence, like all practical reason, entails both cognition and

16. Pieper, *Faith Hope Love*, 99.
17. Pieper, *Faith Hope Love*, 176.
18. See Pieper, *Faith Hope Love*, 187–89.
19. Pieper, *Four Cardinal Virtues*, 9.

decision and is simultaneously oriented toward reality, volition, and action. Prudent thinking, however, is not theoretical or abstract but oriented toward what is real. The prudent person is thoughtful while the thoughtless person is imprudent. Although making prudent judgments requires deliberation, it should not postpone indefinitely deliberate action; indecisiveness is opposed to prudence. Consequently, the attention of the prudent person is fixed upon the "not yet," so the prudent choice is rarely made with absolute certainty. Moreover, a prudent person does not allow the ego to get in the way of making a decision and acting upon it in a just manner. Placing the ego off to the side exposes the link between prudence and justice, because people who attend only to themselves ignore reality and thereby cannot be just. Most importantly, deliberative prudent action "transforms knowledge of reality into realization of the good."[20] This transformation requires such aptitudes as deliberation, courage, candor, simplicity, and bold decision making. Love is therefore the form that prudence must take.

Justice is generally a habit that seeks to render what is due a person. This habit is expressed negatively when we react unfavorably to treatment that we feel we do not deserve. For the Christian, justice also entails being a servant of God; through justice we love and serve our neighbors. Similar to love, justice is always relational. I cannot treat myself justly or commit an injustice against myself, but I can treat others justly or unjustly. The virtuous person desires justice as an obligation or debt owed to neighbors, many of whom are strangers. Justice, then, is a communal enterprise that is realized within specific human associations, and there are three basic forms for realizing this virtue in these communities: reciprocal (relations among individuals), ministering (relations within community), and general (social relations). As Pieper notes, late-modern societies, in both individualistic and collectivist forms, largely ignore the validity of these nonpolitical associations, effectively rendering justice inoperative or irrelevant.[21] Moreover, these societies strip justice of any virtuous standing, confining it to pragmatic policies and actions undertaken by the state. Institutional procedures and precautions, however, cannot offer an adequate substitute for justice. The idea that a perfected political system can guarantee justice is a deception perpetrated by a late-modern technical rationality. Only a just government consisting of virtuous leaders can render justice.[22]

Fortitude is the virtue that enables us to overcome natural fears and vulnerabilities. Stated positively, fortitude is the prerequisite of courage—for,

---

20. Pieper, *Four Cardinal Virtues*, 22.
21. See Pieper, *Four Cardinal Virtues*, 73–75.
22. See Pieper, *Four Cardinal Virtues*, chap. 6.

ironically, without weaknesses no one could be brave. "An angel cannot be brave," Pieper writes, "because he is not vulnerable. To be brave actually means to be able to suffer injury. Because man is by nature vulnerable, he can be brave."[23] Fortitude is also related directly to the other cardinal and theological virtues. Without prudence and justice, for example, there can be no fortitude, because fortitude serves a just cause and prudent judgments are required for its implementation. Fortitude is not synonymous with fearless-ness, for love is always accompanied by vulnerability. Fortitude, then, enables a person to be not only courageous but also patient. And it is, in its fullest sense, a gift of the Spirit.

Pieper regrets that the meaning of *temperance* has been largely reduced to moderation in eating and drinking.[24] The virtue is more expansive and significant than that. Temperance entails discovering an order within oneself, a process of self-discovery that is ordered to truth—the truth of God and of being God's creature. This virtue, then, inspires humility, for in finding the order within ourselves, we also see the truth of our dependence on God and neighbor. According to Pieper, "The ground of humility is man's estimation of himself according to truth."[25] Consequently, the humility engendered by temperance is more an attitude than a behavior, and we catch a glimpse of this virtue through the gift of humor, especially the self-deprecating kind.[26]

Recovering Aristotelian and Thomistic accounts of virtue has received considerable attention in contemporary moral philosophy,[27] and a number of Catholic and Protestant theologians have drawn upon and contributed to this recovery.[28] Yet there are a number of contrasting and complementary voices employing Platonic and Augustinian sources that need to be noted briefly.[29]

Gilbert Meilaender, for instance, accepts the basic distinction between the theological and cardinal virtues, although he renames them, respectively, the "Christian" and "Platonic" virtues.[30] He does not deny that these virtues are central to living the good life, for people must first be good before they can live lives that can be said to be good. Rather, his concern is with the center of gravity in the process of habituating the virtues. He worries that too much confidence is placed in the will and in the ability of individuals to make them-selves virtuous. Despite Thomas's proviso on the necessity of divine assistance

23. Pieper, *Four Cardinal Virtues*, 117.
24. See Pieper, *Four Cardinal Virtues*, 145.
25. Pieper, *Four Cardinal Virtues*, 189.
26. Cf. Buckley, *Morality of Laughter*, 42–46.
27. See, e.g., MacIntyre, *After Virtue*.
28. See, e.g., Porter, *Recovery of Virtue*; and Hauerwas, *Community of Character*.
29. In addition to the authors discussed below, see Gregory, *Politics and the Order of Love*.
30. See Meilaender, *Theory and Practice of Virtue*, chap. 1.

in mastering the virtues, there is nonetheless an implicit confidence that humans possess an innate capability to become good by doing good deeds. But this confidence does not adequately safeguard against the sinful tendency to indulge in self-justification, thereby distorting the subsequent practice of the virtues. The capacity to practice the virtues rightly should be seen as more akin to infusions of divine grace that reorient and amplify natural proclivities than to exercises of the strength of one's own will. The virtues are not techniques to be mastered; rather, they collectively form a moral vision over time. The virtues are divine gifts that enable us to see more clearly and, in gaining clarity, to act more fittingly. "Virtue is not finally or simply a possession; it is a quest for what can only be received."[31]

The work of Jonathan Edwards is also enjoying renewed interest among virtue theorists.[32] For Edwards, "True virtue most essentially consists in benevolence to being in general. Or perhaps, to speak more accurately, it is that consent, propensity, and union of heart to being in general, which is immediately exercised in a general good will."[33] Virtue is akin to the beauty of acts to which praise or blame are assigned. Virtue, then, is grounded in one's disposition, will, and heart; the virtuous person has a truly beautiful heart that is benevolently disposed toward the wellbeing of others. We should seek the particular good of others because it is consistent with being in general.

Since being in general is the source and object of true virtue, God is the origin of virtue since God has the greatest quantity of being. But how do we know concretely the content of divine being, and how is it related to human or creaturely virtues? Humans, after all, interact with particular beings and not with being in general. Edwards's solution to this epistemological conundrum is the incarnation. Cochran explains, "Christ's divine nature is the moral archetype for true virtue, and his human nature is likewise the moral archetype for the human virtues that are excellences particular to creatures."[34] Christ reveals both divine and human nature, and thereby both divine and human virtue. We can only know virtue through Christ's revelation and grace.

Edwards adopts a dyadic understanding of virtue. True virtue is inherent only in the nature of God. Despite the ravages of original sin, humans still possess a natural faculty to recognize God's superior excellence, and some are drawn, through grace and the leading of the Holy Spirit, to emulate it (albeit in a limited and imperfect manner).[35] Even depraved creatures want

31. Meilaender, *Theory and Practice of Virtue*, 19.
32. See, e.g., Cochran, *Receptive Human Virtues*.
33. Edwards, *Dissertation Concerning the Nature of True Virtue*, loc. 19117, Kindle.
34. Cochran, *Receptive Human Virtues*, 62.
35. This special grace and spiritual guidance are given only to the elect.

to follow good examples. Although this emulation gives nothing to God, in benevolently promoting and rejoicing in the happiness of others, we uphold God's glory. The person who supremely loves God is at least in touch with the source of true virtue.

Humans also have innate natural proclivities that resemble virtue. This is not true virtue, however, because it is driven by self-love rather than general benevolence. Self-love is the love of one's own happiness and is oriented toward one's private interests. "Thus, that a man should love those who are of his party, and who are warmly engaged on his side, and promote his interest, is the natural consequence of a private self-love."[36] These private or inferior virtues, however, should not be despised. "In many of these *natural affections* there appears the *tendency* and *effect* of benevolence, in part."[37] Gratitude, friendship, marriage, and parenthood are examples of these natural affections. "Thus these things have something of the *general nature* of virtue"[38] and in their limited way are beautiful and efficacious. The problem is not these private affections and virtues per se, but that we are tempted to restrict the moral life to them and ignore God, and thereby the nature of true virtue. With the infusion of God's grace and leading of the Spirit, however, some (the elect) are enabled to resist this deadly temptation and align their lives with a general benevolence.

Although the Aristotelian-Thomistic tradition is the dominant voice in contemporary accounts of virtue ethics, Platonic and Edwardsian themes offer important emphases and insights often neglected by the dominant tradition. Yet one need not choose one option to the exclusion of the other. I am not suggesting that any easy synthesis can or should be attempted. Rather, there are complementary themes from these traditions that can be utilized to provide a richer account of the virtues and of the virtuous life. For the purpose of this book, I am defining virtue as an innate or divinely infused quality or faculty that, with the aid of God's grace and leading of the Holy Spirit, can be practiced and habituated in ways that align one's life with the good. Moreover, mundane actions and relationships, somewhat akin to Edwards's private virtues, initiate and help sustain the more formal practices of habituation that are manifested in one's character.

Before examining this relationship among the mundane, virtue, and character, we must first visit the problem of vice.

36. Edwards, *Dissertation Concerning the Nature of True Virtue*, loc. 19579, Kindle.
37. Edwards, *Dissertation Concerning the Nature of True Virtue*, loc. 19979, Kindle (emphasis original).
38. Edwards, *Dissertation Concerning the Nature of True Virtue*, loc. 19994, Kindle (emphasis original).

Vice

Vice has traditionally been understood as a corruption of virtue through either deficiency or excess. Consequently, every virtue has two corresponding vices. For example, the virtue of courage is accompanied by the possible vice of cowardice (a deficiency) or recklessness (an excess). The truly courageous person has habituated the mean between deficiency and excess. The virtue of courage enables one to master fear without succumbing to cowardly behavior that surrenders to fear—or to reckless behavior that ignores it. In this respect, people who habituate vice may be said to be vicious, because their moral conduct is either deficient or excessive. It is important to keep in mind that this potential plagues not only the four cardinal virtues but also the theological virtues described above.[39] According to Rebecca Konyndyk DeYoung, there are seven "capital vices" or "deadly sins": envy, vainglory, sloth, avarice, anger, gluttony, and lust.[40] Rather than describing each briefly, I will concentrate on sloth to illustrate the broader problem of vice.

Sloth is not laziness; it is much worse than that. Sloth is basically malevolent and ultimately deadly inaction. As Karl Barth contends, "But as reconciling grace is not merely justifying, but also wholly and utterly sanctifying and awakening and establishing grace, so sin has not merely the heroic form of pride but also, in complete antithesis yet profound correspondence, the quite unheroic and trivial form of sloth."[41] This slothful form of sin denies the incarnation in particular, because it prevents human creatures from acknowledging their own exaltation in the exaltation of Jesus Christ. Sloth displays ingratitude and distrust, leading to a withdrawal from God into oneself. This withdrawal in turn is a refusal to shape one's life in relation to God, neighbors, the created order, and the limits of time. For Barth, sloth is simply stupidity that "loves to make itself out to be either the pillar of society or the sacred force of revolutionary renewal!"[42] Such stupidity disfigures us into inhuman creatures capable of committing inhumane acts against neighbors, either willfully or through casual neglect. The pillar exudes an unwarranted moral superiority that despises the inferiority of lesser mortals, while the revolutionary sweeps away recalcitrant opponents as little more than human debris.

Michael Raposa offers a subtler insight into sloth than Barth's, but the consequences he identifies are equally deadly. *Acedia* is a "medieval term for spiritual

---

39. The one exception is the love for God. One can have too little love for God, but never too much.

40. See DeYoung, *Glittering Vices*.

41. Barth, *Church Dogmatics* IV/2, 403.

42. Barth, *Church Dogmatics* IV/2, 414.

sluggishness, dullness in prayer, boredom with the rituals of devotion."[43] It is similar to William James's idea of the sick soul.[44] Raposa asserts that acedia, this "demon of noontide," is rooted in a "powerful boredom."[45] All significant forms of boredom "have something to do with the awareness of death, the recognition that all things must pass away in time. Another way of putting this is to say that boredom has something to do with 'nothing,' the nothingness that lurks behind and threatens each person, every project, each moment."[46] This lurking nothingness leads to a numbing indifference and emptiness that paralyzes the will, over time becoming a habitual sadness and refusal of love. In short, sloth prevents one from finding or having any meaning in life.

More expansively, acedia can plague not only individuals but also societies. R. J. Snell, for example, contends that acedia permeates late-modern culture. "Burrowed to the roots of our culture's self-understanding and metaphysical dreams, sloth is enmeshed in our very way of being, our vision of what it means to be human."[47] The slothful person cannot engage, or even tolerate, the real, for the "weight of reality is viewed as an insufferable demand, as oppression, an illegitimate restriction of freedom."[48] A comprehensive artifice is thereby proffered as a less demanding substitute for a hefty reality, a substitute requiring no meaning since there is none to be had anyway. The preferred sin or vice of late moderns is, perhaps, sloth rather than pride.

It is easy to see why sloth is often confused with laziness. If the nothingness of life is devoid of any possibility of meaning, then one collapses in on oneself. Since nothing really matters, why do anything at all? Returning again to John Banville's *The Sea*, the narrator copes with the reality of his wife's impending death and its aftermath by not dealing with them. Rather, he turns deeply inward, cutting himself off from other people and activities that would draw him outward, and in the process shrinking to almost nothing in the face of life's lurking nothingness. This strategy, however, displaces him, so he is never connected to any particular place at any particular time. "Being here is just a way of not being anywhere."[49] Acedia creates free-floating specters that never land anywhere.

Counterintuitively, sloth can also promote frenetic activity. One strategy for dealing with the reality of life's nothingness is to stay on the move to avoid

43. Raposa, *Boredom and the Religious Imagination*, 2.
44. James, *Varieties of Religious Experience*, lectures 6–7.
45. See Raposa, *Boredom and the Religious Imagination*, 20.
46. Raposa, *Boredom and the Religious Imagination*, 34.
47. Snell, *Acedia and Its Discontents*, loc. 47, Kindle.
48. Snell, *Acedia and Its Discontents*, loc. 186, Kindle.
49. Banville, *The Sea*, 143.

or evade it for as long as possible. Since nothing ultimately matters, then one activity is as good as any other. There is no purpose to action other than to be active. The fading author in *All the Sad Young Literary Men* asks Google to change its algorithms to produce more hits, especially for his earlier, obscure articles. Google declines. For this author, writing is no longer about having some important meaning to convey to readers; it has become simply identifying keywords, the more the better, to be identified by a search engine.[50] Sloth can cause one to collapse into the self, and it can also scatter so there is no self to be collected. In either case, sloth entails constructing a fantasy that despises the weight of reality.

Habituating sloth forms a despairing person, one ultimately cut off from God, the world, and other people. The result is a misshaped character, a disoriented and distracted person driven by disordered desire. Similar patterns could be traced in respect to the other capital vices, but the point is that in habituating a vice or vices we become vicious people. Consequently, one of the principal tasks of moral formation is to habituate the cardinal and theological virtues so that one becomes a virtuous person: one, for example, who is faithful, hopeful, and loving. This habituation requires disciplined practice, a conscious effort aided by grace and the leading of the Spirit to exhibit supremely—in thought, word, and deed—the love of God and neighbor. Practices over time shape a virtuous character.

But one cannot suddenly choose to become virtuous; there must be some prior orientation that directs one's attentiveness to be good and to seek the good of others. In other words, how are the virtues properly related to ordinary living? How should the virtuous life evolve from and draw upon the mundane?

Character

Character is shorthand for the kind of person one is. It involves *being* and *doing* not as discrete domains that are easily divisible but as two angles from which to view a seamless, whole person. Being is doing, and doing is being; the unity of the two is one's character. It is through character that, over time, we are known and assessed by others. We come to be known as reliable, kind, and truthful or as untrustworthy, cruel, and deceptive. And others come to treat us accordingly. For instance, we do not share confidences with those we know to be habitual gossips but only with those we trust will keep our information confidential. Moreover, most moral decisions and acts flow directly from one's

---

50. See Gessen, *All the Sad Young Literary Men*.

character. Sometimes we have the time to deliberate carefully about a moral decision we must make. Should I authorize the removal of a ventilator from a dying loved one? Should I confront a friend about his marital infidelity? But many, probably most, moral decisions and acts do not afford us the luxury of time for deliberation. We are confronted with a pressing set of circumstances requiring an immediate response. In response to an embarrassing accusation, do I tell a lie or the truth? Do I laugh or not at a joke told to belittle another person? How we respond in these kinds of situations is not thoughtful but reflects one's character; the kind of person one is. When pressed, we react courageously or cowardly, temperately or intemperately, faithfully or unfaithfully, and with little thought.

This does not mean, however, that character is thoughtless. Rather, a good deal of thinking should occur regarding the habits forming one's character. It may be said that character demonstrates one's alignment with the good. For Christians, this good *is* God. The virtues of faith, hope, and love—with the aid of grace and the work of the Spirit—orient and order our lives toward this greatest good. We are infused with a divine love that is both our beginning and our end. This love becomes our being, who we are. And we need to think long and hard about which habits promote and which prevent this love from shaping who we are becoming and aspiring to be.

This love, however, is not limited to God but includes our neighbors. Neighbor love also becomes habituated and shapes a person's character. The supreme love of God orders all our lesser, but nonetheless important, loves. To love a neighbor, not as an abstraction but as another person, requires that we know what his or her particular good might be. And to know the good of the other requires, as Iris Murdoch insists, unselfing in order to be truly attentive to the needs and good of the other. But how can we become habitually unselfed? The mundane is, or can be, remarkably proficient in forming attentive habits, because of its routine and repetitive qualities. Through common relationships and activities, we prepare ourselves to practice the virtues required of neighbor love.

The chapters in part 2 and part 3 examine some of these ordinary relationships and activities, but briefly noting one of each may serve to illustrate at this juncture how the mundane may prepare and exhibit neighbor love. First, friendship is a common relationship. Most people have at least one or two friends. A friend is not an object to be manipulated or exploited. We do not, or at least should not, choose our friends solely on the basis of how they might benefit our ambitions. Friendship entails mutuality; it is a reciprocal relationship of giving and receiving. Such reciprocity, however, is not an exact exchange: I'll give you a compliment if you give me one. Rather, over time friends come to know each other through a mutual unfolding of themselves as disclosed in conversations, deeds, and shared activities. To understand this unfolding, and over time to contribute to it, requires attentiveness, an unselfing to allow the other to be other. Over time, an ordinary friendship may evolve into a relationship of deep trust and steadfast caring, preparatory work for practicing the virtues.

Second, there is the mundane activity of shopping. Shopping is often disparaged as profligate self-indulgence. Admittedly, there is little to praise in the mindless consumerism seemingly driven by the mantra "I shop, therefore I am." But shopping is not as hedonistic as its critics often charge. Shopping is never an entirely self-gratifying activity. Even the most self-indulgent shopper benefits others. When I buy that most exquisite single-malt whiskey, I help keep distillers, distributors, and merchants employed; I make a modest contribution to their material wellbeing as I indulge my epicurean longing. Shopping always benefits more than one party, and in the absence of shopping, our material wellbeing would be greatly diminished. Moreover, we do not always shop for ourselves. Buying a gift for someone is an obvious example. When we purchase food, we may have a number of other people in mind, such as members of our household or dinner guests. We buy clothes and toys for children, or spend money to repair plumbing to keep the house comfortable for everyone living in it. And in these exchanges, we not only attend to the physical needs of others but also try to obtain something for them that they will enjoy, perhaps even treasure. We take the time to find just the right gift. Shopping can be a small act of neighbor love, and preparation for practicing the virtues that make us habitually loving people.

Common relationships and mundane activities help us adopt a perceptive and receptive locus. In attending to a relationship or activity, attention is directed toward the other or the task at hand rather than toward oneself. We perceive what is required of us in this attending, and in turn receive the outcome of our perception: a need is met; the good of the other is recognized. It is a stance that invites one to unself. At least momentarily, the ego shrinks, allowing one to escape, however briefly, the self-absorbed enclave. Instead of trying to master a situation or another person to satisfy oneself, a space is created that allows the self and the other to simply be.

What I described in the previous paragraph is similar to Oliver O'Donovan's idea of being at rest. It is worth quoting him at length. To be at rest requires

restraint of competitive self-assertion, acceptance of others' activities and initiatives, flexibility in waiting upon them, and readiness to give them time and space. They describe a moment when the urgent need to act is postponed in the interests of others' actions. This is a practical disposition, not one of inert passivity, but one of self-restraint rather than initiative, affirmative encouragement rather than competition. It is not that the sphere of action has been left behind for contemplation; rather, inaction has been drawn into the scope of the active disposition, which now extends its scope to include the activities of other people.[51]

This space that encourages unselfing is akin to what Edwards identified as general benevolence and to what O'Donovan calls "'resting in' others' labors."[52] To be at rest is to be in a field in which the virtues—especially the theological virtues of faith, hope, and love—may take root and bear fruit.

Counterintuitively, being at rest permits us to play or to be playful. The importance of play should never be underestimated. Historically, play has been offered as an antidote to acedia because play draws us out from ourselves.[53] Being playful requires give-and-take, freeing ourselves from obsessively pursuing an interest. Moreover, play pervades virtually every aspect of life. In addition to being inherently enjoyable, playing encourages social interaction rather than solitude, depends on imagination, undergirds formative mythologies, and is foundational to a civilization.[54] Most importantly, playfulness aligns us properly with what is serious. That which is most serious (God, for instance) should be responded to playfully. Johan Huizinga writes, "Play is a thing by itself. The play-concept as such is of a higher order than is seriousness. For seriousness seeks to exclude play, whereas play can very well include seriousness."[55]

Admittedly, play is often centered on competition. Competing is not necessarily a brutal or combative enterprise. Good play is ordered to rules, however formal or informal they might be. The rules provide a structure enabling competitors to be properly playful. Although playing is ideally liberating, it nonetheless requires order to be efficacious. Granted, competition entails winners and losers, and here a cautionary note must be raised. The purpose of playing is not to win but to play. "The passion to win sometimes threatens to obliterate the levity proper to a game."[56] To play *only* to win is to impose a seriousness that excludes playfulness. The rise of modern sport has prompted a decline in play. What could be genuine play often becomes one more exercise

51. O'Donovan, *Entering into Rest*, 2–3.
52. O'Donovan, *Entering into Rest*, 3.
53. See Raposa, *Boredom and the Religious Imagination*, chap. 3; and Snell, *Acedia and Its Discontents*, chap. 6.
54. See Huizinga, *Homo Ludens*.
55. Huizinga, *Homo Ludens*, 45.
56. Huizinga, *Homo Ludens*, 46.

in enlarging the fat relentless ego. On the other hand, when one plays for love of the game, there is an unselfing as one is drawn into, or even loses oneself in, the enchantment of playing. To play well requires adhering to rules, practicing and habituating skills, a process not unlike forming a virtuous life. More strongly put: a life cannot be virtuous if it is devoid of play and playfulness; and in this respect, the mundane and ordinary constitute potentially excellent training facilities.

This training underlies much of Iris Murdoch's fiction. Murdoch has a keen ability to describe the contours of daily life in meticulous and engaging detail. The ordinary items in a room and simple actions of a character that could easily be overlooked are given a subtle prominence. These details drive her plots. In the words of David Gordon, "Murdoch is a wonderfully gifted storyteller but a storyteller of a special kind, one who not only delights us with an abundance of sensuous details, finely observed and resourcefully invented, but also makes the ideas come alive as she does so. The most distinctive quality of her fiction is the way it mythicizes everyday life, making 'spiritual significance' out of imaginary characters and dramatically exciting action."[57] In paying attention to the details, her stories disclose a realistic world populated by ordinary people. "Despite all the beguiling particulars of characterization with which she delights us, her true strength lies in the creation not of lovable characters but of fable-like plots through which a religious vision is articulated."[58]

This vision captures and portrays the mundane circumstances where people spend most of their time and the equally mundane characters who are weak, vulnerable, and morally clumsy. Consequently, one does not frequently encounter wicked characters in her stories. This does not mean that evil is absent from her stories. To the contrary, it unfolds as the most conspicuous feature in all her novels. But it results from deeply flawed, self-absorbed characters who cannot see the world or their neighbors with much clarity: cave-dwellers who see only shadows and illusions, people enslaved to their fat relentless egos. In short, evil results from the kind of people we encounter daily—including, sometimes, in the mirror.

But there are also some rare characters who are genuinely good, and who are also the least visible. These characters "live as if their being is quietly compelled by an inner necessity; they face a contingent world without hungering for form and meaning; they lack self-consciousness and a sense of self-importance; their influence on others is so unapparent as to make them

---

57. Gordon, *Iris Murdoch's Fables of Unselfing*, 1–2.
58. Gordon, *Iris Murdoch's Fables of Unselfing*, 23.

seem almost invisible."[59] These atypical characters are invariably associated with common pursuits such as preparing and sharing meals, with acts of unexpected and gratuitous kindness, with playful detachment. And they are invariably minor characters, floating through the plot, largely unnoticed and unappreciated. Unsurprisingly, they are also the most unselfed characters.

Visiting briefly Murdoch's novel *The Nice and the Good*, we catch a glimpse of these contrasting characters.[60] In this story there are many nice characters. Octavian and Kate Gray, for instance, appear to be a gracious and generous couple who open their spacious estate to guests and residents that they lavish with fine meals and parties. Yet the people they rope into their lives are objects of their imposed self-improvement projects or sources of amusement and gossip. John Ducane is a respected scholar and lawyer and a dedicated public servant. He tells himself that he wants to be good, but he carelessly perpetuates and then clumsily ends an affair with a much younger woman, whom he professes to love but does not know how to love. Octavian, Kate, and John cannot see or treat the other characters as others because they cannot escape themselves. The other is effectively a source of nourishment for egos that must constantly be fed. They are not malicious characters; they are actually quite nice. But they are not good because they cannot see the good of others.

But there are a few good, or almost good, characters. Mary Cassie is a widowed housekeeper. Although she resents her affluent sister and can be a bit cynical at times, she has cared tirelessly for her dying mother, and she enjoys preparing meals for the household, for "they were times of communication, ritualistic forgatherings almost spiritual in their significance."[61] Willy Kast is a refugee scholar living in a cottage on the Gray estate. Having spent the war in Dachau, he is melancholic and often irascible, demanding, and unapproachable. Yet he nonetheless offers insight into the nature of the good, and a scathing indictment of the nice: "'Happiness,' said Willy, 'is a matter of one's most ordinary everyday mode of consciousness being busy and lively and unconcerned with self. To be damned is for one's ordinary everyday mode of consciousness to be unremitting agonizing preoccupation with self.'"[62] Theo is Octavian's older brother. Earlier in his life he gained some clarity about what the good is and what it requires. In response, he tried to become a Buddhist monk but failed miserably, a failure that haunts him. He now lives a quiet and aloof life in search of a single, unifying truth—an overriding love of the good. Theo finally knows the good (a rare occasion in a Murdoch novel), but

59. Gordon, *Iris Murdoch's Fables of Unselfing*, 33.
60. Murdoch, *The Nice and the Good*.
61. Murdoch, *The Nice and the Good*, 14.
62. Murdoch, *The Nice and the Good*, 187.

he is a minor, barely noticeable character. Finally, there are the nine-year-old twins, Edward and Henrietta. They spend much of their time wandering the estate, collecting stones and playing with their dog. When they interact with the other characters, however, they bring a spontaneous jocularity to the scene that eases the heavy burden of unremitting self-awareness that pervades the story. For a few moments, the nice people are unknowingly unselfed.

I conclude this chapter with the twins because playfulness is a vital ingredient of the moral life. Without the ability to play, one cannot be virtuous, for play represents a proper response to what is seriously good. This does not mean that virtue is merely playing a game; rather, it means that vice cannot be effectively resisted in the absence of play. In many respects, vice is an inert, self-absorbing, and self-diminishing seriousness, as seen in the previous discussion of sloth (or acedia). Play draws us out from ourselves. Consequently, if the habituation of the virtues requires playfulness, then one's character cannot be properly formed in its absence. In short, a life that can be said to be good includes being attentive to playing. And good playing requires rules and order, the topic of the next chapter.

CHAPTER 4

Ritual and the Ordering
of Time and Place

On Belonging

I ended the preceding chapter by insisting that play or playfulness is a crucial component of the moral life. I must now explain why. As I mentioned, play requires rules and practicing requisite skills. This ordering, however, does not occur in a vacuum but in specific contexts involving time and place. Playing takes time. If I play a game with someone, I must devote time to the activity. Playing requires a place. I must be somewhere to play a game—even an online game requires that I be some place to use my device. Play makes explicit the inextricable relation between time and place.

This inextricability, in turn, requires ordering. I must set aside time to play a game, which means that I cannot devote time to other activities, such as napping or reading a book. A place must be prepared to play a game: a simple table will do for Scrabble; an elaborate field is needed for baseball. While the game is on, these are devoted places. While people are playing Scrabble, the table cannot be used to prepare a meal; while people are playing baseball, the field cannot be used for parking cars.

The ordering of these times and places often includes informal and formal rituals or ritualistic behavior that simultaneously expresses memory and anticipation. Saturday afternoon, for example, is the designated time for the household Scrabble match. Throughout the preceding week, contestants anticipate being victorious while also recalling previous defeats, an anticipation and recollection expressed, perhaps, through rituals of friendly banter before the game. There may also be the more formal ritual of setting up the table and assigning seats for the competition. For an approaching big baseball game with a notorious rival, in anticipation of winning the game while also remembering past victories and losses, players and fans may repeat activities or dress in ritualistic ways that are almost superstitious. The game itself may be initiated through the formal rituals of announcing the starting lineups and standing and doffing caps to sing the national anthem. In the time and place of play, we remember and we anticipate.

This ritualistic ordering of playful remembrance and anticipation discloses a much broader aspect of human life, for much of our lives are centered on the ordering of time and place, and rightfully so. In the following two sections I say more about time and place and how they are (or should be) related. In the final section I argue that in properly, and therefore playfully, ordering time and place we find our belonging.

Time

As finite and mortal creatures, humans experience time in a linear manner. There is the trajectory of past, present, and future that carries each of us along in its wake. Each person is born, lives awhile, and dies. Each of us has an allotted time, and it eventually runs out.[1] Linear time is a universal reality, although its significance or insignificance is interpreted in myriad ways. To be human is to acknowledge, albeit in differing ways, the linear trajectory of time.

As finite and mortal creatures, humans also experience time in a cyclical manner. Time repeats itself, though imprecisely. Each week begins with a Sunday and ends with a Saturday, week after week, fifty-two times a year, year after year. And each year comprises four repetitious seasons. The cycles of time predate us and will continue on when we are gone. Cyclical time is another universal reality, although its importance or unimportance is deciphered in various ways. But to be human is to acknowledge the cyclical recurrence of time.

Since time is a universal reality, experienced by all people in all times and places, one might presume that it is a commonly understood phenomenon. Not quite. As Saint Augustine discovered, we assume we know what time is until we start to think about it, and then it becomes terribly muddled.[2] Past, present, and future, for instance, appear obvious: what has happened, what

---

1. I owe much of my understanding of our allotted time to Karl Barth. See *Church Dogmatics* III/2.47.
2. See Augustine, *Confessions*, book 11.

is happening, and what will or may happen. But is there really a present? While typing this sentence, I am presumably doing something now, yet every keystroke quickly becomes part of the past. In addition, I am not concentrating on the now because my goal is to finish the sentence, and eventually the paragraph. If there is a "present," it is fleeting—an ephemeral membrane between past and future. There is no substantial present in which we may immerse ourselves. Rather, we live in a murky and shifting mixture of what has been and what shall or may be.

A similar ambiguity pervades cyclical time. We experience time as repetition: we regularly go to sleep, and we regularly wake up. Repetition, however, is not synonymous with exact duplication. No two family dinners, for example, are precisely the same. Yet we place a family dinner in a different category than that of a business dinner with a client. Why? What is the difference? Recurrence and similarity. Family dinners recur, and in doing so establish familiar patterns of similarities. A family dinner often occurs at a prescribed time and place, and expectations emerge regarding what are acceptable topics of conversation. Yet a family dinner does not replicate its predecessors. Menus and conversations vary, but there are sufficient similarities that establish familiar patterns that make each meal identifiable as another family dinner. A dinner with strangers lacks (forgive the pun) a family resemblance. Contrary to Nietzsche, cyclical time is not the eternal recurrence of the same;[3] it is more akin to the recurrence of the similar.

Despite the ambiguity of linear and cyclical time, we must nonetheless order time, otherwise we would have no continuity of identity. But how do we pursue such ordering if there is no real "present" separating past and future and no exact duplication of recurrences? The short answer is *imagination*. To imagine is not to fantasize. Imagination entails the interpretation of real experiences that have occurred or are anticipated. In this respect, memory and expectation are interlocked and mutually informative. Past and future constantly intrude on each other. These imaginative interpretations are admittedly constructs, but they are constructs of something and not invoked ex nihilo.

In the provocative words of David Hogue, we are constantly "remembering the future" and "imagining the past."[4] By this I take him to mean that we do not remember past events in a precise manner, as if we are watching the same film over and over again. Rather, we interpret and revise the past imaginatively. Moreover, our anticipation of the future is pointless if it is cut off from these imaginative interpretations and revisions of the past. According to Hogue,

3. See Nietzsche, *Gay Science*, book 4.
4. See Hogue, *Remembering the Future*.

"life and identity are not limited to the events of history; we constantly live on the cusp between the past and the future."[5] Consequently, memory and imagination are inseparable. "Our imaginations are as essential when we are recalling the past as when we are speculating about or planning for the future. And without memories, our dreams for what may yet be would be empty and impossible. We imagine the past and we remember the future."[6]

I draw upon Hogue in the remainder of this section (perhaps, I fear, even in ways that I do not recognize and acknowledge precisely). Rather than contrasting an imagined past with a remembered future, however, I focus on the past as remembrance and the future as anticipation. Our sense of past is largely one of interpreted memories, recalling and retelling that which has been. But what do we recall and retell? I suggest that it is largely a series of fulfilled and frustrated anticipations. We recall and interpret episodes that fulfill our anticipations (in expected or in surprising ways) and those that frustrate our anticipations (either because of our failures or because of chance events). As Hogue makes clear, this recalling and retelling is subject to constant revision over time because we are always seeing and interpreting events in a new light—often in emotive ways ranging, for instance, from joy and gratitude to regret and bitterness. Cumulatively, over time, these interpreted memories shape our identities. In this respect, remembrance is *recalled anticipation*.

Identity, however, does not remain encased in the past. We also wish to project ourselves into the future; the person I am is not necessarily the one I wish to become. We strive to reshape our identities by undertaking actions or responding to events in which anticipated outcomes may or may not be satisfied for a variety of reasons. These unfolding episodes are added to our reservoirs of (re)interpreted remembrance. It is important to stress that our anticipations of future actions and their outcomes may be new but are usually not novel. Rather, anticipation grows out of remembrance. When we work or play, for example, we remember similar situations, although we anticipate what we judge to be better outcomes than what occurred in the past. This simply affirms the observation that all intentional action attempts to somehow improve one's life, and the outcomes cannot be measured in the absence of memory. What is superior can be assessed only in comparison to what is inferior. Granted, this assessment may prove inaccurate or delusional, but that is due to faulty interpretation. In this respect, anticipation may be understood as *anticipatory remembrance*.

5. Hogue, *Remembering the Future*, 4.
6. Hogue, *Remembering the Future*, 4.

This interplay between recalled anticipation and anticipatory remembrance reinforces the fluidity of linear time as it advances from past to future and the recurrent but inexact similarity experienced in cyclical time. In short, whenever we think about the past, our attention is redirected, in part, to the future because there is no sharp demarcation between these two domains. And, conversely, whenever we anticipate the future, our attention is directed, in part, to the past for the same reason. In cyclical time, we experience the accumulation of recurrent similar events, but we reinterpret their significance over time. In these recurrent cyclical episodes, we encounter both continuity and discontinuity within linear time. For instance, I assume that many readers of this book have participated in a number of Christmas mornings. Over time, how we interpret the significance of this recurrent morning changes; our joy and wonder as a child is not the same as what we experience as we grow older. Additionally, innovations, both chosen and not, in how Christmas morning is celebrated add a dissimilar component: the family may choose to sing "Jingle Bells" instead of "O Come, All Ye Faithful"; the illness or death of a loved one may create a jolting absence. In cyclical time, we encounter both continuity and discontinuity between remembrance and anticipation in linear time.

But how do recalled anticipation and anticipatory remembrance help us to order time? We may turn to Christian thought and practice, and to the more mundane experiences of aging and the life of a household, to gain some helpful hints.

In Christian theology, *eschatology* refers to "last things." It is, of course, a highly speculative branch of theological discourse, since no one other than God knows the destiny of creation in any detailed way. It is nonetheless an essential area of doctrine because it addresses the end or *telos* of the gospel. Yet if there are last things that should command our attention, then there are also first things and things in between that are equally important. Christianity is a religion deeply grounded in linear time or history, such as the history of Israel and the church. This helps to account for the largely narrative structure of the gospel, for it is an unfolding story of origin, destiny, and what lies between. According to Paul Ramsey, "The Prologue of St. John's Gospel is the Christian story of creation, our chief creation story, primary over Genesis."[7] Christ, as the incarnate Word of God, is the Alpha and Omega, the beginning and end of God's creation (see Rev. 21:6). This incarnate origin and destiny summarizes the extraordinary acts of God noted in chapter 1, and it infuses the virtues of faith, hope, and love in the trajectories of created order

7. Ramsey, *Speak Up*, 21.

over time (as summarized in the preceding chapter). Anything we might say speculatively and incompletely about creation's Omega point forces us to remember Jesus's anticipatory life, death, and resurrection. And, conversely, anything we might say interpretively about Jesus prompts us to look ahead to what he anticipated in his teaching and ministry. As Christians, we move through time toward its end. In an admittedly insufficient analogy, the gospel is somewhat like a symphony being directed by God through its movements and to its eventual finale.

There are some rough parallels with the more common and less grandiose experience of aging. A lifetime takes place in linear time. To restate the obvious: every human being has a beginning and an end, and a relatively short or long passage of time in between. We all have personal histories that unfold in the flux of remembrance and anticipation. Moreover, we have a sense, either vague or intense, that our personal histories are parts of a larger one that both precedes and outlasts us. As Hannah Arendt puts is, "To be alive means to live in a world that preceded one's own arrival and will survive one's own departure."[8] If in linear time there is a "present," perhaps it is the time of being alive, and the past is that time when we were not, and the future is when we will be no longer be. As human beings, we move through our allotted time toward its appointed end. Ironically, it is in being attentive to the common traits of one's finitude and mortality that we catch an iconic glimpse of creation's extraordinary origin and destiny within a time bracketed by eternity. Within this symphony, we each play an instrument, well or badly, for a while.

Within this linear trajectory we also experience time in a cyclical manner. The church's liturgical calendar captures this repetition. The church year begins with the expectation of Advent and joy of Christmas, which anticipate the solemnity of Lent and joy of Easter. Year in and year out, Christians revisit and recall the pivotal moments of their faith. The church calendar ends with the longest season of Ordinary time. It is also the season that receives the least amount of theological attention. I am not a liturgical theologian, but I suspect that one reason for this inattention is that unlike the other seasons, Ordinary time is neither festive nor solemn. Its lessons and hymns focus on themes that are, well, ordinary. It is the season of the long, hard grind of waiting. We learn to wait for the *parousia*, and we learn this lesson through liturgical enactments of recalled anticipation of the incarnation and anticipatory remembrance of Jesus's promised return.

The rhythms of a household also capture the repetitive cycles of time. Sustaining a household requires daily, weekly, and periodic activities. Clothes

8. Arendt, *Life of the Mind*, 1:20.

must be washed, bathrooms cleaned, meals prepared, appliances maintained. These are dull, monotonous activities that are nonetheless crucial, because attending to the basic material needs of household members helps them to flourish. In the absence of these repetitive, mundane activities, a household is not a suitable habitat for its inhabitants. And through recurring activities we learn to wait—not to wait for the end of a household, but to wait on its members.

Cyclical time discloses the need for ritual and ritualistic behavior for ordering time more broadly. The liturgy utilizes formal rituals—spoken, sung, and embodied—in denoting the emphasis of a season or particular service. There are good reasons why hallelujah is not uttered during Lent and why the Eucharist is not celebrated without prior confession and forgiveness. Although ritual recurs, it is not mere repetition. We experience the season of the ecclesial calendar differently as we grow older, and how rituals are performed changes over time. Unlike the symphony of linear time, cyclical time is more like a fugue: recurring rhythms in the background are accompanied by slight variations in the foreground.

Households also have their rituals, albeit often less formal ones. How clothes are washed and how meals are prepared often follow prescribed patterns of repeated behavior. There are certainly variations in routine: eating at seven rather than six, washing the clothes on Thursday rather than Wednesday. But you nevertheless eat meals and wash the clothes day in and day out, week after week. Some readers may object that, given their highly mobile lifestyles, they have no time or need for such ritualistic behavior. But even the most mobile person has rituals. Think of the rituals performed at the airport, in the hotel room, during meetings, and upon returning home for however brief a time. These commonplace household rituals are somewhat akin to jazz. There is plenty of improvisation, but it all takes place against a steady beat or rhythm.

All this talk about time, however, is incomplete or even vacuous in the absence of place. For we can experience linear and cyclical time only by being in place.

Place

By *place* I mean a physical or material location. A place may be a natural object, such as a mountain or beach, or it may be a human artifact, such as a building or garden. Place is a fixed locale that delineates where we are. Moreover, we are in place within time, and time is marked by being in place. The passage of linear time within a place may be relatively brief (as in an afternoon hike through the woods) or relatively lengthy (as in living in a home). Cyclical time is also experienced while being in place: worshiping in the same church each Sunday morning or the annual Thanksgiving dinner at grandmother's house. Place and time are inseparable, because we cannot mark time without being in some place and we can only be in a place at some time.[9]

The incarnation reinforces the inseparability and necessity of place and time. The Word became flesh in a particular place, a Roman province in what is now called the Middle East, and at a particular time, a little over two thousand years ago. It could not be otherwise if God was to enter a temporal creation, for place and time are prevalent features of the domain where mortals dwell. Yet subsequent Christian teaching and practice inspired by the incarnation make a surprising move. Rather than solidifying a static understanding of place and time, Christian teaching and practice emphasize their variability and malleability. Christians, for instance, are not permanently in a fixed place. They can be anywhere, for Christ is present wherever two or three are gathered in his name. But they gather somewhere, and although they may gather at any time, they gather at specific times.

In short, humans live out their lives by being in time and in place. It is time and place that situate finite and mortal creatures within a temporal and material creation. Much of this being situated is centered on the ordinary. Again, the incarnation affirms the mundane quality of creaturely life. Although the incarnation is an extraordinary event,[10] its aftermath is remarkably fixed on the commonplace. Jesus is born, an occurrence he shares with every person. He interacts with others in such ordinary places as the marketplace and the household. His teaching, especially in the parables, often focuses on the mundane: parental love, work, caring for others, flowers.[11] Most of his miracles are performed with commonplace outcomes in mind. Although a few of the miracles attributed to Jesus are out of the ordinary,[12] most are directed toward basic needs, such as feeding the hungry and healing the sick,[13] events we often witness without assigning any miraculous significance to them.

I think, perhaps, we have a tendency to interpret Jesus's life and ministry in overly dramatic terms, effectively making him a larger-than-life character, cut off from the very creaturely life in which the Word he embodies became incarnate. And in doing so, we lose much of the iconic and formative significance

9. See Casey, *Getting Back into Place*.
10. See chap. 1.
11. See, e.g., Luke 15:11–32; Matt. 20:1–16; Luke 10:25–37; Luke 12:27.
12. See, e.g., Matt. 14:22–33.
13. See, e.g., John 6:1–14; Matt. 15:29–31.

of the mundane. Through Jesus's life and ministry, we catch a glimpse of divine grace, and in following Jesus we become habitually gracious people. Perhaps in the Gospels, the mundane is not background but an understated foreground in which the gospel itself unfolds.

Once again, the rituals of the liturgy and ritualistic practices of the household can direct our attention toward this understated foreground. The eucharistic liturgy, for example, is focused on the body and blood of Christ and the attendant acts of eating and drinking. Eating and drinking: nothing could be more conventional. The music, words, and bodily movements of the rituals employed direct our attention to this central mystery of our faith that is given to us through the undramatic vessels of bread and wine. And if our attention wanders, then we miss the iconic moment of seeing in these commonplace elements a divine love and grace that permeates the entire created order from beginning to end. Through a loaf and chalice, we catch a glimpse, however fleeting, of what Michel Quoist calls the "long throb of love towards Love eternal."[14]

Frequent participation in the eucharistic liturgy is also formative. The rituals surrounding this sacrament repeat a steady pattern of confession, repentance, forgiveness, and absolution. Through our repetitive and ritualistic participation in this pattern, we (hopefully) become habitually forgiving people—people who generously offer forgiveness to our neighbors and eagerly and gratefully receive it as well. In the eucharistic liturgy, we are reminded that as finite and mortal creatures we are situated in time and place, complete with all the mundane details this status entails.

The household is also an understated foreground that is, at least potentially, formative and iconic. The daily chores required in maintaining a household are insufferably dull and repetitive. Although they usually do not demand sustained concentration, a modicum of attention is nonetheless needed. Without due attentiveness, the task at hand may be done poorly or haphazardly. In preparing a family meal, for instance, ease and nutrition are certainly considerations, but so too are the tastes of those sharing the meal. A dinner composed of unpalatable dishes is not an event to be savored, nor is it likely to promote fellowship around the table. Additionally, one must attend to the preparatory details. I know from personal experience that allowing one's mind to wander while reading a recipe can result in something inedible, and, more ominously, given the lethal potential of most kitchen utensils, there is the risk of wounded fingers. To maintain a household, you need to pay attention to what you are doing.

14. Quoist, *Prayers*, 16.

We undertake these chores largely in response to the necessities endemic to being embodied creatures. The condition of physical environments matters, not only for the sake of surviving but also for the sake of flourishing. People tend to do better in habitats that are clean and tidy rather than dirty and messy. There is much to be said in favor of making the bed every morning and cleaning the bathroom regularly. Admittedly, we often accomplish mundane tasks for the sake of our own wellbeing, especially if there is no one else willing or able to clean up after us. We attend to our own needs, and there is nothing selfish or wrong about that. But, at least in part, we are also attending to the wellbeing of neighbors, those with whom we share a home, or guests. The ubiquity of the mundane is inescapable for finite beings who together are situated in time and in place.

Although it may be conceded that the mundane forms useful habits enabling human flourishing within a temporal realm of necessity, how can it possibly be iconic? Do we catch a glimmer of something more significant while making the bed or cleaning the toilet? Yes, or at least the potential is there. In being attentive to the commonplace activities that promote our own flourishing, we may also be tending to the wellbeing of others. Consequently, the daily, mundane tasks we routinely undertake are acts, albeit modest acts, of neighbor love. In being attentive to the ordinary, we discover that we are bound to one another in countless ways, and these bonds constitute our being. The long throb of love to Love eternal that Quoist mentions is intertwined with a throb of love to neighbor. This is why our lives as finite and mortal creatures in time and in place are incomplete without also including belonging.

Belonging

We are not created to be alone. The biblical creation story is quite clear that Adam is not complete until joined by Eve (see Gen. 2:18–24). To be always alone would make one less than fully human. Humans are creatures who flourish in the company of others. Without the third person plural, our lives are indescribable and unimaginable. Being alone, however, is not synonymous with solitude. Indeed, a capacity for solitude is necessary for healthy personal and social development.[15] But solitude is a temporary withdrawal or distancing from others rather than their absence. Even in our solitude, our thoughts are often of others, both living and dead. Our solitude acknowledges and affirms our need and desire for fellowship; to be with and present to others. Humans belong with one another.

15. See Turkle, *Alone Together*.

What exactly is this belonging? First and foremost, it entails mutuality. As hinted above, we do not find ourselves in ourselves, but in our interactions with others. We find ourselves in our unselfing. But this does not mean that we can or should ignore our personal wellbeing or soul care. A vital inner life is crucial to our mutuality.[16] Yet the core of our personal being is formed, or should be formed, in relationship to God and neighbor. For how else could we fulfill the two great commands? Our lives are interwoven in a myriad of differing relationships: spouses, parents and children, friends, colleagues, strangers, producers and consumers, fellow citizens. Although each of these spheres of affiliation differs in respect to purpose and enduring commitment, they all involve mutuality and reciprocity—a give-and-take appropriate to the relationship, at times roughly symmetrical and at times highly asymmetrical (for reasons that range from valid to capricious). Without these affiliations, however deep or shallow they might be, we cannot belong—for there are no points of reference demarcating the social bonds that define, at least in part, who we are and aspire to become. Without these bonds, we become, in effect, free-floating specters rather than the embodied and finite creatures we were created to be.

Belonging is timely. There are two principal connotations to how I am using *timely* as a concept. First, the word *timely* connotes immediacy. We belong with others over time within shared places. The length of time may be relatively long (such as with parents, children, or spouses) or relatively brief (such as with friends, workplace colleagues, customers, or clients). In both instances, this mutual belonging changes over time: a married couple celebrating their golden anniversary is not quite the same as they were on their wedding night, and friends have come and gone over their fifty years of marriage. The fluidity of belonging also appears in a given place, again for relatively long or short periods of time. A married couple may have lived in the same house for fifty years or may have moved often; one woman may work in her family business for her entire career, while another changes jobs frequently throughout her lifetime. Human flourishing depends on immediate and countless interactions with others on a timely basis, interactions that are often unacknowledged and unappreciated but are nonetheless vital. Humans were created to belong with one another through a series of given and chosen relationships, and in the absence or neglect of these relationships, the quality of human life is diminished. There is no more destructive falsehood pervading late modernity than the lie that humans are autonomous beings and that,

---

16. See Murdoch, *Metaphysics as a Guide to Morals*, esp. chap. 9; see also Arendt, *Life of the Mind*, vol. 1, chap. 4.

therefore, whatever belonging they may enjoy or exploit is nothing more than a fabrication for which time and place are irrelevant. Hence the lie that the internet and, especially, social networks promote human flourishing.[17]

Second, the word *timely* connotes both continuity and discontinuity. Although relationships endure over time within shared places, the character of such immediacy does not remain fixed. Although the generational structure of the parent-child relationship, for instance, cannot be altered, the relationship between parents and offspring changes. Adult children should not be treated by their parents as if they were still in grade school. Moreover, levels of reciprocity and dependency change as parents and children grow older or face debilitating illnesses or injuries. Parents and children relate differently over time, but they always remain related as parents and children.

There is a similar pattern of continuity and discontinuity with respect to work. Most people spend most of their adult lives working either inside or outside the household (and their work almost always involves at least a bit of both). Work seems to be a necessary given of the human condition. But how we work changes, often in reaction to technological innovations or other economic forces beyond our control. Punching a clock may give way to telecommuting. More dramatically, those whose livelihood once depended on repairing typewriters were forced to learn a new trade. And within some households, vacuuming is now done by a robot. As humans, we spend a great deal of time working, but what we do and how we do it evolves in unexpected ways.

In the preceding paragraphs, I have argued that time and place are crucial factors in the promotion of human flourishing, because as embodied creatures our belonging is necessarily mutual and timely. I must now add an important caveat: although time and place are crucial, they are *not* absolutely essential to our mutual and timely belonging *in Christ*. Scripture and doctrine are clear that humans are social creatures who belong with one another. Yet we are often surprised by the people with whom we belong for either short or lengthy periods of time. We may, for example, choose our spouses and friends, but we do not choose our parents, children, siblings, fellow workers, and fellow citizens, or the strangers we encounter. And learning to love people not of our choosing is both the exquisite wonder and the vexing challenge of being human, encapsulating both the grace and the tribulation of neighbor love lying at the core of Christian belief and practice. That is an important message to remember and exhibit in a culture that often succumbs to the falsehood

---

17. See Carr, *Shallows*; Ferguson, *Great Degeneration*; Jackson, *Distracted*; and Turkle, *Reclaiming Conversation*.

that human flourishing is predicated on unfettered choice. Humans need to be fettered by people they do not choose.

Additionally, as embodied and social creatures, humans belong somewhere, but almost anywhere will do, as attested by Scripture and doctrine. Even in its Diaspora, Israel remains a covenant people. And Christians have never been a territorial people. Rather, Christians are a pilgrim people, never entirely at home at any time or place because their eventual destination is on the other side of eternity. Consequently, they are free to traverse the world in response to God's calling concerning where they should be and with whom they should belong for however short or long a period of time might be required. On this lifelong pilgrimage they might be accompanied by other pilgrims, but they will certainly encounter a wide range of neighbors that God commands them to love. In acknowledging the proper significance of time and place in respect to belonging, we discover that although human life necessarily occurs in particular times and places, human flourishing ultimately depends on water and the Spirit rather than blood and soil. This, again, is the challenge of neighbor love, and remembrance and anticipation, as discussed above, goes a long way in helping us to order this love as pilgrims.

This assistance can again be seen in the ritualistic structure of both liturgy and family. The liturgy portrays events whose significance is timeless and universal yet grounded in time and place. For instance, Christmas focuses on the unfolding story of the incarnation (the Word is made flesh) while the crucifixion is the centerpiece of Holy Week (Jesus, the bearer of the incarnate Word, dies for the sins of the world). For Christian faith, both seasons encapsulate and portray key theological themes that are valid for all people always and everywhere. Yet Christmas would lose its evocative power if no mention were made of a baby born in Bethlehem during a census taken by the emperor Tiberius, and Holy Week makes little sense in the absence of a trial and execution conducted under the authority of the Roman prelate Pontius Pilate. Remembrance and anticipation are deeply embedded in both of these seasons. Christmas recalls the anticipation of Advent while also directing attention toward Holy Week, which in turn is bracketed by the hope of both Advent and Easter. Although these pivotal pieces of the story are thoroughly enmeshed in particular events that occurred at particular times, they have been celebrated for over two millennia by Christians almost anywhere and everywhere at the appointed times.

A similar, albeit less dramatic, ritualistic structure of remembrance and anticipation is embedded in a family. Many, if not most, families have experienced pivotal events that helped shape a shared identity, in respect to both who family members have been and to who they hope to become. Some of these formative events involve joyous occasions such as weddings, births, or major accomplishments at school or work. Others may entail great sadness or a sense of loss: divorce, prolonged illness, debilitating injury, or death. Each of these events incorporates anticipation and remembrance that merge and evolve over time. Parents, for example, might anticipate who their new child will become in what for them is the future, and their grandchildren might in turn remember who that child—their own parent, now dead—became in what for them is the past.

Birth and death are commonplace experiences, shared by all people everywhere. It is important to emphasize that where these formative familial events occurred is not important, but also to be attentive to fact that they happened somewhere at some time. Family stories do not begin with "once upon a time" but with a particular occasion that occurred at a specific time and has reverberated ever since, perhaps even across the generations, forming a lineage. The coming to be and passing away of generations within a family is strikingly mundane. Yet in their ritualistic ordering they also become, however fleetingly and puzzlingly, icons disclosing the pervasive love at the origin and end of creation.

We may visit, briefly, Marilynne Robinson's Gilead quartet[18] to gain some greater clarity on how the interaction between time and place and remembrance and anticipation shapes a sense of belonging. The setting of these three novels is Gilead, a small town in Iowa. The story is about the relationship within and between two families, those of the Reverend John Ames and the Reverend Robert Boughton. John and Boughton are both in their seventies and have been lifelong friends. Except for some stints away at college and seminary, both have lived and worked their entire lives in Gilead. When John was young he was married for a few years until his wife died in childbirth, along with his daughter. He has recently married a much younger woman, Lila, and they have a six-year-old son. Boughton is now a widower after a long and happy marriage, and he has several grown sons and daughters.

The principal lightning rod of the story is Jack Boughton, Robert's son. Jack was born shortly after the tragic loss of John Ames's first wife and daughter. Boughton had named his son after his friend to comfort him. But Jack has never been much of a comfort. John is not fond of his namesake, finding him devious and untrustworthy. Jack was always a bit of a miscreant, bringing grief to his family, especially his father. As a young man he left Gilead under a scandalous cloud. Jack is now in his early forties and estranged, against his

---

18. This quartet consists of the books *Gilead*, *Home*, *Lila*, and *Jack*. But as I have yet to read *Jack*, I will limit my discussion here to the other three volumes.

will, from his common-law wife and their child. He is attempting to return to Gilead, presumably to make amends with his family—or, more likely, to fulfill his mother's prophecy that he "was born to break his father's heart."[19]

More than one heart is broken in Jack's attempt to return home, and the story of this unsuccessful prodigal is told from three different perspectives. *Gilead*, the first novel, is narrated by John Ames. John is feeling the physical strains of growing old and knows that for him time is running out. He wonders why a pretty, young woman married him; and they both wonder why he has to be "so damn old."[20] He envies Lila because she is much more at peace with the world than he is. John is also writing a diary for his son, whom he will never see become a man. It is a mixture of anecdotal family history, observations on his son's daily activities as a child, and advice. John warns his son, for instance, to stay away from Jack, for "he is not a man of the highest character."[21] John is not at all pleased that Jack has returned. He worries what ill effect this might have on his friend Boughton, who is in poor health. His conversations with his namesake have been short and icy, and when Jack attends a Sunday morning service at John's church, he is offended by the sermon because he feels it is directed against him personally.

The narrator of the second novel, *Home*, is Glory, Jack's younger sister. Glory has already returned home, partly to care for her father, but she is also destitute. Glory had left Gilead to attend college and stayed away for thirteen years, teaching English literature. She was engaged, but her fiancé left abruptly, taking all of Glory's savings with him. She worries about what she has done with her life. When she was young, Glory believed she shared a special bond with Jack, but that feeling has faded over time. Jack calls to tell her he will be returning, and she is angry with her brother for all the work that will be required to get the house in shape for his impending stay, and for the upset the anticipation is already causing for their father. Yet she controls her anger in the hope that some reconciliation might be achieved to end twenty years of estrangement between father and son. It is a vain hope, however, for her father's growing senility prods unrealistic expectations, and Jack is in no condition to receive the kindness that has been prepared for him. Jack's stay creates, as feared, a great deal of emotional turmoil. The relationship between Jack and his father grows increasingly tense, and Jack is deeply hurt by a perceived slight that he detects in one of John's sermons. Jack finally tells Glory that he has sent for his "wife" and child, because Iowa permits

19. Robinson, *Home*, 56.
20. Robinson, *Gilead*, 50.
21. Robinson, *Gilead*, 125.

interracial marriage, but he knows they cannot remain in Gilead and he must leave. Despite the trouble Jack creates, Glory cannot remain angry with her brother, and she is heartbroken when she tells her seriously demented father that Jack has left—again.

The final story, *Lila*, is told from Lila's perspective. Lila stumbled into Gilead with no intention of staying very long. She was a neglected and abandoned child and has spent most of her life on the road, finding temporary employment and equally temporary friends. Yet one Sunday morning she walks into John Ames's church and finds herself listening attentively to his sermon. Lila keeps coming to church each Sunday and talks with John a great deal in between. Eventually John baptizes Lila, and, much to her surprise, she falls in love with this old preacher, they are married, and shortly after they have a son. She is hard-pressed to explain how this happened. Lila spends a good deal of time learning the mundane details of running a household and being a mother, skills she knows will serve her well when she becomes, probably sooner rather than later, a single parent. She is also a bit perplexed by the congregation and community she now finds herself to be a part of. The natives are mostly friendly, or at least courteous, but they do not quite know how to relate to this unconventional preacher's wife, and Lila is equally at a loss, for she has no history with this place where she now finds herself, and there may or may not be a future there as well. Lila knows she can leave anytime she chooses, and she finds such knowledge reassuring; staying in place is unfamiliar and at times uncomfortable.

These personal misgivings and troubled relationships are punctuated by the monotonous routines underlying the lives of the characters. John spends most of each day, except Sundays, praying, studying, preparing an upcoming sermon, napping, writing the dairy for his son, sharing a meal and spending time with Lila. Except for an occasional pastoral visit with a parishioner, this pattern is rarely interrupted. Glory performs the daily tasks required for running a household: cleaning, washing, cooking. But she also has other habits, such as daily Bible reading, that structure her day. For Glory, faith is largely unreflective habit, loyalty, and reverence. She does not describe herself as pious, yet "she did not know what it meant to be pious. She had never been anything else."[22] Lila spends most of her time learning the new and unaccustomed skills of being a wife, mother, and homemaker. She is often perplexed and bemused by both the irksome and the reassuring patterns emanating from a steady life. She especially enjoys gardening. Jack's life is ostensibly devoid of any daily continuity. He seems to bounce from one crisis to the next.

---

22. Robinson, *Home*, 109.

It might appear that Robinson's quartet is bleak and boring reading, little more than a failed and stilted sequel to the prodigal son parable. Not true! The stories are laced with unexpected moments of love and grace. For example, Jack eventually tells John about his wife, Della, and their son. But they are not legally married because she lives in a state that prohibits interracial marriage, and her family loathes Jack because he is White. They have found another man willing to marry Della and adopt her son. Jack admits that his return to Gilead had been a silly attempt to set things right, and he has never confessed this story to his father and sister. It will be left to John to tell them after Jack leaves and ask them not to judge him. But why not judge him, since once again he has hurt those who love him? In that relatively brief encounter with his namesake, John learns something about grace that reduces life to its essentials. He discovers that grace manifests itself in a variety of ways. No one should be as lonely as Jack. John is sitting with Jack waiting for the bus, slips him some money, and offers a blessing: "'Lord, bless John Ames Boughton, this beloved son and brother and husband and father.' Then he sat back and looked at me as if he were waking out of a dream."[23]

There are other such moments and insights interwoven throughout Robinson's quartet, which collectively help illumine the human condition, or at least some of its important aspects. Two observations concerning these disclosures, particularly in respect to love and grace: First, these insights are recognized because of prior habits predisposing one to see these unexpected moments. It is the repetitious nature of the mundane that enables it to also be iconic. John's daily study of the Bible and theology helps prepare him to see grace in a concrete way, and Glory's unnamed piety serves as a similar lens. The most poignant scenes in this three-part story do not so much disrupt the commonplace patterns of daily living as grow out from and reinforce them. These formative habits help the characters see what others in the story need or require, and these habitual actions sometimes reveal something deeper and unexpected that would not be recognized in the monotonous and mundane. Collectively these habits and practices help fashion "an earned innocence . . . which is as much to be honored as the innocence of children."[24] It is telling that the one character who is never able to see that he is loved or to accept forgiveness, and who in turn is clumsy in offering love and forgiveness, is Jack.

Second, these revelatory insights are embedded in particular times and places. The town of Gilead is the background that makes the quartet explicable. The histories and aspirations of the characters are deposited in this

23. Robinson, *Gilead*, 241.
24. Robinson, *Gilead*, 40.

place over time. John and Boughton were born, lived, and will presumably die here. Glory's pious habits help her remember her home, where she is from.[25] Even Lila, who was not born in this place and has been grafted into its time only recently, has chosen to make her lot in Gilead—at least for the time being. Again, it is Jack who is most estranged from this place and who cannot find the wherewithal to reenter it. Yet even his exilic status cannot sever entirely his bonds, for it is from Gilead that bonds of love and grace from Glory and John radiate and continue to embrace him wherever he might wander. As Glory discovers, hope and patience take a lot out of her, but she nonetheless insists that "the soul finds its own home if it ever has a home at all."[26] That is her hope, her prayer, for her brother.

Gilead, however, should not be romanticized. It is not a perfect place. John and Boughton often display a parochialism that drives Lila, at times, mad. Glory is horrified when she learns that she will inherit the family house when her father dies. She has no desire to live the remainder of her life in Gilead, but she cannot sell the house, or even change it in any way, because of her siblings' expectations. She will be stuck in Gilead, and she is afraid she will never have a life of her own. It is not entirely Jack's fault that he has been exiled from Gilead and forced to become a nomadic wanderer. He, and John, know he can never return to Gilead, at least not with his wife and son; they would not be welcomed. Years ago, Gilead had a Black community, but this community quickly left after one of its members was accused, falsely, of some crimes. Although Gilead provides a place for mutual and timely belonging, there are limits to who can be included.

I have lingered for a while in Gilead because it offers a fitting transition. In this chapter and the preceding ones, I have argued that humans are not autonomous beings but are bound together by myriad social bonds. These bonds are exercised through our callings and vocations, our practicing and habituation of the virtues, and our mutual and timely sense of belonging. Most importantly, we come to fashion these bonds through the common-place and ordinary workings and rituals of daily life, and these formative habits and acts teach us such important lessons as the need for unselfing in serving our neighbors. Through the mundane we also gain some clarity on the extraordinary gift of love that God has given us in creation, incarnation, and resurrection. Gilead reminds us how ordinary and fragile are the bonds that make us human and humane. And Gilead also reminds us that they are bonds of imperfection. In this earthly life we are not bound together with

25. See Robinson, *Home*, 101–2.
26. Robinson, *Home*, 282.

angels, but with fellow sinners who often frustrate and disappoint. Yet I am suggesting that in these same, imperfect bonds lies both the challenge and the joy of being the human creatures that God has created and redeemed, and it is in and through the mundane that we are both formed, in part, to take on the challenge and to be occasionally embraced by joy. I am cognizant that to make this suggestion convincing, I need to say much more about the commonplace and mundane. And I intend to do just that in the remainder of this book.

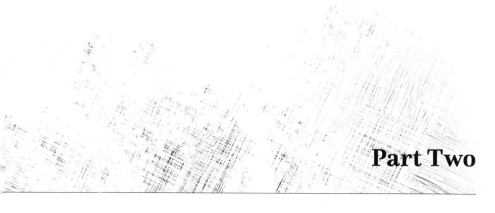

Part Two

EVERYDAY RELATIONSHIPS

CHAPTER 5

Neighbors

Neighbors are unexceptional; we see them every day. But who exactly is my neighbor? As Scripture demonstrates, this is an old and elusive question. When Jesus is asked this question, he doesn't answer it directly; rather, he tells the Good Samaritan parable (see Luke 10:25–37). This familiar story nonetheless offers some helpful insights into neighborly relations—that it includes, for example, the mutual meeting of needs. All neighbors, whoever they might be, are in need, and good neighbors address those needs when they are able to do so. Yet this insight does not go very far in defining who exactly my neighbor is. Nor is any precise definition forthcoming in this chapter, because the very concept of neighbor is vague. There are many different types of neighbors. Some are in close proximity, and others are far away. Some are known to us, and others are unknown. Some of our neighbors in need are within our power to help, while others are not. And so on. Virtually anyone and everyone is potentially a neighbor. It is impossible to make all these particular people fit into one definition. Nevertheless, God commands us to love our neighbors. In what follows I examine some general themes regarding what this command requires of us, setting the stage for the following chapters that concentrate on relationships with particular kinds of neighbors.

Neighbors Everywhere

Every day we are awash in a great sea of neighbors. This defies common sense. The range of people we, as late moderns, regard as neighbors is not very large; it is a small pond at best. Neighbors are those people who live in our neighborhood or apartment building, and we may expand that net to include some friends, workplace colleagues, and fellow church members. We tend to assume that neighbors are a small collection of people who share either a nearby locale or a common set of interests. Our neighbors certainly include this small cadre, but this cadre reflects an impoverished understanding of what being a neighbor means, for it excludes such people as strangers, enemies, those we would prefer to ignore, and those we have never met. These categories, however, do not make the people we place in them any less our neighbors. Being a neighbor does not necessarily depend on physical proximity, shared interests, familiarity, or likeability.

Karl Barth captures, rather nicely, the expansive range of neighborly relationships.[1] According to Barth, relating to neighbors, in conjunction with marriage and parenthood,[2] is an important avenue to finding one's freedom in fellowship. Beyond the family, there are broader spheres of affinity in which humans define their being. Humans, however, are related to one another not only generally but also specifically through particular associations and societies. Consequently, we routinely encounter familiar, often nearby neighbors and unfamiliar, often distant neighbors. These encounters are simply part of being human, for they form bonds of mutual and timely belonging.

More importantly for Barth, it is engaging unfamiliar neighbors that expands both human fellowship and human freedom. Encountering unfamiliar people imposes constraints. One must be cautious in the face of new patterns of conduct, customs, values, and the like. The encounter may also lead to "homesickness," a longing to be with one's own people.[3] Barth admits that such a longing is natural and understandable, but it must not block God's command to love our neighbors, especially distant and unfamiliar neighbors. We must understand formative historical and geographical features in dynamic rather than static terms. "One's own people in its location cannot and must not be a wall but a door."[4] Paradoxically, it is through both immersing ourselves in our own people and walking through the door that we differentiate ourselves from other neighbors, both strengthening our fellowship with others and enlarging our scope of freedom. "The one who is really in his own people, among those near to him, is always on the way to those more distant, to other people."[5] It is in loving one's own that we are drawn to love others.[6]

1. See Barth, *Church Dogmatics* III/4, 285–323.
2. See Barth, *Church Dogmatics* III/4, 116–285.
3. See Barth, *Church Dogmatics* III/4, 293.
4. Barth, *Church Dogmatics* III/4, 294.
5. Barth, *Church Dogmatics* III/4, 294.
6. See selected references in Grant, *Lament for a Nation.*

Three caveats must be considered in regard to Barth's account of near and distant neighbors. First, Barth does not specify how widely the door between societies should be opened. He admits that distances will vary over time and that occasionally the door may need to be shut, but it should never be permanently barred. He would prefer that, in response to the command to love one's neighbor, the borders separating nations and people be fluid, so that individuals may pursue genuine exchange. But Barth is reluctant to stipulate how fluid the borders should be, and he admits that there are no given forms to follow for enacting God's command in this respect.[7] In short, Barth cannot be invoked to support policies of either closed or open borders in any sweeping way. Rather, his principal concern is promoting fellowship among near and distant neighbors, and venues for faithfully pursuing this command will be adjusted in response to changing social and political circumstances.

Second, Barth contends that a nation is predominantly a fellowship of shared history, soil, and race. In many respects the political association growing out of this fellowship is a vital factor in shaping one's identity and belonging, for it is largely in national settings that we discover and affirm who are our own. There is nothing inherently wrong with a sense of national identity and belonging. Yet it can become a toxic nationalism that sees all other nations as inferior, thereby effectively barring the door permanently and preventing any extensive fellowship with distant neighbors. There is nothing wrong with love of country so long as it is not predicated on the disparagement of other countries. In this respect, fellowship with near and distant neighbors requires a patriotism that is based on a love of one's own, but a love that extends out to others, rather than a nationalism that seeks to impose one's own ways on other people.

Third, Barth is correct in insisting that fellowship with unfamiliar and distant neighbors is predicated on a love of one's own. This is why the task of properly ordering marital, familial, and political associations is such a crucial one.[8] The proper ordering of these familiar neighbors should not lead to insularity but to openness to the other. The paradox of these associations is that they expand the scope of our freedom through a series of relationships that are largely not of our choosing but nonetheless endure over time. Our most familiar neighbors are given rather than chosen; we may choose our spouses, but we do not choose our children, siblings, or fellow citizens.

---

7. See Barth, *Church Dogmatics* III/4, 300–304.

8. For a more extensive inquiry into such ordering, see Waters, *Family in Christian Social and Political Thought*.

But in late-modern societies, who exactly is our own? This question does not stem merely from the decline of marriage and family and from the withering of national loyalties within the contemporary political landscape.[9] Rather, it reflects a larger cultural shift, increasingly on a global scale, toward a strong preference for relationships that are chosen instead of given. It is now often thought that the former enables one's freedom and mobility while the latter is an impediment best avoided. It is expected that relationships should exist as much as possible among consenting individuals with shared interests or goals, and that relations are ideally temporary and easily deconstructed and reconfigured as needed or wanted. There is little desire to be affiliated with one's own unless such affiliation can be understood as a transitory construct that one wills or chooses. But if given familiarity is shunned, how can unfamiliarity be tolerated, much less embraced?

Neighbor Love

The concluding question of the preceding section is, I believe, one of the most pressing tasks of Christian moral theology in the contemporary world. If there is no given fellowship of familiar neighbors that can or should be the accepted starting point, then there are two bleak alternatives. On the one hand, the door separating societies might be left wide open or unhinged, and any sense of national identity prohibited as a vestige of privilege and oppression. Individuals would then be free to wander where they will either to pursue their respective self-interests or to cobble together temporary alliances with other like-minded people. As a shorthand, this may be called the "progressive" option. On the other hand, in response to the endemic nihilism of late modernity, the doors separating societies might be shut tightly and locked before it is too late, and the nation would always be privileged, in the pole position for the hearts and minds of its people. One's own would then largely be defined by who is not one's own. This may be regarded as the "reactionary" option.

Both of these options have their respective attractions. The progressive option seemingly provides a wide range of individual choice that presumably compensates for the loss of given communities in which one is born. Accidental neighbors are replaced with chosen ones. In contrast, the reactionary option restricts the scope of individual choice in order to strengthen the bonds of prior identities into which one is born—identities supplied by history, geography, tradition, or race. Familiarity is simply valued over unfamiliarity, and

---

9. See Waters, *Just Capitalism*, chap. 3.

the apparent lack of personal freedom is well worth the cost of maintaining communal solidarity.

These "attractions," however, are largely illusory and potentially destructive. The freedom championed by progressives degenerates into collective identities defined by ideology, religion, race, gender, class, and the like. And unfamiliar neighbors are defined in similar ways. These imposed categories become, effectively, rigid givens that dictate certain perceptions, commitments, and behaviors for groups that are often intolerant of deviation. Freedom is mutilated into a conformity that is shaped by neither tradition nor custom, but rather by the will and power of those defining the group identity. More destructively, opponents are placed in constructed categories of identity that justify their curt dismissal, castigation, violent confrontation, and eventually willing or unwilling incorporation into the progressive community through the coercive imposition of its core values. Barth's door is swung wide open, not to engage the other but to bring the unenlightened into the fold. This is, in short, an imperious strategy.

Reactionaries largely embrace a series of givens such as shared blood, soil, and history as the principal factors that shape and express the corporate identity of a people. These constraints both define the range of individual freedom that is permitted and enable its permitted expression. Yet unlike the progressive strategy, the eventual goal is not the inclusion of the forcibly converted but the exclusion of unfamiliar neighbors. The operative tactic is to identify who is not like "us" in order to preserve the purity of the community through their exclusion. The range of neighborly engagement and affection is narrow, and often receding, for no one is needed beyond one's own—again, a goal that is shared with progressives but is here achieved through exclusion rather than inclusion. The door is closed tightly, and in some cases barred to prevent contagions from unfamiliar neighbors. This is, in short, a xenophobic strategy.

Neither of these options is good or compatible with the gospel. Loving our neighbors, both near and far, familiar and unfamiliar, is not a suggestion but a command. Nor do Christians have the luxury of choosing which neighbors they shall love and which they shall not love. The command is not selective but universal: All neighbors are to be loved, and the practical expression of that love is not predicated on the efficacy of either inclusion or exclusion. Neighbors are to be loved simply because they are neighbors, though we encounter them in a variety of ways—as family, friends, fellow citizens, strangers, and enemies—and in each instance we are required to treat them accordingly. We are to treat them as they are, and not as we might wish them to be.[10] Indeed,

---

10. This does not preclude, however, opportunities for evangelism and conversion.

our many callings and vocations, as well as their accompanying virtues (described in part 1) are predicated on encountering and serving the neighbor as an other requiring our unselfed attentiveness.

The best way to solve the dilemma of the progressive and reactionary options entails recovering a healthy tension between what is given in the ordering of human life and the freedom that is inherent to the human creature bearing the *imago Dei*. I do not attempt to either formulate a solution or offer a detailed exposition of this tension in this book because of its particular purpose and limited scope. Rather, I explore some suggestive ways this tension might play out in respect to the different kinds of neighbors we encounter on a daily basis. I begin by examining some of the mundane expressions of neighbor love in the following section.

Mundane Expressions of Neighbor Love

Since we encounter a variety of neighbors on a daily basis, it is to be expected that we will treat them in largely ordinary ways—commonplace ways that we give little, if any, thought. Unlike friends or enemies that require a more immediate or sustained reaction, we treat most of our neighbors with casual indifference. We don't wish them ill, but neither are we attentive to their good. There is nothing necessarily wrong with this indifference, so long as it is civil. A presumed intimacy with every neighbor would prove intolerable. The indifference I have in mind, however, is not a functional invisibility, treating a neighbor as if she were not there. What is incumbent upon one in acknowledging neighbors who require a fitting response? What kinds of practices are needed in order to learn how to treat certain neighbors with an appropriate indifference?

To answer these questions, I focus on what I call "gray relationships" with neighbors.[11] Some contrast may help clarify what I mean by gray relationships. There are some neighbors we will never know—a troop of obvious tourists on a street corner or workers for an internet firm from which items or services are purchased. Our relationships with these kinds of neighbors are perfunctory, often defined by customary etiquette or standards of behavior. I do not yell insults at tourists or knowingly enter misleading information on a website. There are neighbors, such as family and friends, with whom we share long and close relationships, relationships that are far deeper and more complex than those we have with all other neighbors. Finally, there are some

---

11. To alleviate any fears or misgivings the reader might have, I do not have fifty shades in mind.

neighbors, known as enemies, who wish to do us ill. And we may at times be obliged to take measures to protect ourselves or other neighbors from them.

The gray neighbors I have in mind are not practically invisible, immediate, or intimate. But due to physical proximity or other factors, they are people we do not choose to encounter but nonetheless do encounter fairly frequently. What kinds of practices should we adopt in order to treat these neighbors in fitting ways? To answer this question, I examine three types of gray neighbors: nearby residents, colleagues, and strangers. In each instance I identify a corresponding practice. Collectively, these three explorations shed some light on an appropriate indifference that some neighbors require and provide a base for subsequent chapters that examine how a greater range of neighbors should be regarded and treated.

First let's consider *nearby residents*. Most people live in relatively close proximity to others. Very few people live in isolated locales. Mostly, we live in cities, suburbs, towns, villages, or hamlets. Within these jurisdictions, we cluster in areas such as boroughs, zones, precincts, and communities. And within these smaller areas, we live in particular buildings on particular streets; in other words, we live in neighborhoods.

In its early usage, a *neighborhood* referred to a small geographic area where people resided closely to one another. There was also a social expectation of frequent face-to-face interactions accompanied by friendly or at least affable behavior. A neighborhood consisted of nearby and familiar people. These connotations still linger, but neighborhoods are now highly variable. A neighborhood might be tiny: a few houses on a cul-de-sac or a few apartments in a small complex. Or it might be expansive: large estates or high-rise condominiums. Some neighborhoods are close-knit, and best friends live next door or across the hall; others are aloof, and interactions are limited to occasional waves by nameless fellow residents. Some neighborhoods comprise a heterogeneous mixture of families, singles, and people of different races and ages; others are largely homogeneous with respect to these characteristics. Some neighborhoods are safe and secure, while others are threatening and dangerous.

Neighborhoods are wildly diverse, but all of them share two similar attributes. First, nearby residential neighbors are rarely chosen. Although Americans, for instance, admittedly tend to gravitate toward neighborhoods with other residents who resemble themselves in terms of race, values, and political commitments, they rarely decide to move next door to their relatives or best friends. Most often they move into neighborhoods where they are not chosen or invited by the residents, nor do they invite newcomers to become their neighbors. Second, residential neighbors cannot be ignored, at least not indefinitely. Neighborhoods have people who pursue their daily living with different mixtures of courage and fear, hope and despair, good health and illness. These myriad factors often remain opaque but nonetheless help shape the neighborly or unneighborly conduct of those living near one another. Regardless of how close-knit or aloof a neighborhood might be, its residents may behave in ways that are objectionable or unobjectionable, obtrusive or unobtrusive; they may irritate, amuse, delight, disappoint, and inspire.[12] Our nearby residential neighbors are there. We see and recognize them, and we must deal with them for who they are.

So what makes a good nearby residential neighbor? Robert Frost's aphorism about fences is not as useful as it may once have been, but *forbearance* goes a long way. In contemporary parlance, forbearance is closely associated with debt relief. For example, a student loan may be temporarily suspended under the terms of a forbearance policy. The word, however, has a much broader and deeper meaning. To forbear is to exhibit self-control, restraint, or reticence—especially in a situation where one would be clearly within one's rights to confront or reprove an offending neighbor. Despite all my previous polite requests, I might, for instance, be justified in finally telling my neighbors off for frequently playing their music too loudly, or in calling the police if they are violating the township decibel code. I might feel momentarily vindicated, but I doubt whether this is a good strategy for building neighborly relationships.

To be clear, I am *not* suggesting doing nothing—an approach that often fuels a simmering resentment or an unjustified martyr complex. As Howard Thurman observed, such resentment can become a precious, personal hatred that deeply distorts one's identity and sense of wellbeing, and the unjusti-fied martyr is always seeking ways to suffer the misdeeds of others.[13] Both reactions illustrate a failure to love the neighbor, because both strive to ma-nipulate the neighbor as the source either of one's righteous indignation or of one's victimization. So I am not encouraging doing nothing in response to offending neighbors. Rather, I am urging an initial forbearance in order to learn why our neighbors offend us, and to determine whether their behav-iors are genuinely offensive. To forbear, then, is to reject an initial reaction of judgment and condemnation in favor of understanding. In this respect, forbearance is an exercise of unselfing. Or, in biblical terms, it is ensuring that I have removed the plank from my own eye before attempting to remove the speck from my neighbor's.

12. My firsthand experience of neighborhoods is admittedly limited. Mostly I have resided in bucolic suburbs that are peacefully uneventful. I don't know what it is like to live in a violent or crime-ridden neighborhood.

13. See Thurman, *Jesus and the Disinherited*, chap. 4.

But why exactly is forbearance a good starting point for dealing with nearby residential neighbors? Again, to be clear, it is not a stance promoting perpetual inactivity. Eventually, a neighbor in the wrong may need to be confronted. But that is a possible outcome rather than a goal. To adopt an initial response of forbearance as an exercise in unselfing is to identify and seek the neighbor's good, thus fulfilling the command to love one's neighbors, even those acting in unlovable ways. Forbearance, then, orients us toward the possibilities of trust and charity. In endeavoring to know why neighbors are behaving in certain ways, we may learn of needs and distresses that require a response of kindness and generosity on our part rather than judgment and condemnation. That obnoxious teenager down the road, for example, may be grieving a dying parent. Forbearance orients us toward preserving the fragile bonds of love that we share as neighbors. Forbearance helps us to learn that there is a profound difference between hating sin and loving sinners. As the Gilead quartet (described in the previous chapter) illustrates, an unselfing forbearance helps form bonds of love with those whose actions we cannot and should not commend. Forbearing neighbors help make a good neighborhood.

We also have *colleagues*. A colleague is a fellow worker, particularly within a profession. Since I am a seminary professor, for instance, the other members of the faculty are my colleagues. This simple definition, however, is too restrictive. Colleagues certainly share certain goals and objectives, but these need not be limited to a shared employer. Even extending collegiality to a larger network is still too confining. My colleagues in my scholarly discipline extend far beyond the seminary that employs me, but even that does not exhaust the possible range of collegial relationships I might have. Others with whom I voluntarily associate, say at church or elsewhere in the community, in the pursuit of shared tasks or goals are also my colleagues.

As the closely related word "collegiality" implies, there is a great deal of collaboration, reciprocity, even harmony involved in accomplishing shared endeavors. Colleagues are all on the same team. (If only this ideal were always true in our experience!) Cooperation is obviously required if colleagues are to successfully pursue their shared interests. This cooperative veneer, however, hides a number of often troubling behaviors that may effectively undercut collegiality. Competition, for example, is also prevalent in the workplace, and among the professions and volunteer organizations. Business firms compete with one another in selling their goods and services, and NGOs compete for the money, time, and expertise of potential donors. There is nothing inherently wrong with such competition, and it often proves beneficial for both producers and consumers. Cooperation and competition are not antithetical but complementary—at least ideally.[14]

Sometimes competition turns unprincipled, cutthroat, or vicious. Employees of a rival firm are not seen as competitive colleagues but as more akin to enemies who must be defeated by any means possible. Stealing trade secrets, spreading rumors, or otherwise undermining the credibility of competitors are justified for the sake of winning. Nor is such unscrupulous conduct confined to the for-profit sector. Schools may denigrate competing institutions to attract students or faculty. Collegiality may also be weakened within particular organizations. Colleagues compete with one another for promotions, for the attention of superiors, or for prestige. These goals are most often achieved as rewards for superior performance or talent, but sometimes people adopt strategies designed to diminish the achievements or sabotage the work of their colleagues. The workplace, professional organizations, NGOs, local PTAs and congregations—all have their machinations and petty jealousies.

The obvious problem with this behavior is that it erodes or destroys the cooperation presupposed by collegiality. If colleagues share common goals, then diminishing one another weakens the prospect of achieving these goals, effectively lessening colleagues' individual wellbeing in the process. There is much wisdom in the observation that a house divided against itself cannot stand. Even cooperating to diminish an external competitor in a dishonest manner is ultimately unproductive, for breaking the "rules of the game" is a disservice to the wider society that such competition is designed to serve.

What is a practice that exhibits and supports a proper attitude toward and treatment of colleagues? *Courtesy*. By *courtesy* I do not mean a feigned politeness that masks disdain or ill will, nor do I mean flattery meant to curry favor. Courtesy is not synonymous with a skillful display of good manners. Polished self-promoters and skilled assassins of character often appear well-mannered. In contrast, genuine courtesy promotes respect and civility.

Respect exhibits an unqualified regard for the ontology of others. Every individual possesses an inherent dignity in virtue of being a fellow person. Respecting the being of one's neighbor, however, does not mean refraining from disagreements or criticism. Colleagues may forcefully disagree over how best to accomplish a goal they hold in common, and one colleague may rightfully criticize another for failing to execute a duty or responsibility, thereby letting everyone else down. This is where civility comes into play, for it sets parameters on how potentially contentious moments among colleagues may

---

14. For a more expansive account of the relationship between cooperation and competition, see Waters, *Just Capitalism*, chap. 2.

be navigated in a mutually respectful manner. Civility helps direct attention toward the proper object of a dispute. For example, in resolving a disagreement over what course of action should be taken, the object is not who will win the debate but what the best course of action is. Arguing in a civil manner helps keep this focus in mind by reminding colleagues of shared objectives. It is to engage in an exercise of unselfing in which colleagues, in and through their disagreements and criticisms, help each other determine the mutual good they are pursuing. Courtesy thereby promotes a mutual respect and civility that simply has no need for personal aggrandizement that is achieved at the expense of colleagues.

I suspect that the reader at this juncture may raise (at least) two objections. First, I am naive. What I have described is an idyllic setting cut off from the hard reality of how things get done in the real world—a deficient perspective stemming, no doubt, from my perch in the ivory tower of academe. Things get done through rough-and-tumble competition in which the best rise to the top of the heap. There is simply little time or need for courtesy. Perhaps. But I question whether the discourteous and even brutal competition that seems to be often taken for granted is really necessary for getting things done in the "real world," or whether it reflects a laziness that is unwilling to give respect and civility a serious try. It is shrewd, even safe to assume the worst in others, and much riskier to be attentive. To be attentive is risky because to be attentive is also to be vulnerable, to let one's guard down in order to see the other more clearly. Some colleagues will take advantage of such a perceived weakness. Yet it is through taking risks that trust becomes possible and valued among colleagues, and trust is the first outcome of courtesy. If this is naivete, so be it, for the uncertainty of trust is preferable to the certainty of a so-called realistic mistrust.

Second, courtesy may be prone to emphasize rhetoric over action, which in turn could stunt effective leadership. With its emphasis on respect and civility, courtesy would seemingly require spending an inordinate amount of time on maintaining cordial relationships with colleagues. Wasting time assuaging the tender feelings of sensitive colleagues impedes good leaders. The decisive leader is rightfully unconcerned about how colleagues might regard her, and respect can be earned in other ways than by courtesy and civility. Would I really prefer a polite but incompetent leader over a rude but capable one? This objection is valid but hard to address, for the choice as presented—between polite incompetency *or* uncivil competency—is overly simplistic. History is replete with examples of foolish leaders who were courteous and with others who were arrogant. History is also replete with effective leaders who were ill-mannered and effective leaders who were genteel. The choice is not always a straightforward either-or.

Nonetheless, if we are faced with the dilemma of choosing between uncivil competency and civil incompetency, which is preferable? Context is not determinative, but it goes a long way in helping answer this question. For example, a discourteous but highly competent political leader is preferable to a polite but ineffectual one. But the sphere of politics is not the same as that of the workplace or voluntary association, for it involves the ordering of love among citizens, and at times enemies, rather than colleagues. Although civility, and therefore courtesy, are not unrelated to good political governance, it is ultimately exercising power rather than promoting collegiality that is operative in serving the citizenry—a topic that is visited at greater depth in chapter 10.

In ordering the love of neighbors who are colleagues, however, it is virtually impossible to separate good leadership from courtesy. Unlike politics, collegiality is based on trust and cooperation, and leaders who fail to create respectful and civil environments that promote trusting and cooperative behaviors also fail to properly serve their colleagues who are their neighbors. Moreover, the courtesy extended to and received by colleagues also promotes conditions in which forgiveness is more easily given and received. The distrust stemming from disrespectful and uncivil treatment has a spiraling effect over time that promotes not only mistrust but also a thirst for vengeance, in both subtle and overt ways. Yet it is hard, if not impossible, to imagine that a love of neighbor can exist and be expressed in the absence of forgiveness—hence the need for courtesy among colleagues that through the mutual respect and civility it inspires makes forgiveness more rather than less likely. Consequently, loving colleagues is also a school for learning to love a more expansive range of neighbors.

Finally, let's consider *strangers*. Although chapter 9 is devoted to examining neighbors who are strangers, a few preliminary comments are in order. Strangers are the most common and ubiquitous neighbors we encounter over a lifetime. But, oddly, we tend to give strangers little moral regard or attention, even though our material and physical wellbeing are often utterly dependent on them. We rely on grocers to sell us food, on bankers to complete our financial transactions, on carpenters to build our homes, and on doctors and nurses to care for us when we are sick. Mostly these services are provided by strangers and not by intimates or friends. We are sometimes literally at the mercy of strangers.

How should we regard strangers, especially in light of the command to love them as neighbors? There are two bad options that could easily be adopted. On the one hand, we could treat every stranger with an uninformed or simplistic trust. We could assume that when we trust the unknown neighbor this act of good faith will be reciprocated in kind and that, therefore, we need not worry about being taken advantage of or harmed. In many, if not most, instances strangers are not menacing and our trust in them is not misplaced. There are, however, many instances in which such trust is not warranted, in which trusting a stranger would result in harm being inflicted that could have been easily avoided.

On the other hand, we could treat every stranger with unrelenting suspicion. We could assume that unknown neighbors should never be trusted and that it is therefore prudent to take precautions against them. Admittedly, there are some, perhaps many, instances in which such precautionary mistrust is in order. But such deep-seated suspicion would create toxic environments of mistrust and aggressive ill will, a greatly diminished social life not unlike Hobbes's state of nature.

Both of these options are misplaced. Practically, both are ineffectual and potentially dangerous. A simplistic trust in strangers is foolhardy because it is reckless rather than prudent, heedlessly subjecting oneself and perhaps others to potential dangers that could have been easily avoided or prevented. Unremitting suspicion is also foolhardy because it is unduly cautious. Human flourishing requires the risk of trusting strangers, for without such trust there could be no civil society, given the countless interactions and exchanges required to maintain it.[15]

More importantly, both of these options violate the command to love one's neighbors—in this case, neighbors who are strangers. To treat strangers with simplistic trust is to assume an unwarranted familiarity that is anything but loving. We assume that we already know what the stranger needs, effectively treating her with willful indifference. The neighbor is no longer an other requiring our attentiveness. Unremitting suspicion reduces the neighbor to little more than a potential enemy, an object of fear and hostility. Such a neighbor does indeed require our attentiveness, but an attentiveness more akin to surveillance than to ascertaining the good of the other. In both instances, we do not encounter neighbors, but our projections of what we think these others are.

Strangers should be treated with an initial hospitality. Although more is said about hospitality in chapter 9, I will offer a brief definition at this juncture. Hospitality entails the amiable reception of guests and strangers. The reception is amiable in that it initially treats the stranger neither with an assumed familiarity nor with suspicion. Rather, the stranger is perceived as a neighbor

---

15. See Fukuyama, *Trust*; and Seabright, *Company of Strangers*.

about whom little is known. But the stranger is received rather than effectively ignored or warily surveilled. The stranger is an unknown neighbor requiring our appropriate or fitting attentiveness, an attentiveness guided by prudent judgment as an act of love.

An important caveat should be noted regarding such prudent judgment. To receive a stranger hospitably does not necessarily mean providing entrance or access to places or spaces that might imperil other neighbors. One's calling to extend hospitality to neighbors who are unknown strangers is tempered by one's duties to neighbors who are known. To use two admittedly extreme examples: hospitality does not require allowing an unknown person to linger in the workplace or allowing one to use your house while you are away on vacation.[16] These acts could imperil colleagues and nearby residents. Moreover, such imprudent or rash judgment does not exhibit an appropriate love of neighbor but creates a potential moral hazard for the neighbor one is attempting to serve. Hospitality does not include unwittingly tempting the unknown neighbor. Since we know little or nothing about the unknown neighbor's history or proclivities, we should be careful about the circumstances in which we attempt to attend to the good of this neighbor. Loitering or unsupervised living space may trigger, for some strangers, behavior that is self-destructive or harmful to others. Love of both unknown and known neighbors often requires restrictive prevention rather than careless inattention.

In this chapter I have built a basic skeleton of neighbor love by concentrating on the "gray relationships" of nearby residents and colleagues, those relationships that are neither intimate nor anonymous. In the following chapters I add some flesh to this skeleton by focusing initially on the more intimate neighborly relationships between friends, spouses, and family members and returning later to the more distant neighborly relationships between strangers and fellow citizens.

---

16. In regard to allowing a stranger to use one's house, I am not referring to a contractual relationship that one might make with a house sitter or with short-term renters who have been vetted.

CHAPTER 6

Friends

Almost everyone has at least one or two friends. Friendship is a commonplace relationship to which we usually give little sustained thought. Indeed, it is difficult to define exactly what it means to be a friend. Most often the term refers to a person with whom we are more familiar and whom we hold in higher esteem than a stranger or a casual acquaintance. These perceptions are subjective and variable. For example, we might have friends whose company we enjoy but whose behavioral quirks we do not always admire. Time and intimacy are also not definitive features of friendship. Some we call friends we have known for decades while others we have known for only a few months or even weeks. One might have a best friend who is also a spouse and, at the same time, have other friends with whom few intimate details are known or shared.

As late moderns, we may spend time thinking about friends, remembering good times or regretting harsh words—but we tend to spend little, if any, time contemplating the meaning and purpose of friendship. This lack of contemplative reflection helps explain, in part, why the idea of friendship grows steadily more trivial and banal for many people. The designation of *friend* is now largely and casually self-determined. A friend may be a person one knows, or a name added to a list on a website in response to a request to be "friended," or a pet, or even—in a few cases—a houseplant or inanimate object. Increasingly, there are robotic and virtual friends. Such friends, however, can be easily discarded. A person can be ignored, a name unfriended with a mouse click, an inconvenient pet dropped off at a shelter, boring robots and virtual reality programs turned off. We tend to regard friends as those we pick and choose at our convenience. This does not mean that we necessarily treat our friends badly, but we tend to ignore friendship as a morally formative relationship.

It was not always this way. The ancients placed a high premium on friendship as a key relationship in practicing the moral life. Consequently, they believed friends should be chosen wisely and cautiously. Choosing well was beneficial while choosing badly might prove corrupting. Ideally, friendship was a schoolhouse for learning the values of loyalty, reciprocity, and mutual accountability. To overgeneralize, one was only as good as the company of friends one kept.

I do not think it is possible, practical, or desirable to try to recover an ancient understanding of friendship in any direct way. The settings of, say, ancient Athens and contemporary London are too remote for any direct transfer from the former to the latter. Moreover, ancient concepts of friendship incorporated certain assumptions that should not be replicated. The elitism of ancient accounts of friendship, for instance, diminishes the moral significance of friendship because it is incompatible with Christian convictions about neighbor love. But this does not mean that there is nothing about how the ancients understood friendship that we may profitably plunder. The following section identifies some ancient, as well as some early modern, conceptual resources that we may use to recover the moral significance of friendship that is also relevant to our contemporary circumstances. This survey is neither comprehensive nor systematic. Rather, some prominent themes are summarized and then further developed, and some are pointedly avoided.

Conceptual Friendship

It needs to be admitted at the outset that although classical pagan philosophers were interested in the topic of friendship, early Christian theologians were much more concerned about charity. Both of these interests are grounded in a love of neighbor, but their respective emphases are in tension. Friendship is based on *philia* and is therefore preferential: some neighbors are chosen as friends rather than others. This, in turn, emphasizes mutuality and reciprocity. In contrast, *agape* is foundational in loving one's neighbors, and meeting their needs is non-preferential, disinterested, and nonreciprocal. Furthermore, *philia* does not value work because work is irrelevant in enjoying the company of a friend, whereas vocation and work play central roles in practicing *agape*.

The differences between classical friendship and Christian charity, however, are tendencies rather than absolute and incompatible distinctions. *Phila* and *agape* are not necessarily incompatible, and one need not be chosen to the exclusion of the other. Consequently, I am not arguing for the superiority of *agape*; rather, I will use both *philia* and *agape* in constructing a Christian account of friendship in this chapter. Admittedly, there is a tension between ancient understandings of friendship and charity—but it is a tension that, when properly ordered, promotes the significance of friends for living the Christian moral life without diminishing charity, on the one hand, and without forgoing friendship for the sake of meeting the needs of neighbors, on the other.

Plato and Aristotle offer two highly significant but competing portrayals of friendship.[1] For Plato, friendship is part of a universal love that grows out of particular relationships. Although love makes one vulnerable to disappointment and heartache, it must nevertheless be affirmed, and its dictates should be followed. The soul can only claim or regain its proper status through love. Beauty is the starting point for achieving this goal, for the beloved object beckons us to embrace and be embraced by beauty. An undisciplined soul, however, may cause us to clutch at beauty in the wrong way. Consequently, desire must be properly formed and controlled if love is to have its way, resulting in philosophy as a shared, universal love among friends of wisdom. Sentiment, therefore, is foundational to friendship.

The chief strength of Plato's account of friendship is the foundational role that love plays. An expansive range of neighbors can be embraced as potential friends. Moreover, the sentiment at the core of friendship at least implies attending to the needs or the good of friends. And this echoes the concept of unselfing examined previously (which is not surprising since both Weil and Murdoch are Platonists). The principal weakness of this account, however, is Plato's restricted understanding of love. It is beauty rather than the friend that is ultimately loved, and this reduces friendship to a means instead of an end. Plato comes dangerously close to regarding a friend as someone to be used in a quest for beauty, effectively blinding one to the actual person who is claimed to be one's friend.

In contrast, Aristotle contends that particular friendships reflect a prior universal love. Within his hierarchical scheme, only equals can be friends. This is why there are no real friendships between masters and servants—or between husbands and wives. Consequently, choice displaces sentiment as the most important feature of friendship. Friendships, then, are always preferential and restricted, intended more to exclude than to include the range of moral obligations that are shared among equals. For instance, justice does not incur obligations that are owed to strangers, and this is why violating the trust of a friend is a grievous denial of justice.

---

1. The following discussion of Plato and Aristotle draws heavily on Meilaender, *Friendship*, chap. 1.

The principal strength of Aristotle's formulation of friendship is its clear connection with morality and broader questions of social and political ordering. We choose our friends wisely because they help us become more virtuous, an objective that is best achieved through rational reflection rather than left to a sentiment that cannot always be suitably controlled. Moreover, friendship, since it involves a relationship among equals, provides a solid foundation for a political order that is also moral. Aristotle likens citizenship to a kind of civic friendship in which justice is the preeminent shared value. Yet ignoring moral obligations owed to those who are not friends, such as strangers or enemies, effectively denies them justice because they are not included within the sphere of civic friendship. Christianity's commitment to universal benevolence calls this exclusion into question. The Good Samaritan, for instance, presumably had an obligation to help the neighbor in need. It is the neighbor, not the friend, that is the principal object of ethical concern. Had the Samaritan ignored the neighbor in need, he would have betrayed their common humanity, thereby committing an injustice.

Saint Augustine tried to reconcile the tension between preferential and particular (*philia*) and non-preferential and universal (*agape*) accounts of love. For Augustine, a friend is only loved properly in relation to God. *Agape* thereby transcends *philia* but does not negate it. Friendship is akin to a school of love, preparing one to embrace a universal vision. Moreover, a friend is not a matter of choice but a gift from God, and as a gift, the friend's particularity cannot be ignored or discounted. Consequently, preferential love is not opposed or unrelated to more expansive forms of love. For it is only in the particular that the universal can be practically expressed. God calls people to forge and maintain particular friendships as a principal means of learning *agape*. In this respect, friendship plays a role in ordering God's creation, for in learning to love and care for our friends, we learn to love and care for humankind. We need friends and particular relationships to learn the content of love, but even within these particular constraints, we love our friends in relation to God.[2]

The chief strength of Augustine's portrayal is the friend as gift. Accepting a friend as a gift goes a long way in countering an understanding of friendship as primarily a means to achieve some larger end or a tendency to choose a friend who is in a position to benefit us. Yet over time such a friend might no longer prove useful, presumably bringing the friendship to an end. But is such lack of loyalty over time compatible with a love of neighbor in which

---

2. For an expansive overview of Augustine's concept and practice of friendship, see McNamara, *Friendship in Saint Augustine*.

friendship is presumably grounded? A friend is valued not exclusively for utility but also for alterity.

Although the imagery of a gift helps in capturing a less-expedient understanding of friendship, it may not go far enough. It is not clear how a "gift" secures the mutuality and reciprocity entailed in *philia*. A gift can be easily possessed, becoming the property of the owner—hardly a fitting relationship between friends enjoying and sharing an ontological equality in relation to God. Although Augustine's moving descriptions of friendships disclose or suggest profound insights into mutuality,[3] Augustine provides little explicit theological discussion of how *philia* should be ordered within the Christian moral life. Although a shared love of God is the content of Christian friendship, there is little explicit direction on how this love should be given and received between friends, weakening its link to a more universal love.

As might be expected, Saint Thomas Aquinas understood friendship as a way of practicing the virtues. Following Aristotle, Thomas refers to friendship as a habit. But what is habituated that Thomas finds worthwhile? The moral import of friendship is that it is essentially predicated on desiring the good of the other. A friend, however, is not simply a means of self-improvement, but also a recipient of one's loving actions. Desiring the good of the other includes concrete actions designed to help the other achieve that good. Moreover, such friendship cannot be other than mutual and reciprocal, for it involves two people desiring the good of each other. What exactly is this good? God. The rightly ordered love of God in turn promotes the virtuous life, since the habituation of the moral and theological virtues orients one toward God. Consequently, the Christian moral life is utterly dependent on friendship,[4] for it draws believers toward friendship with God. In this respect, friendship embodies, at least to a limited extent, charity itself.

Thomas seemingly relives much of the tension between classical and Christian understandings of friendship. Since friends should orient us toward friendship with God, the purported differences between *philia* and *agape* are presumably transcended and made one in God. To love God is simultaneously to love one's neighbor, and vice versa. True, but there is an important omission. In aspiring to a transcendent friendship with God, Thomas says nothing about the commonplace activities of ordinary friendships, an omission he shares with almost every ancient philosopher and Christian theologian. Such an omission, however, results in a stilted portrayal of friendship, which in turn robs friendship of a significant moral and theological contribution—namely,

3. See Augustine, *Confessions*.
4. See Wadell, *Friendship and the Moral Life*; and Wadell, *Becoming Friends*.

how friends reinforce the incarnation so that the quest for a transcendent friendship with God does not become divorced from the physical and material creation that God created. Before developing this crucial aspect of friendship in the next section, a few more theological voices need to be briefly considered, to note both some of their contributions that can be employed profitably and a pitfall or two that should be avoided.

Most of the preceding inquiries into friendship begin with the reality of particular friends and work their way up to a transcendent source of *philia*, or even to friendship with God. Jonathan Edwards reverses this direction. As seen previously in respect to virtue,[5] Edwards begins with a general benevolence and then works down to concrete behavior that, with the aid of grace, may be described as virtuous. Similarly, God is the source of love that filters down in and through human relationships. We cannot truly love our neighbors until we first love God. Until we acknowledge the true source of love, we cannot see our friends as they really are—namely, as sinful neighbors condemned and redeemed by God. To be faithful to God, then, requires faithfulness to the neighbor. Edwards highlights the role that mutual fidelity plays in friendship. Friends are faithful to God and to each other, and such fidelity assists people in fulfilling their respective callings and vocations; the love of God and the love of neighbor cannot be separated. Edwards's scheme, however, is question-begging: Do the ordinary patterns of friendship, that are seemingly far removed from any transcendent source, teach us nothing about the love of God and neighbors bearing the divine image and likeness?

Jeremy Taylor defines friendship as essentially charity extended to the world.[6] Through general friendship we learn something about divine love for the world, and friendship is therefore compatible with Christian teaching so long as it benefits all humankind. A good man or woman is a friend to the whole world. Taylor admits, however, that most friendships are necessarily limited and particular. These particular friendships, however, are compatible with a more general friendship, because "friendships are nothing but love and society mixed together, that is, a conversing with whom we love."[7] Taylor contends that virtue strengthens friendship, but perfect friendship is not reducible to virtue, for it entails a "union of souls"[8] that cannot be confined to a set of prescribed practices. Nonetheless, Taylor cannot resist the temptation to offer practical and pastoral counsel, admonishing the reader to avoid such untoward conduct as revealing a secret or bitterly admonishing

5. See chap. 3.
6. See Taylor, *Nature, Offices, and Measurers of Friendship*, 302–3.
7. Taylor, *Nature, Offices, and Measurers of Friendship*, 306–7.
8. Taylor, *Nature, Offices, and Measurers of Friendship*, 325.

a friend. Taylor's emphasis on a general friendship permeating the broader community and manifested in particular friendships is to be welcomed. It is nearly impossible to imagine a flourishing civil community that is devoid of particular friendships. Additionally, although Taylor's counsel may appear quaint, it nonetheless serves to remind us that friends are accountable to one another rather than being endlessly indulgent. As we see in the next section, mutually accountable friendship makes an important contribution to flourishing communities.

Søren Kierkegaard is an admittedly brilliant philosopher, but he makes some peculiar claims about love.[9] For Christians, he argues, *agape* is clearly superior to *philia* (and *eros*), and any attempt at reconciling these loves is doomed to fail. Consequently, Christians should avoid friendships as they are commonly understood. The primary weakness of friendship is its close relation to passion. Passion diverts one's attention from knowing and loving God. This is why nowhere in the New Testament is friendship celebrated. Rather, we are commanded to love our neighbors in a dispassionate way. Kierkegaard sees little value in friendship because it lacks any substantial moral content. Since friendship entails preferring some neighbors over others, it is essentially a disguised form of self-love since we tend to prefer those who are similar to us. The friend is another self that I love, expressing little more than self-esteem. In contrast, Christianity is essentially a life of self-denial, especially as encapsulated in the love of neighbor. The neighbor should be loved dispassionately and non-preferentially, without any thought of reciprocity, thereby negating the need for friends. Yet, as argued below, this negation of friendship, and more broadly of *philia* (and *eros*), effectively diminishes love as the principal source for vocational formation and practice that is crucial in serving the neighbor.

Another weakness in Kierkegaard's account of love is that he effectively concocts a strategy to avoid disappointment.[10] In the absence of any expected reciprocity, neighbors, especially friends, spouses, and offspring, can never disappoint us. Such invulnerability, however, is the denial of love, as C. S. Lewis recognizes.[11] Love, in any of its forms, is never safe. "To love at all is to be vulnerable. Love anything, and your heart will certainly be wrung and possibly broken."[12] Only in hell is one safe from love. Lewis portrays friendship as a highly vulnerable expression of love because it is the "least *natural*

---

9. The remainder of this paragraph summarizes Kierkegaard, *Works of Love* 2.2.
10. See Meilaender, *Friendship*, 44–45.
11. See Lewis, *Four Loves*.
12. Lewis, *Four Loves*, 121.

of loves,"[13] for it is not driven by any natural or biological necessity. Rather, friends are chosen for a variety of reasons, such as shared interests or beliefs or providing mutual support in response to crises or social hostility. Moreover, friends cannot be made; they are embraced. Coming into a new friendship is more akin to receiving a gift than to fabricating an artifact. The friendship is a safe and graceful haven in the midst of an indifferent world. This is why friendship is vulnerable, for it depends on the shared interests or expectations of individuals, and these change over time, and often not in complementary ways. It should not be surprising that friendships wax and wane and sometimes become extinct. Yet despite the risk inherent in *philia*, friendship is vital to human flourishing, both individually and collectively.

Particular Friends

Saint Augustine is correct when he insists that a friend is more gift than choice. But what is entailed, and what is required of us, in responding to these gifts that God brings into our lives? In answering, partially, this question, I draw on the resources identified in the preceding section while also trying to avoid some of the traps. In the following analysis, I concentrate on persons as friends rather than on abstract or theoretical understandings of friendship.

Friends assist each other in broadening and deepening their shared love of the good. For Christians, the supreme good is, of course, God. And friends help one another obey the first great commandment. To be candid, however, even the attention of the most pious friends does not remain perpetually fixed on God. Indeed, one's attention cannot remain transfixed by the transcendent and eternal without ignoring the friend, thereby denigrating the ordinary and temporal qualities of the created order. I do not deny the crucial importance that transcendence and eternity play in shaping and living out the moral and spiritual life. But for the purpose of this chapter, I am more concerned with the commonplace sensibilities and activities shared by friends that are formative and habitual and therefore preparatory in making one receptive to the transcendent and eternal. In this respect, there are five crucial features of friendship: fidelity, accountability, vocation, community, and mutuality and reciprocity.

Fidelity. Friends are faithful and loyal to each other. Such faithfulness and loyalty are not feeble and fleeting but steadfast and enduring. Friends support each other through thick and thin. William Tecumseh Sherman once said of his friend, "Grant stood by me when I was crazy, and I stood by him when

---

13. Lewis, *Four Loves*, 58 (emphasis original).

he was drunk, and now we stand by each other."[14] Deceiving or betraying a friend is a hateful act because it destroys the trust that is fundamental to all civil behavior. If we cannot depend on our neighbors, especially our friends, we are back in Hobbes's state of nature. Good friends, then, learn valuable lessons from each other about love and courage, and—more expansively— about loyalty and fidelity to God.[15]

Accountability. The fidelity owed a friend, however, is not absolute. We are not entitled to assume that our friends will endorse and defend everything we say or do. Such a presumption would fail to acknowledge that friends are bound together by a fidelity to a more expansive truth and goodness. Friends are thereby mutually accountable in honoring these larger commitments, requiring that they speak truthfully regarding their own and each other's failings. To persistently indulge a friend's deplorable speech or conduct, for example, is to effectively disparage friendship itself. This does not mean that a friend is abandoned when she fails the true or the good, but that the fidelity offered by a friend is in support of the sinner and not the sin committed. When friends call one another to account, they learn important lessons concerning faith and measured judgment. In short, a good friend is immeasurably loyal but not incessantly forbearing—someone who tells us what we need to hear and not necessarily what we want to hear.

Vocation. Friends help each other pursue their respective vocations. This assistance is both direct and indirect. A friend is a neighbor whom I am called to serve. To serve this neighbor requires that I discern what my friend needs to promote his good. Consequently, friendship is an ongoing, though often unacknowledged, exercise in unselfing. Friendships, however, are not enclaves secluded from larger social contexts. Learning to serve our friends may also equip us to better identify and serve the needs of neighbors, for instance, who are strangers. In this respect the preferential *philia* and non-preferential *agape* are not opposed or mutually exclusive; the former prepares and feeds into the latter. Indeed, a good friend may hold me accountable by insisting that my scope of neighbor love is too constricted and needs to be enlarged in order for me to faithfully fulfill my calling and vocation.

Community. As implied in the preceding paragraph, a friendship is not an isolated island but something more akin to a favored, shared locale, just slightly hidden from public view. The hustle and bustle of society is always a few steps away and never entirely out of earshot. Friends claim just enough privacy to sustain their mutual fidelity, a privacy deserving the respect and

14. Brockett, *Our Great Captains*, 162.
15. See Royce, *Philosophy of Loyalty*.

support of the larger community because the larger community is itself composed of and benefits from friendships. It is impossible to envision a genuine community devoid of friends. The two most prominent forms of social ordering that discourage or squash friendships are totalitarian regimes[16] and hell.[17] Well-ordered communities—those dedicated to securing the shared goods of freedom, peace, and justice—promote human flourishing, and such promotion is best enabled by mutually faithful and supportive friends pursuing their respective vocations.

But there is an important caveat to this. A community should never succumb to the equivalent of a club of like-minded friends. A member of a community is not synonymous with a crony. At times, a community must hear the hard truth, even prophetic judgment that it is failing to honor its shared goods for all its members. And faithful friends, faithful members of the community, do not try to shield one another from either truth or prophecy. Yet such accountability is always accompanied by fidelity, a forbearance in which condemnation is not damnation but an invitation to amendment of one's life and to strengthen the bonds of community. A hard truth is not heard when it is spoken with smug self-righteousness or hatred, and the prophetic is never effective when it is severed from the pastoral.

Mutuality and reciprocity. Contrary to Kierkegaard, there is nothing incompatible about friendship and Christian faith. The love that created and was given to human beings was never designed to make them invulnerable to disappointment or suffering. To love is to risk, and to never risk is to forever forgo the abundant life—to settle for surviving instead of flourishing. Friendship is predicated on taking a chance, for friends can and do fail us. Why? Because friendship is all about mutuality and reciprocity between sinners (not between angels). Friendship is necessarily about give-and-take, for it is not a one-sided relationship in which one is always taking and the other giving. Despite the need to unself, a self must also be sustained to be undone. To use a crude analogy, friends feed each other spiritually and emotionally, but it is a mutual and reciprocal giving and receiving, and not a dance between predator and prey.

As noted previously, however, the bonds shared by friends are fragile and can weaken or break, negating the goods of *philia*. Noting a few of these vulnerabilities will suffice to illustrate how the love shared by friends may prove ineffectual or may even fail. A friend may prove unfaithful. For example, after

16. See, e.g., Arendt, *Origins of Totalitarianism*, part 3.
17. See, e.g., Lewis, *Screwtape Letters*; and Lewis, *Great Divorce*. See also Buckley, *Morality of Laughter*, chap. 5.

a while we may no longer prove useful in helping a friend achieve her professional goals or meet her emotional needs and so she may turn her attention to another person, one who is better positioned to help her, prompting in us a response of jealousy, a sense of loss or even of betrayal. Or, rather than taking the time or effort to hold a friend accountable for conduct that is hurtful to himself or others, we may find it easier to avoid the awkward conversation and indulge him without regard for his reputation. Friends may also ignore the assistance they can provide each other in pursuing their respective vocations, concentrating instead on enabling each other's self-indulgent desires. Friends may also spend their time denigrating the larger community and its members, effectively turning their relationship into a small gossip club that does nothing to promote the common good. Finally, friends may fail to honor their mutuality and reciprocity: one "friend" is expected to constantly feed the ego of the other "friend," receiving little or nothing in return. Any thought of unselfing is dismissed as a useless encumbrance in a friendship that is not unlike emotional vampirism. In short, despite the good of friendship, the actual behavior between friends may leave much to be desired.

The reader may object that my description of friendship is stilted, divorced from how friends actually interact. How often do we wake up in the morning and say to ourselves, in effect, "I hope Jack will help me with my vocation today" or "I trust Jill will hold me accountable for that stunt I pulled at work yesterday"? Rather, friends simply enjoy each other's company, spending their time in fun and games rather than trying to identify each other's so-called good. We take joy and pleasure in our friends as they are. As I have admitted, a friend is a gift, and like any gift, we get what we get—a package that both disappoints and delights. We properly think about our friends as real persons and not as representations of an abstract ideal of friendship. Additionally, friendships are not as vulnerable or fragile as I contend but are resilient and survive over time, albeit often in new or subdued ways.

The objection is correct. We should focus our attention on actual friends rather than on the idea of friendship, otherwise friendship becomes a rather tedious exercise in contemplating a love devoid of flesh and blood. Yet the characteristics of friendship, such as fidelity and reciprocity, help us be better friends by providing a kind of summary of the qualities of friendship that are gleaned over time. In other words, we do not begin with theoretical constructs of friendship and then try to make individuals conform to the model, but out of actual relationships the good qualities of friendship find a fertile field in which to grow. Friends *are* gifts, and some are delicate while others are hardy, some are conventional while others are eccentric—and each needs to be treated accordingly in respect to the goods that gifted friends embody. In this respect, friendships are exercises in unselfing, whether we recognize them as such or not. Theoretical understandings of friendship, then, provide useful rules of thumb for unselfing, provided they are seen as a means rather than as an end. Friendship is the background supporting the foreground of friends.

Perhaps my stilted rhetoric can be enlivened a bit by visiting an actual friendship. C. S. Lewis and J. R. R. Tolkien were friends for more than three decades.[18] I will not offer a detailed description of their long friendship, since much has already been written on it.[19] Rather, I will highlight selected aspects of their friendship to illustrate some of the more prominent features.

The two were faithful friends. They met frequently, spending time talking about a wide range of subjects. Lewis encouraged Tolkien to keep working on his fiction and was helpful in finding a publisher for *The Hobbit*. Tolkien initiated Lewis into Norse mythology, was a central figure in his conversion to Christianity, and was instrumental in securing for him an endowed chair at Cambridge. Their friendship, however, had its rough patches, and they grew distant especially toward the end. Lewis frequently withheld personal details from Tolkien, was often absorbed in grieving his wife Joy's death, and was dealing with his failing health, exacerbated by his frequent commutes between Oxford and Cambridge. Tolkien was apparently irked by the attention Lewis devoted to Charles Williams when the latter joined the Inklings,[20] was dismissive of Lewis's books on popular theology, and disapproved of his marriage to Joy Davidman. As the two men grew older they also grew apart; meeting infrequently, their conversations became more forced and inconsequential. Their friendship weakened, but it did not die. Lewis never spoke ill of his friend to others, and Tolkien was devastated by Lewis's death, afterward often defending his friend from what he believed were unwarranted attacks by critics. As reflected in *The Chronicles of Narnia* and *The Lord of the Rings*, both prized and practiced the virtues, such as loyalty, that originate in and support friendship.

They were accountable to each other. As professional colleagues they assisted each other's scholarly pursuits and collaborated on curricular reforms at Oxford. In both instances they were also critical, holding each other to high standards and expectations, and in this respect they aided each other in pursuing their professional callings. A similar pattern took shape in their

18. They first met in 1926, and Lewis died in 1963.

19. See, e.g., Duriez, *Tolkien and C. S. Lewis*.

20. Charles Williams was an editor with Oxford University Press whose own literary works and interests captivated Lewis when they first met. The Inklings was an informal "club" of men who shared a range of literary and intellectual interests. See Carpenter, *The Inklings*; and Zaleski and Zaleski, *The Fellowship*.

personal lives and vocations, especially in matters relating to their shared Christian faith. This does not mean, however, that the mutual accountability they practiced was always on target or helpful. Lewis, for instance, was perhaps too exuberant in his praise of Tolkien's work, tended to discount his friend's Catholicism, and virtually ignored Tolkien's life as a husband and father. Tolkien was much less reticent to challenge. His criticism of *The Chronicles of Narnia* and of Lewis's theological books was often scathing, and he was not shy about making known his displeasure with Lewis for marrying a divorced woman. Yet despite these awkward attempts at supporting and admonishing, they nonetheless helped each other remain faithful to the truths they held in common. Without their friendship, I think the quality of their respective literary works would have suffered, and, much more speculatively, I believe their respective spiritual lives would also have been diminished.

Their friendship was formed and sustained in relation to larger communities. Although Lewis and Tolkien enjoyed what could be described as a long and close friendship, it was not like a fortress that kept others out but was frequently on public display. Both spent a great deal of time with fellow Inklings, with university colleagues, and with members of scholarly guilds. Both served their nation as army officers in the Great War and played supporting roles as civilians in the Second World War. Both helped shape public opinion through their extensive writing and public speaking. These interactions with a variety of communities provided a range of both similar and dissimilar experiences that enriched their lives as both individuals and friends.

These communities grounded their friendship by offering places where it could grow and flourish. It is impossible to conceive of Lewis and Tolkien as friends in the absence of the Eagle and Child,[21] Oxford, and England. These communities gave much to both Lewis and Tolkien that helped their friendship to flourish. And both gave much back to these communities. But communities are also flawed, and they failed these friends at crucial moments. For instance, Tolkien was eventually forbidden to read any rough drafts of *The Lord of the Rings* at Inklings meetings because one member was tired of elves.[22] Oxford never bestowed on Lewis an endowed chair despite his decades of service as a student, tutor, and fellow; his popularity as a lecturer and writer was not well received by his less-gifted faculty colleagues.

21. This was the pub where the Inklings often met (also known as the Bird and the Babe, or the Bird and Baby).
22. This hurt Tolkien a great deal and discouraged him from writing fiction. It was roughly at this point that Lewis's support and encouragement became much more pronounced, even extravagant. See Duriez, *Tolkien and C. S. Lewis*, 128–29.

Underlying all these qualities of friendship was a sustaining mutuality and reciprocity, a generous giving and receiving of time and attentiveness. Lewis and Tolkien paid attention to each other, coming to know one another at a depth shared with few other people. They consoled one another and grieved together, and—more often—shared a whimsical humor. They were mutually attuned, often putting the needs of their friend before their own. But not always. At times they failed to identify the needs of the other or misread what was required of a friend. Despite the decades of a reciprocal unselfing that seemed to come naturally and effortlessly to both, their respective fat relentless egos were never entirely undone. Nonetheless, they formed each other in countless ways through the routine give-and-take that good friends master over time. Any biography of either Lewis or Tolkien that excluded their friendship would be woefully incomplete.

One crucial factor in this friendship is difficult to describe: namely, the activities that sustained Lewis and Tolkien as friends. The difficulty results from how ordinary and routine these activities were, but how easily they can be missed or overlooked. The two spent a lot of time walking together, drinking at a pub, sharing a meal. Admittedly, these are terribly mundane activities. So why are they crucial? They force people to be in a shared place, thereby enabling a mutual attentiveness. Over time, at a deliberate pace, individuals become friends by being in place together. This is an important reminder in a culture that has come to believe that friendships can be built and sustained on the run. All that is needed is posting a photo, texting or tweeting a message. But these are not adequate substitutes for time-consuming, face-to-face encounters in a shared physical place. Without this basic physicality, it is difficult to imagine how so-called virtual friendships enable humans to flourish as embodied beings. In an age when "friends" are casually regarded as artifacts easily created and discarded, the slow, painstaking process of receiving and caring for the gift of a friend is a much-needed antidote.

Since friends choose to make themselves vulnerable to each other, friendship is also an important setting for learning important lessons about grace and forgiveness. Without the grace to embrace the other as he or she is and to forgive that other when one is wronged, no friendship could survive, or perhaps even get started. There were many times when Lewis and Tolkien learned these lessons, often by failing to be graceful and forgiving when it was required. This need for grace and forgiveness in the ordinary relationships of everyday life becomes more pronounced when we turn our attention to a more intimate friendship in the next chapter.

CHAPTER 7

Spouses

There is nothing unusual about being married. There are a lot of spouses in the world. Virtually every society—ancient, modern, and contemporary—has some institution, legal recognition, or acknowledged relationship that can be called marriage. There is, not surprisingly, a great deal of cultural variability regarding the customs and forms surrounding marriage, but there are also striking similarities. Often, one does not need to be deeply steeped in a foreign culture to recognize who is married to whom. Even informal cohabitation arrangements often appear similar to marriages.

Within the Christian tradition, marriage has been regarded as a special kind of friendship.[1] Saint Augustine established marriage as a genuine, although inferior, vocation alongside continent singleness.[2] Among the three goods of marriage is a mutual fidelity shared by husband and wife.[3] This ideal of mutual amicability was further developed by subsequent generations of both theological and secular writers.[4] Moreover, friendship expresses and solidifies the love underlying marital vows and covenants.[5] Although the phrase "I married my best friend" can often sound overly sentimental, it nonetheless captures an essential truth.

Authors are shaped and limited by their personal experience. Despite their best efforts to imagine what others are undergoing, the exercise often

---

1. See Wong, *Beginning from Man and Woman*, 160–69.
2. See Augustine, *On the Good of Marriage*. See also Brown, *The Body and Society*, chap. 19; and Ramsey, "Human Sexuality."
3. The other two goods are offspring and sacrament.
4. See Witte, *From Sacrament to Contract*.
5. See Wong, *Beginning from Man and Woman*, chap. 5.

proves, at best, incomplete. I am no exception, so two disclaimers concerning this chapter: First, my portrayal of marriage may seem unduly idealistic. I have been happily married for over forty-five years, and marriage is, to use an old word, an estate I easily and unreservedly commend. But I know that not everyone has the same interest in or experience with marriage. For a variety of reasons many have chosen not to marry, and even more have found themselves married to indifferent, cruel, or hellish partners. Second, same-sex marriage is gaining public and ecclesial acceptance, as well as legal regulation and protection. I have no desire to enter the moral, theological, and political debates swirling around this innovation. But my experience of marriage has been quite traditional, and I am not certain how easily my thoughts on marriage translate. I acknowledge the reality of both of these circumstances that are unlike my own, and I admit that I don't have a "feel" for them. Consequently, the following words have been chosen to address as many readers as possible, and I hope my efforts will succeed more often than they fail.

Cleaving

Marriage is a special kind of friendship. How so? Because it involves cleaving. Admittedly, the word *cleaving* (or *cleave*) is antiquated. But it should be dusted off and used again, because it is a good word for characterizing marriage. Genesis 2:24 in the King James Version of the Bible states, "Therefore shall a man leave his father and his mother, and shall *cleave* unto his wife: and they shall be one flesh" (emphasis added). Jesus commends this passage in his teaching on marriage and divorce (see Matt. 19:5; Mark 10:7). To cleave is to adhere, cling, hold fast, attach oneself; it is to remain devoted, faithful, and steadfast. The word connotes two becoming one. Alas, this connotation is archaic and has fallen out of use; it is replaced in modern translations with such terms as "united," "bonds," or "joins." It is understandable why contemporary words have been employed in recent translations. The Bible is a vessel revealing the living Word of God and should therefore be easily accessible to readers. Language changes over time.[6] Our daily parlance no longer includes such antiques as *forethink* or *verily*. Granted. But most of the substitutes in this case are wanting, methinks, because they fail to capture both the depth and the breadth of cleaving.

Many of the substitutes are cautious and tentative, suggesting mutual consent tempered by a lingering suspicion. The connotations are primarily

---

6. See Lewis, *Studies in Words*.

conditional and contractual: two individuals joining in an agreement that is not necessarily assumed to be permanent. The two remain two. This contractual understanding of marriage may accurately reflect emerging, even dominant, cultural trends, but it is a deeply diminished understanding of what biblical teaching on cleaving entails.

Additionally, the substitutions fail to capture the ominous side of cleaving that I have not yet mentioned. To cleave also means to divide, split, pierce, or tear apart.[7] The term *cleaving* serves to remind that love is fragile and vulnerable. Love binds together, but the bond can also be broken; that which is cleaved together can also be cleaved apart. This is, perhaps, why love and its failure are experienced so intensely in marriage, because of marriage's inherent intimacy. Spouses see each other at their best and worst, in some instances strengthening their covenant while in others weakening or destroying it. Some couples who once pledged their undying love to each other are consumed by unending acrimony. *Cleave*, archaic word that it is, needs to be recovered, for it depicts love rather vividly, both as a power that binds and as a fragile gift that requires mutual attention and care. In short, cleaving is another exercise in unselfing.

In the remainder of this section, I examine two proclivities that may help promote cleaving as a constructive practice. The ensuing examination is not exhaustive but illustrative. *Fidelity* is the first proclivity. As mentioned in chapter 6, fidelity or faithfulness is indispensable to any friendship, and marriage is no exception. Marital fidelity is often popularly understood as refraining from having sexual relations with anyone other than one's spouse—or, more succinctly, from committing adultery. It is certainly that, at a minimum, but in biblical and traditional Christian teaching marital fidelity means much more. One could avoid committing adultery yet nonetheless be unfaithful to one's spouse. How? By withholding physical or emotional intimacy that restricts the one-flesh unity of marriage or by sharing certain confidences with others that violate the exclusivity of the spousal relationship.

This is not to suggest that a spouse can or should bear the burden of meeting every need a partner might have, but neither does this limitation suggest a so-called open marriage.[8] Spousal friendship is different from other forms of friendship because of its limited scope of participants. We may choose various friends to satisfy, in part, a variety of interests, but we do not choose various spouses to satisfy a range of more intimate physical and emotional needs. Cleaving is a two-person activity, not a group activity.

---

7. *Cleave* appears thirty times in the King James Version, mostly with positive connotations.
8. See, e.g., Nelson, *Embodiment*, chap. 6.

Although one may find being married fulfilling, marriage is not a means of self-fulfillment. Rather, it is predicated on a self-giving mutuality, entailing a reciprocity that is roughly equivalent over time. Exchange is at the heart of marriage. If one partner always receives while the other only gives, it is difficult to see how such a relationship can be regarded as truly marital. Granted, the exchange is not always meticulously equal. There are times when giving and receiving are necessarily unequal but nonetheless reflect the genuine depth of love that makes two one: for instance, the care given by one spouse to another during a debilitating or terminal illness. Friends or even strangers may provide such extended caring, but there is no compelling expectation that they should do so. In marriage, by contrast, such care is expected, and according to the traditional vows, promised. This is why, in part, positive law regards and enforces marriage as a contract, because of the promises that are exchanged between two people. But a theological account of marriage employs the terms of lifelong covenant or sacrament to capture the more binding qualities of mutual faithfulness. Marriage is an exercise in mutual unselfing in which one comes to know and enable the good of the other, and in doing so also graciously and thankfully receives the gift of love that is offered by the other.

Trust is the second proclivity. We trust strangers; otherwise we could not conduct many routine financial transactions or economic exchanges. We trust friends; otherwise we would not tell them secrets. But spouses are trusted in transparent ways that transcend all other relationships, save that with God.[9] Again, to employ an out-of-date biblical word, spouses know each other in ways that each cannot (or should not) be known by any other. Such mutual knowledge is not only physical but also emotional and spiritual—in short, a deeply personal knowledge approaching the totality of the being of the other. Spouses see each other at their best and worst, and they trust that such knowledge will not be used in manipulative or destructive ways, but to strengthen bonds of love and affection. Ideally, spouses trust each other not only with their wellbeing but, at times, with their very lives.[10]

Trust differs from but complements fidelity. If faithfulness solidifies the marital bond, then trust encapsulates the risk and vulnerability of marriage. Trust can be misplaced or violated. For instance, one may place her confidence in a spouse who proves incapable of being faithful. Or trust can be violated by a spouse who willfully deceives or abuses. Yet trust is often rewarded in

9. Even in the most close or intimate marriage, neither spouse ever entirely "sees" the soul of the other, for such sight (insight?) is reserved to God alone.

10. For example, in living wills approved by married individuals, the vast majority assign durable power of attorney to their spouses rather than to other possible designees such as parents, siblings, offspring, friends, or lawyers.

marriage. Spouses can and do remain faithful to each other, their mutual vulnerabilities remaining undisturbed. And on those occasions when spouses fail each other, the presumption of trust makes forgiveness and reconciliation easier. It is easily granted that to trust is to also take a risk. But what is risky can fail, and the consequences of that failure can hurt, especially when one fails at loving another person. Perhaps, then, it would be prudent to refrain from risk-taking, to make oneself as invulnerable as possible. This strategy is admittedly tempting—but it is ruinous. The cost of invulnerability is to forgo love, not only of a spouse but also of any genuine friends. It is the attempt to inoculate oneself against fellow humans with whom one was created to be in fellowship. As C. S. Lewis suggested, only in hell are we free of risk-taking, because there we are entirely isolated and devoid of any company.[11]

Together, fidelity and trust help disclose love as the centerpiece of the human condition, because as creatures created in the image and likeness of the triune God we were created *by* love and *for* love. In mutual faithfulness, two are bound together in love, but a love that cannot be taken for granted or ever fully domesticated. Love is always accompanied by risk and cannot be otherwise, for it would no longer be directed toward someone who is genuinely other and who will always remain at least a bit opaque. This implies that one cannot be truly fulfilled if one refuses the possibility of having one's heart broken. Humans were created to be risk-takers. This does not suggest a divine endorsement of recklessness, but it serves to remind us that we are stewards rather than masters of our lives. It is the risk-averse steward, who hides the single coin entrusted to his care, who is condemned (see Matt. 25:14–30).

Together, fidelity and trust are two distinct but related contours of love that help shape a marital identity over time. It is the identity of two becoming one. This is not an appealing image to late moderns because it ostensibly diminishes the individuality they prize so deeply and work so diligently to devise and express. After all, we are subjected to the daily mantra that we are all unique, self-made persons, as witnessed by the burgeoning market of self-help products and services.[12] Two becoming one would divert attention from one becoming a better and more self-loved one. Yet it is often in intimate and enduring relationships such as marriage that we discover who we are. Counterintuitively, the strong individual is not a self-made artifact but a creation resulting from a mixture of self-giving and receiving from another self. A good marriage does not destroy individuality but builds it. To use an

---

11. Lewis, *Four Loves*, 121.

12. Curiously, late moderns turn to the assistance of others, especially so-called experts, to help them manufacture their unique identities.

admittedly simple example, marriage is a singular story about two principal characters. It is, ideally, a story of two remaining two as they become one, for in lifelong fidelity and trust they also discover their mutual belonging, and in that belonging are found their respective marital vocations.

Belonging and Vocation

As mentioned above, marriage is a lifelong covenant. Two people pledge that for the remainder of their earthly lives they will remain faithful and committed to each other, despite whatever unforeseen circumstances might occur. Spouses remain married for better and for worse. This is a sentiment that late moderns find both unrealistic and unattractive. People change over time, so how can we expect them to be bound by promises they can no longer keep if they are to be honest to themselves as autonomous persons? If people, for instance, can fall in love, they can also fall out of love. Wouldn't it be more honest to admit that a once-living love has died and to discontinue a now farcical relationship? As Jacques Ellul contends, such frank, even brutal honesty is the spirit of our age, which contends that we should place ourselves first and above others to avoid conforming to stifling customs and commonplaces that prevent self-fulfillment.[13]

To be clear, the possibility of dissolving a marriage cannot be ruled out on theological or moral grounds. As Karl Barth notes, some marriages fall under God's judgment.[14] Yet the permissibility of divorce does not detract from the Christian teaching that marriage is ideally a lifelong and indissoluble covenant.

Ellul is correct that the priority of the self is a dominant presumption of late-modern anthropology. This priority is a commonplace that is nearly always center stage and is rarely questioned, a self-evident truth requiring no further justification.[15] It is, however, a "truth" requiring justification, and it cannot bear much scrutiny—for, as we found in the preceding two chapters, it presupposes an autonomy that is little more than a fabrication, and a destructive one at that. We live in a world of neighbors. We become who we are in the company of others (such as parents, siblings, friends, and spouses). Ironically, without others we would not become individuals because we would have no one with whom we could contrast, or differentiate, ourselves. Humans belong with one another; they were not created to be alone.

13. See Ellul, *Critique of the New Commonplaces*, 49–55.
14. See Barth, *Church Dogmatics* III/4, 204–33.
15. See Ellul, *Critique of the New Commonplaces*, 3–27.

Marriage is one relationship where many people find a significant, if not predominate, sphere of mutual and timely belonging—spanning, often, the majority of a couple's lifetime. As noted above, marriage is mutual because it entails the fidelity and trust of two people. It is also timely, not simply because it endures for a period of time but also because it is a locale in which spouses find they belong together within a temporal creation. As creatures they are not free-floating spirits but embodied beings requiring the attention of others. Humans live out their appointed times not in trying to avoid each other but in embracing their creaturely interdependence as a gift rather than a curse. Hell is not other people, but their prolonged absence.

Marriage not only encapsulates mutuality but also entails particularity. People are not married in general but are bound to specific persons. *This* woman, for instance, is married to *that* man; these two particular persons belong together. This particularity exposes both the depth and the challenges of neighbor love. The vast majority of neighbors we encounter in a lifetime are strangers, and often invisible or unknown ones at that. Our interaction with these neighbors is often brief and utilitarian, but it is nonetheless accompanied by certain obligations, such as courtesy and respect. Yet there are also more compact spheres of neighbors, such as colleagues, friends, and families. These spheres require acts of love that are not requisite when we encounter strangers. Indeed, it would be unsuitable to treat a stranger with the familiarity of a friend, and likewise wrong to treat a friend with the cursory utility usually reserved for a stranger. Neighbors should be treated in ways that fit with the ways love both requires and restricts.

Within this spectrum, marriage is the most intimate expression of neighbor love. Although friends and family are loved with greater intensity than strangers and colleagues, they cannot match the intimacy shared by spouses, for spouses know each other in body, soul, and spirit. Marriage is a unique relationship that cannot be replicated by any other pair of neighbors. Consequently, the mutual belonging of marriage is also exclusive. The spheres of family and friends can be expanded, but not so that of marriage, because of the mutual fidelity and trust that bind a couple together. As the traditional vows make clear, cleaving requires forsaking all others.

This is not to say, however, that a married couple is somehow isolated or cut off from other forms of human association. To the contrary, marriage can and does provide a stable base from which broader associations of belonging may be encountered and embraced. For example, in the next chapter we will see how marriage is related to family and how the familial household is, or should be, a hospitable place. But this is to anticipate, and at this point it is important to remain focused on marriage, especially as a calling and vocation.

The vocation of marriage entails a wide range of activities, habits, and virtues too numerous to mention in this chapter. For the purpose of what follows, however, I ask the reader to keep in mind that the vocation of marriage embodies the fidelity and trust associated with cleaving, and the mutual and exclusive belonging that is shared and deepened by spouses over time. In cleaving to and belonging with one another, a married couple becomes one over time, and in becoming one the two become more substantial respectively. How can this be? The marital calling prompts one to love the other as other, requiring that the familiarity gained over time not diminish the mystery of otherness as a consequence. Marriage creates and maintains, so to speak, a proper distance in which the two become one while remaining two. In their cleaving and belonging, the other becomes bound to the other while remaining other. The imagery of cleaving implies a kind of clinging, but this is not a smothering embrace. To use a simplistic metaphor, a couple is better able to walk through life together holding hands than hugging. This is only a half-truth, for it suggests that marriage is primarily frenetic activity, constant movement over time. But marriage includes stopping, simply being and belonging in each other's company.

What I have in mind is again similar to Oliver O'Donovan's notion of "entering into rest" as the predominate mode of communicating love among people. In communicating the good of love, people are bound together, albeit imperfectly, through a series of both restraints and freedom to act. O'Donovan's concept is acutely pertinent to marriage, and it is worth quoting him at length:

> Negative or positive, these features of love move round a well-described circle: restraint of competitive self-assertion, acceptance of others' activities and initiatives, flexibility in waiting upon them, and readiness to give them time and space. They describe a moment when the urgent need to act is postponed in the interests of others' actions. This is a practical disposition, not one of inert passivity, but one of self-restraint rather than initiative, affirmative encouragement rather than competition. It is not that the sphere of action has been left behind for contemplation; rather, inaction has been drawn into the scope of the active disposition, which now extends its scope to include the activities of other people.[16]

The love that we communicate, that we share with each other, is familiar and yet also more than familiar, affirming our dependence on one another. Love is expressed through what we do for each other and what we refrain from doing.

16. O'Donovan, *Entering into Rest*, 2–3.

Charity, in particular, is a focused love of the world and of the persons we encounter in the world. Love does not displace faith and hope; rather, they are concrete expressions of love.

According to O'Donovan, communicating love is crucial to human flourishing, so one might expect that he would describe it in rather grand, even grandiose theological terms. This is not the case. Here is a partial list of activities that sustain communication: preparing and sharing a meal; celebrating the accomplishments of friends and family; housework; mind-numbing, tedious chores. The word *caring*, however, appears most frequently: acts of kindness attending to the physical and material needs of family, friends, strangers; loving our neighbors. It is daily, common, and ordinary acts that sustain communities, and it is within community that the moral life has its greatest depth, for it is also in communicating that we fulfill our callings and vocations. In O'Donovan's words, "Our practical calling is to respond to the meaning of the world and the presence of the neighbor, and that will take us far beyond the boundaries of anything we call work, into the life we share with family and friends, into one-off acts of care shown to other people, into acts of reflection, meditation, and worship. These, too, are our calling."[17]

I know of no better word than *caring* to describe married life at its best. It is in caring for each other that two people discover their mutual and timely belonging with an exquisite intensity. To illustrate, Wallace Stegner's novel *Crossing to Safety* is a story about two married couples who are best friends. Sid and Charity have had a long and somewhat tempestuous marriage, one in which she has asserted nearly total control over her husband and large brood of children. Larry and Sally have also shared a long marriage, but early on Sally contracted polio and Larry has devoted himself to caring for his disabled wife. At the end of the story, Charity is dying of cancer, and she calls together her friends and family to be with her during her last few days. Yet Charity closes Sid out despite his protests, preferring the company of her daughters and Sally. Out of frustration and in embittered compliance with his wife's final command, Sid tells Larry that he takes pleasure in seeing that Larry is as addicted to and dependent on his wife as Sid is, and that neither could possibly be "unchained."[18] Larry admits to himself that this is true, but he also thinks, what Sid "doesn't understand is that my chains are not chains, that over the years Sally's crippling has been a rueful blessing. It has made her more than she was; it has let her give me more than she would

17. O'Donovan, *Entering into Rest*, 110.
18. Stegner, *Crossing to Safety*, 339.

ever have been able to give me healthy; it has taught me at least the alphabet of gratitude."[19]

What Sid perceives as chains are the bonds of imperfection that bind finite and mortal beings together. In tending to Sally's physical needs, such as helping her to get out of bed or stand up and sit down, Larry also perceives the depth of the love that they share, because caring is not always or even often a one-way street, but an exchange. Giving and receiving care is reciprocal, exposing the reciprocity that binds us together and also the depth of one's own life within that shared bond. Larry reflects, "You can't be close to the mortality of friends without being brought to think of your own."[20]

There is much that could be said about this story. One could, for instance, criticize Charity for closing Sid out while dying. How could she refuse her husband's wish to be at her bedside as she dies—a final act of love? We should not be too quick to judge. As Larry reflects, Charity is "capable of a noble generosity, and of cramming it down on the head of the recipient like a crown of thorns."[21] She knows that her husband is not a strong man, and he will need time and distance to deal with her passing, for otherwise he will wallow in self-pity. Charity also knows that Sid is incapable of creating this necessary distance on his own; she needs to push him away for his own sake. Larry wonders whether she was "thinking ahead for [Sid], breaking him away from her by an act of cruelty and preparing him for healing"?[22] Is Charity aptly named?

The ending of this novel is admittedly dramatic. But it is only a small piece of an otherwise ordinary story about two married couples. Most of the story is about falling in love, courting, exchanging vows, raising children who keep one awake all night when ill, and coming to terms with childlessness that deprives one of such loving sleep deprivations. There are hours spent keeping the house clean, running errands, buying groceries, preparing meals, doing yardwork; there are friends and colleagues who (for a while) edify and others who disappoint. There are moments of career success and moments of failure. It is in many ways a story about two unremarkable married couples who, like millions of other couples, spend a lifetime learning to cleave their lives together in differing ways, at times doing it well and at other times badly. The cumulative effect of these years of mundane activities shaped these characters for the dramatic moment of death that concludes the novel. Ultimately, it is the reader of this story who must judge whether or not they were well

19. Stegner, *Crossing to Safety*, 339–40.
20. Stegner, *Crossing to Safety*, 339.
21. Stegner, *Crossing to Safety*, 340.
22. Stegner, *Crossing to Safety*, 340.

prepared as married couples to face this final hour, whether or not their trust for each other was well placed, whether or not the risk of love was rewarded.

It is through cleaving and trusting over time that marriage forms its bond. It is a bond of promises given and received. Marriage is thereby a vocation, entailing vows that are meant to be kept without reservation. As W. H. Auden observed, "No one can hope to have a vocation, in fact, if he makes a private reservation that, should circumstances alter, he can get divorced."[23] Yet marriage is also a bond of imperfection, despite the solemn vows that are made in the presence of God. Spouses, for instance, come to rely on each other. That reliance is a vow of mutual fidelity intended to endure for a lifetime. Often that reliance is steadfast, but at other times it is weak and fleeting. The calling and vocation of marriage often discloses the capacity for love and affection at its best, and it is also a love that at times fails the beloved. The love that binds a couple together is not an angelic love but a fallen, creaturely love. The vocation of marriage is predicated on the need for frequently offering and receiving forgiveness.

Mutual caring is the hallmark of marriage. It is in and through caring for each other that spouses come to belong with each other, and in their mutual belonging the two become one. Stegner's *Crossing to Safety* is a multifaceted story, but it is a tale about caring. The care binding Larry and Sally together is obvious. They exhibit a tender, uncomplaining response to a physically debilitating polio that would prove catastrophic to many, but to Larry and Sally it becomes an occasion to learn the alphabet of gratitude. The care that binds Sid and Charity is far less obvious; some might even say it is absent. Yet there is no single way of exhibiting care when it comes to particular people. Stegner entertains the possibility that caring must at times be cruel, a suggestion that is not incompatible with Christian faith. Christians affirm that God cares for them, but a caring God does not spare humans the pain and suffering that is inherent in their status as finite and mortal creatures.[24] It cannot be otherwise if humans are to flourish, for love cannot be separated from suffering, and without love humans cannot flourish.

Marriage directs our attention toward the mundane, and that focus in turn helps us identify, solidify, and cherish what is truly most satisfying and worthwhile, what best promotes human flourishing. If marriage were not fixated predominantly on the commonplace needs of embodied creatures it would be a hideous estate, for spouses would simply be used by each other for their respective self-aggrandizement. Marriage, then, provides a potentially

23. Auden, *Complete Works of W. H. Auden*, 2:177.
24. See, e.g., Lewis, *Problem of Pain*.

potent antidote to the incessant and vacuous striving undertaken by many late moderns. To get lost in a relentless quest for self-fulfillment, to indulge a ravenous appetite for the extraordinary, is to lose track of what is genuinely vital. It is to fall victim to the illusion that a good life is only one that is bigger than life. To invoke another antiquated word, it is committing the sin of vainglory.[25] Entertaining this sin results in a deadly reversal of priorities, for it places the illusory safety of isolated autonomy over the risk of love.

Marriage is a crucial and basic calling and vocation grounded in covenant that helps prepare people to participate in larger spheres of human association. If this is true, then care must be taken not to sequester marriage away from public view. Marriage is rightfully a private association of two consenting adults, but that privacy is expressed and protected within broader public contexts. It may be asked, then, What does this expression and protection contribute to the goods of civil society that are broadly shared? One such contribution is that of household hospitality when spouses invite children into their marital fellowship. To speak of marriage, at least within the Christian tradition, presupposes saying something about *family*, the topic of the next chapter.

25. See DeYoung, *Vainglory*.

CHAPTER 8

Parents and Children

Parents and children are everywhere. There is nothing unique about the parent-child relationship. Everyone alive today has parents—every child has two biological progenitors, and most have at least one nurturing parent. Many adults become parents, whether biologically, by adoption, by fostering, or by some combination of the above. The relationship between parents and offspring is ubiquitous because the survival of the human species, and of the civilizations they create, depends on each generation passing on life to the next.

Although the parent-child relationship is commonplace, it also has a deeper connotation. For instance, it is a relationship composed of particular individuals. There are no generic parents and children. This man is the father of that daughter, and this woman is the mother of that son. The intergenerational bonds that are formed, or that fail to be formed, are crucial components of personal and interpersonal development, for good and for ill. This is especially true in respect to young children, who require the affection, attention, and guidance of loving parents as a foundation for subsequent maturation.

Although the parent-child bond is deeply personal and rightfully private, it also has great social importance. Societies comprise not only individuals but also associations, many of which are based on affinity. Families are one such association. This is why, in part, the state and civil society often assist parents in fulfilling their child-rearing responsibilities by providing schools, health care, social services, and the like. Although the family, contrary to some pagan philosophy, is not the foundation of civil society, it is nonetheless a crucial association underlying a civil and political order.

The adept reader will have noted how, in the preceding paragraph, I transitioned from *parent-child relationship* terminology to the terminology of *family*. The switch was intentional. Family connotes a larger association within which parents and children are embedded. Although familial households may be composed of one parent and one child, family also refers to extended affinities of kinship. In addition to parents and a child there may be siblings, grandparents, aunts, uncles, nieces, nephews, and cousins. These extended spheres of affinity help prevent the so-called nuclear family from becoming a secluded enclave, cut off from any substantial contact with other forms of human association. Additionally, these broader spheres of affinity help (or should help) prepare members to relate to larger spheres of strangers and citizens they encounter in civil society and the political realm. In short, a well-ordered family is not oriented solely in upon itself but is also ordered toward interacting with broader spheres of association.

A detailed description of the moral and political importance of family is beyond the scope of this chapter.[1] Instead, I concentrate on three important touchstones that are grounded in ordinary familial relationships and activities. These touchstones are the parental vocation, family as its principal vocational outcome, and the ordering of families in relation to civil society and political governance.

Parental Vocation

Traditionally, Christianity has taught that marriage is the proper moral and social basis for procreation and for the education of children. I find little reason to quarrel with the precept. Recall the previous chapter: in marriage two become one in a bond that is, ideally, lifelong. In their cleaving over time, spouses create a space of mutual belonging in which an exclusive friendship and fellowship may flourish. They belong with each other. It is exclusivity that gives marriage both its relational security and its moral probity. In their mutual trust and fidelity, spouses find a relative safety and security that, as autonomous individuals, they would not have. In becoming one the two create a loving space in a world that is not always hospitable or welcoming.

But there is a danger here that should make us wary. The exclusivity that gives marriage much of its strength can become distorted, turning a marital niche into an insular and secluded enclave. Such a distortion is the very denial of what Christian marriage means. As Saint Augustine taught, there are three

1. For a more detailed description, see Waters, *Family in Christian Social and Political Thought*.

goods of marriage: faith, sacrament, and offspring.[2] Faith refers to the mutual fidelity and charity shared by husband and wife. The sacramental status or qualities of marriage have to do with a permanence that is steadfast and life-long. Offspring direct spousal love out beyond itself, making it more expansive and inclusive. Together these three goods provide the pivotal parameters of a household based on friendship and concord.

God may call spouses to open their marital fellowship to include the gift of children that God entrusts to their care.[3] Most often this calling is fulfilled through procreation. Through their one-flesh unity, a married couple gives birth to a child that they subsequently raise. The emphasis, however, is not on the biological origins of a child but on his or her rearing. The parents with whom a child belongs need not share a bloodline or genetic line of descent with the child. Adoption is an equally valid way of establishing a family. Adoptive parents are not second-best substitutes but are following a paren-tal vocational path that is nearly indistinguishable from one originating in procreation. Whether through procreative or adoptive means, what is most important is creating a household, a place of mutual and timely belonging for all members of a family, regardless of how they are welcomed into its fellowship.[4]

What this ideal of mutual and timely belonging conveys is that although biology cannot (or ought not) be ignored in respect to ordering the relation-ship between parents and children, neither should it be determinative. This acknowledgment counters two proclivities in contemporary moral thought that often distort both philosophical and theological understandings of the family. On the one hand, biology is dismissed as an irrelevant consideration. Parenthood is understood predominantly, or in some instances exclusively, as an act of will rather than as a calling and vocation. Consequently, any tech-nological, market, or contractual means may be utilized to obtain a child. But this effectively reduces children to outcomes of reproductive projects in which a place of mutual and timely belonging is displaced by an implicit concept of ownership. On this view, a child, regardless how she is procured, does not so much belong *with* her parents as she belongs *to* them.[5]

On the other hand, biology (i.e., genes) becomes the overriding factor: fulfilling the desire to become a parent requires that a child carry the genes of at least one parent. Hence the recourse to surrogacy or other techniques to obtain a child of "one's own." Yet this is a curious strategy, particularly

2. See Augustine, *On the Good of Marriage.*
3. Parenthood is a calling, but not all married couples are called to be parents.
4. See Waters, "Welcoming Children into Our Homes."
5. See, e.g., Robertson, *Children of Choice.*

for Christians, since parents do not own their children. Rather, a child is ultimately a gift created by God and entrusted to the care of parents. These parents, in turn, whether they be procreative or adoptive, commend the child back to God through the sacrament of baptism.[6] In this respect, baptism provides an important reminder that lineage is not an overriding consideration; it should not dictate our theological or moral understanding of family. Moreover, preserving a line of genetic descent as the exclusive or premier desire places a heavy burden on children as objects of hope. This burden, however, is unwarranted—especially for Christians, whose hope is not flesh and blood but water and Spirit. Our future is not our children, but Christ our redeemer. This is why, traditionally, marriage and family have been seen as a providential witness (to a good creation) that is complemented by the witness of vocational singleness (to creation's eschatological end in Christ).[7] This does not mean that the vocation of parenthood is not predicated on the love and care of children; it means that children should be loved and cared for as fellow creatures and not as potential saviors. As Hannah Arendt rightfully contends in her account of natality, children serve as important symbols of the hope that something new can occur.[8] But that hope is potentially a gratuitous blessing and not an entitlement.

Genetic descent is the way that humans perpetuate themselves as a species. This is a fact that should not be ignored so that parenthood becomes an act of will, reducing children to artifacts of what is willed. But neither is this fact decisive. Giving birth is not synonymous with being a parent. Parenthood often (though not always) begins with giving birth; the vocation of parenthood, however, necessarily entails the provision of mutual and timely belonging. To pretend that origin does not matter or that it is the only thing that matters is to portray a highly truncated understanding of the relationship between parents and children. Biology and the provision of mutual and timely belonging both matter and are not mutually exclusive.

Adoption illustrates that parenthood is a social and normative construct, while it is also embedded in human biology. How could it be otherwise for embodied creatures requiring the care and fellowship of other embodied human creatures? Adoptive parents provide affection and caring that biological parents are either unable or unwilling to provide. Consequently, we may say, without contradiction, something like the following: a woman who

6. In many churches practicing believers' baptism, children are commended to God through a ritual act of dedication.

7. See Waters, *Family in Christian Social and Political Thought*, chap. 4.

8. See Arendt, *Human Condition*, chap. 5. See also Bowen-Moore, *Hannah Arendt's Philosophy of Natality*.

surrenders her child to adoption after giving birth is the mother of that child, but the woman caring for the adopted child is the mother with whom the child belongs. Marriage and parenthood as vocations oriented toward providing places of mutual and timely belonging serve as important reminders that we humans are embodied creatures; as such, we are biological and social beings who cannot be reduced to either one or the other.

Family

Christian moral theology has consistently taught that marriage is an institution or estate established and blessed by God. From roughly the fifth century on, marriage has enjoyed either a sacramental or a privileged status within a wide range of Christian churches.[9] Concurrently, marriage has been affirmed and supported as the normative context for the procreation and education of children. Although much recent teaching is less condemnatory and may even be supportive of situations failing to meet this norm—for example, single parents and children born out of wedlock—two married parents remains the explicit or implicit preferred standard. There are good reasons for preserving and supporting this standard given the teaching of Scripture, the Christian moral tradition, and human experience more broadly (there is considerable evidence that people, especially children, flourish in what may be described as intact families).[10]

It is surprising that although much has been written about marriage, parents, and children, the idea of family has not found universal support among theologians. Why? There is seemingly a reluctance to give family any unwarranted significance since it is a form of human association grounded in nature. Such grounding, it is feared, highlights the old creation and its dependence on lineage over the eschatological and spiritual emphases of the new covenant in Christ. It is understandable that we love and are drawn most strongly to those with whom we share natural bonds of affinity. And that is the problem. Fixating on those who are nearest and dearest may create suspicion, even hostility, toward a broader range of neighbors that God commands us to love. In short, family becomes a barrier in obeying and following Christ. A similar fear, it should be noted, appears sometimes in secular guise: families are viewed with suspicion or even hostility because they impede one's loyalty to the state or to its political leaders. Consequently, policies are adopted that

---

9. See Witte, *From Sacrament to Contract*.

10. See, e.g., relevant sections of Browning et al., *From Culture Wars to Common Ground*; Browning, *Equality and the Family*.

are designed, explicitly or latently, to simultaneously weaken families and promote the state (effectively as a surrogate parent).[11]

Karl Barth, for example, writes extensively about the relationship between men and women and about procreation, parents, and children in the context of vocational expressions of neighbor love.[12] Yet he avoids the word *family* because it has "no interest at all for Christian theology."[13] This lack of interest results from the family's affiliation with politically organized units such as households, clans, and tribes and their subsequent corrupting influence on issues of social and political ordering. It is understandable why Barth dismisses the family, given the rise of Nazism in his time and its emphasis on blood and soil. The German *volk* had become, effectively, a family writ large, replete with xenophobia and rabid racism. *Family* had been corrupted into a metaphor justifying fear of strangers, especially those from "inferior" races, and thereby preventing an expansive love of neighbor. But it is not clear why Barth finds it necessary to dismiss entirely the theological significance of familial expressions of love. If, as he argues, the fellowship of women and men as disclosed in marriage forms the normative basis of parenthood, then why is the resulting familial association of no theological interest? Moreover, it is hard to imagine the types of marital and parent-child fellowships Barth expounds without presupposing the social context of family, much more to imagine how these fellowships should be related to near and distant neighbors in its absence.

Sadly, Barth's brusque dismissal of family leaves by the wayside of theological consideration a crucial form of fellowship enabling human flourishing. The ordering of marital and parental fidelity is founded on and reveals an *unfolding* and *enfolding* familial love. When, for instance, God calls a woman and man to marriage, a new and more expansive love unfolds in their mutual and exclusive devotion to each other. Their one-flesh unity embodies their fully shared being. Should God call this couple to become parents, a further unfolding of their love occurs in the extension of their fellowship to children entrusted to their care. There is a common thread in the unfolding of familial love, originating in marriage and extending through child-rearing.

The presence of a child does not construct a parallel relationship: a family is not a container for separate spousal, parental, filial, and fraternal relationships. Rather, these relationships are aspects of a shared loyalty, mutual belonging, and common love. We may speak of marital love unfolding into

---

11. See, e.g., Russell, *Marriage and Morals*, esp. chap. 15.
12. See Barth, *Church Dogmatics* III/4.
13. Barth, *Church Dogmatics* III/4, 241.

parental love and of a consequent unfolding of familial love, in turn, enfolding the forms of love preceding it. Although family includes marriage and parenthood, they are not its totality, nor can family be reduced to either of these constitutive elements. As James Gustafson argues, "marriage and family are more than the sum of their individual parts, more than the aggregate of the persons who belong to them."[14] Consequently, marriage is the normative foundation of family because it embodies the natural and social contours of the relationships offering a mutual and timely place of belonging.

The family, then, bears a providential witness to the vindicated order of creation being drawn toward its destiny in Christ, for—at the very least—families involve the ordering of human life over time. Human beings perpetuate themselves through progeny. No generation comes into being ex nihilo, cut off from ancestors and descendants. Every person is a recipient, and many are potential progenitors, of a genetic legacy. People, however, do not merely ride the crest of biological processes, because each generation is brought into being through what may be characterized as a socially ordered particularity. Every child has a particular mother and father, and each parent begets a particular daughter or son. Individuals are not related, either biologically or socially, to a general humanity but to specific people. Although all humans were once children, all the women and men preceding them were not their parents, nor are all children succeeding them their offspring. Without particular biological and social bonds, a sense of continuity between generations is lost. This loss in turn weakens the family's providential witness by effectively denying the vindicated order of creation, because humans do not merely perpetuate themselves as a species but pursue a purposeful transmission of life from one generation to the next. A family embodies a lineage *and* teleological structure that help situate its members within creation's unfolding history.[15]

This lineage and teleological structure are captured in the dynamic character of familial relationships. Families change over time, as necessitated by generational transitions. What preoccupies newlyweds is not the same as what preoccupies a couple after fifty years of marriage. Parents come (or should come) to interact with their offspring as adults rather than as children. Adult children come (or should come) to see their parents in reciprocal rather than dependent ways. Indeed, there is a symmetry in which the dependence of young children on their parents is reciprocated later as children care for aging parents.

14. See Gustafson, *Ethics from a Theocentric Perspective*, 2:162–63.
15. This paragraph and the preceding one were adapted from Waters, *Family in Christian Social and Political Thought*, 192–93. Reproduced with permission of the Licensor through PLSclear.

Granted, many families confront less than ideal situations. Divorce, illness, untimely deaths, and countless other challenges plague many families. Nonetheless, there is a general, commonplace, and often inarticulate expectation that generations somehow pass the torch. Often this transition is accomplished clumsily. An older, aging generation does not wish to admit its growing dependency on a younger, stronger one. And this emerging, dominant generation is hesitant, ill at ease about usurping the authority of those who gave them life. Or they may not want to accept their new responsibilities. Hence the awkward dance adult children and their parents perform in giving and receiving care that is simultaneously necessary to and resented by both. Yet many families find a way to maneuver this passage, and in doing so are reminded that they are embodied, and therefore ordinary, beings with a host of ordinary needs. Much of this generational dance centers on such mundane things as housekeeping, preparing meals, running errands, and ultimately caring for failing bodies.

Families teach us much about the symmetry of care over time, how it is a given and how its recurring reality orders creaturely life this side of eternity. When a family is steadfastly a place of mutual and timely belonging that accommodates itself to changing realities with the passage of time, perhaps the generational dance becomes less awkward or is even replaced with acceptance and consent: a consent to a vindicated created order. But there is something missing in this portrayal of family. A family is not a mini-society unto itself. It exists within a larger social setting which it both receives from and contributes to, and within which it may be supported, neglected, or reviled. It is time to redirect our attention toward this more expansive context.

Families and Society

When Christians say they support the traditional family, they often have in mind what is called the bourgeois or Victorian family, usually composed of two parents and at least one dependent child. There is much to commend in this "traditional" family, but it is a relatively recent innovation, roughly coinciding with modern industrialization. A different model prevailed for Christians for nearly eighteen centuries, and the primary focus was on the household rather than the family. The origins of this model are found in the New Testament's so-called household codes.[16] The normative Christian household consisted of three pairs of relationships: husband and wife, parents and

16. See Eph. 5:22–6:9; Col. 3:18–4:1; 1 Tim. 2:8–15; 6:1–2; Titus 2:1–10; and 1 Pet. 2:18–3:7. See also Dunn, "Household Rules."

children, master and slaves. This model was virtually identical to the one found in pagan households, but with one important difference. In pagan household codes, instruction was given to only the "stronger" member in each relationship: husband, father, and master. In the early Christian codes, the roles of both parties were addressed. Externally, Christian households appeared to be no different from their pagan counterparts—and therefore they seemed to pose no threat to the established social order—but their internal ordering incorporated an equality in Christ (see Gal. 3:28) that tempered the inherent patriarchy of the ancient household. In this respect, the Christian household codes were quietly subversive.[17]

These codes were refined by subsequent theologians. Early Protestants, for instance, retained the basic tripartite structure of relationships. And in both Catholic and Protestant teaching, though it took far too long, slaves were eventually replaced by servants (either employed or indentured). It was also common among Puritans to apprentice children to other households to learn a trade or domestic skills.[18] This household model held a dominant place within traditional Christian teaching, and as late as the early nineteenth century Friedrich Schleiermacher devoted two chapters to the role of servants in his *Christian Household*.[19]

Despite its long and venerable history, however, the household model has been largely displaced, at least within Western cultures, by the bourgeois or Victorian family, or—in more contemporary parlance—the nuclear family. In contrast to the household model, the nuclear family does not consist of three pairs of relationships but is an intimate association of parents and children. This shift in emphasis away from the household to the family occurred roughly in the early nineteenth century and quickly gained strong support among the middle class in Europe and the United States. Why this rapid change of preference? To a large extent, it reflects a reaction to a new economic trend: industrialization. The household became a unit of consumption rather than production. In agrarian and craft-based economies, members of a household worked to sustain themselves through the production and sales of goods and services. A residence and place of commerce were often inseparable. With industrialization, this pattern changed dramatically. Husbands/fathers were routinely employed outside the home, working in factories, stores, or offices, and their salaries enabled wives and offspring to purchase a wider range of goods and services. Additionally, this arrangement "freed" women

17. See O'Donovan, *Desire of the Nations*, 183–84.
18. See Morgan, *Puritan Family*, chap. 3.
19. See Schleiermacher, *Christian Household*.

from productive pursuits to concentrate on managing the home and on child-rearing. In tandem with the development of technologies that made house-keeping less time-consuming and onerous, the need for servants declined and was eventually eliminated in many instances. The home and workplace were effectively split into two unrelated domains. Additionally, many single young men and women were also employees, delaying marriage and offspring given the expenses associated with maintaining modern homes.

The rapid development of the nuclear family is an understandable, and in many respects admirable, response to the advent of modern industrialization. With the pressures of employment, more complex social institutions and structures associated with urbanization, and growing political encroachment into the daily lives of citizens, the family serves as a much-needed bulwark protecting the privacy of its members. The family provides a space of trust and intimacy, in contrast to a larger world that is frequently indifferent or even inimical. Ideally, the competitive pressures of the workplace and marketplace do not come home, and the laws, rights, and duties pervading the public square are replaced by a more familiar and affectionate mutuality. After a long, hard day in the world, who would not want to come home to enjoy the private intimacy of a loving family? Ideally, the family provided a haven in a heartless world.[20]

From a Christian perspective, however, there is, at least, one thing wrong with the preceding portrayal of the nuclear family: namely, the family was never intended to be an entirely private association. Hence the assumption that strangers in the role of servants were and should be regarded as members of the household. Family rightfully provides some solace from worldly pressures, a haven of sorts, but not as an enclave secluded from the social settings in which it is embedded and the other forms of human association with which it interacts. Rather, the family is uniquely situated to help its members negotiate and mediate the private and public.

Richard Baxter offers some helpful guidance regarding how and why this mediation should be pursued.[21] A rightly governed Christian household bears witness to a social order derived from mutual and sacrificial love. Such a family is oriented toward pulling its members out beyond their respective self-interests, preparing them to embrace more expansive forms of human association beyond the family. Spouses help each other in charitable works and hospitality, children are taught useful vocations, servants and masters treat each other fairly for the good of the household and civil society. The

20. See Lasch, *Haven in a Heartless World.*
21. See Baxter, *Christian Directory,* part 2. The discussion on Baxter is adapted from Waters, *Family in Christian Social and Political Thought,* 32–38. Reproduced with permission of the Licensor through PLSclear.

ideal Christian family is a providential witness to the goodness of a vindi-cated created order while also intimating eschatological fellowship—for its members are also sisters and brothers in Christ, an identity that transcends their familial and household roles.

A family and its household should also be an open and outward-looking community. Beginning with marriage, a familial covenant envelops a growing circle of children and servants, prefiguring their oneness in Christ. If there is an element of self-interest in performing one's familial roles, it is inherently linked to one's ultimate fulfillment and fellowship in Christ. The family points beyond itself to a time when, in Oliver O'Donovan's words, "Humanity in the presence of God will know a community in which the fidelity of love which marriage makes possible will be extended beyond the limits of marriage."[22] In this respect a family is not simply a self-referential witness to its opaque privacy, but a provisional privacy anticipating a more expansive and loving society.

A properly ordered family resists turning in on itself. This warning is promi-nent in the extensive attention Baxter devotes to household servants. They are not merely auxiliaries promoting a family's economic interests but play a normative role in domestic governance. A household does not exist exclusively along a shared bloodline but includes fellowship with strangers. Late moderns may object that contemporary economic structures render the household model untenable, yet it nevertheless suggests that a family is incomplete when it is isolated from larger social networks. It would be unthinkable to Baxter to write about the Christian family referring only to spouses, parents, and children, for the family is not ordained by God to provide a haven in a heart-less world, but to be a sign of the world being drawn toward its destiny of universal fellowship in Christ. And that fellowship is *not* a family.

I think it highly unlikely that servants will be reintroduced in forging a neo-household model of the family. Contemporary economic circumstances and social mores virtually preclude any such attempt. Although a growing number of two-income families employ strangers to provide childcare and housework, to shop, and to run errands, these individuals are employed to compensate for a lack of time or interest and there is no thought of including them as members of the household, despite the offer of occasional sentimental and flattering platitudes. Moreover, conceiving of families in the absence of servants is not incompatible with Christian moral teaching, especially in light of the economic and social changes accompanying industrialization.

22. O'Donovan, *Resurrection and Moral Order*, 70.

Nevertheless, families cannot or should not attempt to isolate themselves from the more expansive associations that make up civil society. If a family effectively becomes a secluded enclave, the material, moral, and social well-being of its members is diminished. There are three prominent reasons why.

First, a secluded family becomes less proficient in preparing its members to practice and habituate civic virtues. A well-ordered civil society is composed of individuals who are skilled in cooperating with others in order to promote their respective interests. Such cooperation may entail commercial exchanges between producers and consumers or volunteer activities through charities or clubs. These cooperative ventures, in turn, strengthen the communities and associations composing civil society. People flourish when they live and participate in a setting of thriving businesses, voluntary associations, schools, charitable organizations, and churches. Moreover, these activities and pursuits are undertaken by friends, neighbors, and strangers, requiring at least a modicum of trust. A civil society cannot flourish in the absence of the virtues of cooperation and trust.

Neither can a family and its members flourish in the absence of cooperation and trust. It is easy to imagine how dreadful life in a family would be if its members sabotaged and mistrusted one another. In contrast, more idyllic families master cooperation and mutual trust, and ideally family members take these skills with them into civil society. Granted, the members of a secluded family can also master these skills, but there is little, if any, effort to extend them beyond the home. Familial cooperation and trust are used to create a barricade protecting a family against unwanted encroachments of more expansive human associations. Such families tend to cooperate with and trust one another to support a wariness of strangers, who are often perceived as threats. The principal objective, either explicitly or implicitly, is to isolate family members as much as possible from the contagion of outsiders.

It is understandable why families might wish to insulate themselves from strangers and from civil society more broadly. Strangers are often indifferent, or they may try to mislead, defraud, or victimize—and there are social forces that belittle, denigrate, or even attack the values a family holds dear. In such a threatening world, a family needs a fortress. Although the desire for seclusion is understandable, it is ultimately a futile tactic, which leads to the second reason for rejecting the enclave model: it perpetuates the fiction of autonomy.

People flourish when they admit and order their dependence upon one another. An individual entirely on her own simply cannot survive. A hermit living a subsistence existence has likely brought with him survival skills he learned from others. Some families may be able to live self-sufficient lives slightly above subsistence. But to attain even this level requires collaboration and mutual support, and such families would remain cut off from deeply significant cultural riches, such as art and literature.[23] A so-called self-sufficient family is also a diminished one.

Families tend to flourish when they are supported by a broader civil society. Individuals flourish through a variety of cooperative activities and relationships that a family cannot provide on its own. Families need the assistance of commercial, educational, health care, civic, and cultural organizations to provide and sustain households of mutual and timely belonging for their members. Ironically, it is families that are open to a larger public that are best positioned to protect their privacy. How can this be? Answering this question prompts the third reason for avoiding a secluded family: an open family is better positioned to protect its privacy.

This assertion is admittedly counterintuitive. Yet a family's openness to being related to and to participating in other associations that make up civil society justifies a greater range of prerogatives that are exercised in domestic governance. If it is acknowledged that families not only benefit from but also contribute to civil society, then there is a strong rationale for allowing families to conduct their affairs with minimal interference and regulation, thus preserving familial privacy. When families attempt to become secluded enclaves, however, there is a heavy price to pay that diminishes the privacy of families, especially in respect to parental prerogatives. If families wish to isolate themselves from civil society, then the state is presumably justified in ensuring that their individual members, especially children, receive proper rearing, education, and health care—actions requiring a great deal of intrusion and regulation. Parents are effectively rendered incompetent to raise their children,[24] reduced to overseeing whatever spare time their offspring might have and funding the agencies and experts providing the bulk of their primary care. The residual privacy is greatly diminished and largely restricted to activities the state deems unessential.

Some members of anxious families, especially parents, may object that being "open" to such an intrusive state and corrupt culture is a recipe for destruction. Doesn't a retreat into greater privacy offer at least some resistance for preserving a residue of family cohesion? Why should families open themselves to a culture and to political structures that erode family values and ridicule any moral formation incorporating "traditional" familial loyalties? As already discussed, there are two reasons why adopting a seclusion strategy,

23. Admittedly, some families may be blessed with members who are artists and storytellers. Still, such a family, isolated from the wider world, would enjoy only a rather limited cultural trove.

24. See Lasch, *Haven in a Heartless World*, chap. 1.

however tempting, should be avoided: it is a futile gesture and, more importantly, it deprives families of the social context and supports they require to
flourish. But there is also a third reason. Civil society cannot be healthy and
political regimes grow corrupt, in part, when families become closed and cut
off from the public and political spheres. For, in the former instance, strangers
are perceived largely as potential threats—inspiring a basic mistrust rather
than trust and promoting, in turn, suspicion and uncivil behavior. And in the
latter instance the state intrudes ever more deeply into the private affairs of its
citizens so that politics begins to misshape virtually every aspect of one's life.

The anguish of families being open to a hostile culture and intrusive state
is real and pressing. So how to resist, and to resist faithfully? Such resistance is
needed but difficult, to say the least. The public bridge that household servants
once provided to broader social and political spheres of human association
is gone, and I think rebuilding it is neither feasible nor desirable. Yet some
portal linking families, civil society, and the state in mutually supportive ways
is nonetheless needed. Without some such mechanism society will grow increasingly populated by uncivil factions and isolated individuals, and politics
will become little more than a perverse exercise in sophistry.

It is difficult to overstate the importance of this task. On the one hand,
our families and other human associations are more diverse than they've ever
been, if for no other reason than changing demographics. Yet this diversity is
being expressed and assessed within a culture that is thoroughly conformist.
The progressive elites of this culture try to dictate which values, moral convictions, and religious beliefs are permissible and which are not for embracing
this diversity. And with each dictate, the circle of permissible expressions of
diversity grows tighter while the circle of those excluded grows larger. On the
other hand, the politics of this culture turns to the coercive power of the state
to enforce its prescribed conformity. A growing menu of green, multicultural,
and politically correct recipes, each diminishing the privacy of individuals and
their families, is foisted upon a bewildered and increasingly hostile public.
The current concoction of culture and politics is lethal and should be resisted.

Resistance alone, however, is not enough. An alternative public and political
vision must also be offered, one in which genuinely open families both benefit
from and contribute to the good of civil society. In the following two chapters,
I will suggest a few basic contours of this alternative vision, such as how we
should engage and relate to strangers and fellow citizens. In the meantime,
there is much families can do to faithfully resist by doing what they do best:
pursuing the ordinary tasks of caring for one another. Cleaning the house,
running errands, preparing and sharing meals, playing together, providing for
the material wellbeing of the household, generously sharing love and affection

are all subversive acts, especially when they are extended to and shared with neighbors. They are subversive because their mundane simplicity helps to put culture and politics in their proper place. The denizens of culture think of themselves as the vanguard of intellectual and aesthetic sophistication. Such so-called sophistication, however, is often little more than unintelligent snobbery elevating a personal preference to a universal demand for conformity. And late-modern politicians are often little more than opportunistic sophists who slavishly follow vacillating cultural trends and then claim they are leading by devising laws and policies that effectively erode the ability of citizens to flourish through their own private initiatives. C. S. Lewis expresses this misguided politics succinctly: "The higher the pretensions of our rulers are, the more meddlesome and impertinent their rule is likely to be and the more the thing in whose name they rule will be defiled."[25]

The mundane relationships and activities of families treat the pretensions of cultural and political elites with the casual indifference they deserve, because both attempt to intrude and manipulate where they don't belong. In this respect, the ordinary tasks and activities associated with maintaining a flourishing family also constitute a first step of resistance.

25. Lewis, *They Asked for a Paper*, 118.

CHAPTER 9

Strangers

O f all the neighbors we encounter, it is probably strangers we most regularly meet. We mingle with strangers in the marketplace and workplace. Strangers serve us in stores and restaurants and are also customers we serve in return. And innumerable casual dealings transpire among faceless strangers in cyberspace. Our material wellbeing largely depends on the goods and services provided by strangers. We need strangers to obtain our daily bread, and yet strangers may also at times deprive us of this essential staple.

Who exactly is a stranger? In common parlance a stranger is a person with whom one is unfamiliar or whom one does not know. There is a range, then, of unfamiliarity among the strangers we meet. Some strangers are encountered in one-off events, remaining entirely anonymous and opaque. Other strangers, such as store clerks or bank tellers, are less unfamiliar because we may interact with them from time to time, but we know them only in a casual and utilitarian manner. We mostly trust strangers, otherwise the commerce enabling our material wellbeing would be virtually impossible. We also mistrust strangers: hence laws and contracts prohibiting willful harm or ensuring compliance with promises made. More commonly we simply keep our distance from strangers we judge to be untrustworthy. And our trust or mistrust sometimes proves justified and other times not.

Although we certainly encounter strangers—people unfamiliar or unknown to us—*stranger* is, for Christians, an inadequate designation. Strangers are also neighbors that Christ commands his followers to love. This love requires moral and practical ordering, for not all strangers are the same. Neighbor love is not a generic sentiment or stance that treats all neighbors identically. Strangers should be loved, but not in the same way as friends or family members are loved. How is a love of neighbors who are strangers properly ordered? An adequate answer would be lengthy and multifaceted, but at this juncture perhaps mentioning one challenge might suffice to illustrate what is at stake in loving strangers rightly.

As noted in previous chapters, love always entails risk and vulnerability. Risk, however, is not synonymous with recklessness. Loving strangers does not entail a vulnerability that is appropriately adopted with trusted friends or family members. Ordering a love of strangers requires prudent judgment within a context of particular circumstances. This is especially important in regard to other relationships that are impinged by one's response to strangers. For instance, it is one thing if I live alone and invite a stranger to live with me, for if my trust proves mistaken, then presumably I am the only one who will suffer the consequences of my imprudent act. But it would be another matter entirely if I were to make my family vulnerable through my bad judgment. The need for prudent judgment becomes even more pronounced in broader forms of social and political ordering. It would, for example, be imprudent for rulers to admit into the countries they govern strangers about which nothing is known, subjecting citizens to potentially unwarranted danger.

Additionally, in any deliberation regarding the ordered love of strangers, our role is not confined to that of the always "known and trusted" person judging the person who is *not* known and trusted. We are also strangers to countless others, who will treat us as untrustworthy neighbors despite our best efforts to prove ourselves otherwise. Like all other expressions of neighbor love, the love of strangers often proves inadequate or unjust, or is denied altogether. Love can and does fail in the short term. Nonetheless, since Christians are commanded to love their neighbors who are strangers, it is incumbent upon them to order that love, with the aid of grace, as best they can. We begin our reflection on this challenge in the next section by examining and attempting to balance the love and fear of strangers.

Xenophobia and Xenophilia

How should we treat strangers? This question does not refer to those occasions that require only a casual gesture or a few polite words. Rather, how should we respond to strangers who are in our midst, exhibit no signs of leaving anytime soon, and are implicitly demanding some sort of recognition on our part—if nothing else, a grudging acknowledgment of their existence, their otherness, their strangeness? To be candid, we (to be honest, I) may respond with an embarrassed bewilderment that effectively tries to deflect the stranger's demand. Or there may be a reaction of fear: an attempt to isolate the stranger as a threat. In some instances, this fear may be intense, resulting in an antipathy directed toward strangers, especially foreigners: in short, *xenophobia*. The xenophobe presumes that every stranger is a potential threat, a callous individual who wishes to inflict harm. Consequently, to a xenophobe, strangers are virtually synonymous with enemies whose threat must be countered and protected against.

To treat strangers generally as little more than antagonists, however, is both unrealistic and immoral. It is unrealistic because contemporary economies and modes of sociality depend on relationships among strangers. Strangers provide the goods and services we consume and that in turn enable our material wellbeing. Without such consumption, human flourishing would be greatly diminished. Like it or not, late-modern societies depend on a fundamental trust of strangers. Granted, this trust is sometimes violated, a condition to be expected in a fallen world, but overall, strangers are much more of a blessing than a bane.

An intense hostility toward strangers is also immoral. Instead of xenophobia, the gospel proclaims *xenophilia*—a love of strangers and foreigners. The need for this command is partly altruistic. We can imagine the anxiety, even fear, that strangers or foreigners may be feeling who find themselves in a strange or foreign setting in which traditions, customs, diets, and language are far different from their own. A response of compassion or kindness from one human being to another is in order. The command is partly an act of remembrance and gratitude (see, e.g., Exod. 22:21). We may remember times when we or our ancestors were strangers in a strange land, recalling acts of hospitality, and we gratefully extend this grace to others in similar circumstances. The command appeals, in part, to self-interest. The golden rule reminds us that we should treat strangers in ways that we would wish to be treated by them.

More broadly, we cannot flourish in the absence of strangers. Human beings are not identical clones but unique individuals. In encountering these matchless differences, our lives are immeasurably enriched by the pluriformity of God's created order, and the strangers we meet embody this pluriform character in an intense way. To paraphrase Saint Augustine, in loving strangers we also love the many coming from the one.

Nonetheless, there is a tension between xenophobia and xenophilia that should not be ignored. The fear of strangers contains a grain of truth: not all strangers can be trusted. Some strangers do wish to harm us or our neighbors. The challenge is discerning between trustworthy and untrustworthy and applying protective measures accordingly. Additionally, the love of strangers does not necessarily entail equal treatment in every situation. This is simply the obverse of the preceding observation on a healthy fear of some strangers. Neighbor love requires making discriminating judgments so as not to subject intimates, friends, or other strangers to inordinate risks.

The proper tension between trusting and mistrusting strangers needs to be maintained to prevent naively xenophobic and xenophilic acts from occurring that ultimately weaken the bonds of association promoting human flourishing. Blind trust or blanket mistrust benefits no one. In short, discerning how best to order our love of neighbors who happen to be strangers requires prudence. In the remainder of this chapter, I probe why and how this task might be undertaken.

Ordering the Love of Strangers

Ordering our love of neighbors who are strangers requires that we love them *as strangers*. Strangers are people who we know relatively little, or in some instances nothing, about. This lack of knowledge, however, does not justify a presumptive stance of either fearful antagonism or naive trust. How, then, should strangers be treated, at least initially? What follows are three suggestions. This list is not exhaustive in either breadth or depth, but it sets the stage for further inquiry in the next section.

Civil indifference. Most of our contact with strangers is brief and passing. Although the possibility of future intimacy, friendship, or collegiality should not be dismissed out of hand, it is nonetheless unlikely. Consequently, indifference is an appropriate initial response to many strangers. The reader might object that indifference demonstrates a callous disregard that dehumanizes the stranger. But this is not true if indifference is understood as a way of respecting the privacy of the stranger, of allowing this neighbor to be an other—an opaque other at that. There are details and secrets of a person's life that I have no need or right to know after one or even many contacts. Hannah Arendt is right to insist that we largely encounter others as they wish to present themselves.[1] An indifferent reception of that presentation at least acknowledges the probable mixture of truth and fiction being presented, which is preferable to the fake intimacy and barely disguised narcissism often presented on social media.

Moreover, the qualifying word *civil* is crucial. Indifference is not necessarily synonymous with terms such as *coldhearted* or *unsympathetic*—which indicate behavior that effectively renders the stranger invisible. Rather, the stranger is a neighbor who can and sometimes does make a moral demand

---

1. See Arendt, *Life of the Mind*, vol. 1, chap. 1.

for recognition and action on our part, such as when she is hungry or when he is in need of assistance. The world would be worse off if indifferent Good Samaritans were to disappear.

Realistic trust. Although our contacts with most strangers are brief and passing, they are not always inconsequential, which leads to this second suggestion. As I have mentioned on numerous occasions, trusting strangers is crucial to enabling human flourishing in contemporary societies and economies. This trust is exhibited mostly in routinely obtaining goods and services and in chance encounters. Such trust is generally inconsequential because it does not require disclosing information about ourselves that could be used to substantially harm us. In Arendt's terms, our self-presentation in these instances is not very self-revealing. There are times, however, when more is required of us. On these occasions we should take care to discern whether the stranger wishing to probe behind one's self-presentation has a legitimate need to do so, to disturb our privacy. Consequently, we need to exercise judgment regarding what is owed to this unfamiliar neighbor. Realistically, how should we determine the trustworthiness of this stranger?

The authority of the stranger is another way to conceive of my suggestion of realistic trust. Following Oliver O'Donovan, *authority* refers to what a person is authorized to do by virtue of his or her role or office.[2] For instance, a bank teller is authorized to access a customer's account number, a tax official has the authority to examine financial records, a therapist is permitted to ask uncomfortable questions about a client's beliefs or conduct that would be deeply offensive if asked by another stranger. These strangers in positions of authority normally use the information they obtain in responsible and trustworthy ways, and they are subject to both moral and legal condemnation when they do not—which is why we are being realistic when we trust them. We do not think kindly of bank tellers using our accounts to purchase items for their own use, tax officials posting our personal financial information on nefarious websites, or therapists using us as objects of derision with their colleagues.

There are two relevant aspects of these encounters with authorized strangers that need to be highlighted. First, the relationship is not reciprocal or equal. Bank customers are not authorized to access the accounts of their tellers, taxpayers do not have the authority to examine the finances of tax collectors, clients are (usually) not allowed to ask their therapists uncomfortable questions. Reciprocity and equality are not universal prerequisites for trusting strangers, especially when the stranger is performing a socially or

2. See O'Donovan, *Resurrection and Moral Order*, chap. 6.

politically authorized function. Realistically, there is no need in these instances for reciprocity or equality.

Second, authority limits what the "stronger" stranger is permitted to ask or demand and what the "weaker" stranger is required to disclose. A bank teller is not authorized to obtain a customer's health care history. A tax official may not probe into the romantic life of a taxpayer. A therapist does not (usually) have the authority to examine the financial assets of a client. Authority, then, limits what "stronger" strangers should know about their "weaker" counterparts, thereby helping to order neighbor love among strangers. In short, exhibiting xenophilia does not require a broad disclosure of private or intimate details, and thereby honors the opaque other (and oneself) as other. Or, more prosaically, loving strangers does not entitle one to be inordinately nosey.

Hospitality. Neither of the preceding suggestions is particularly welcoming to the stranger. Rather, they counsel behavior that treats the stranger with a benign courtesy. That is far preferable to exhibiting contempt—and fitting, as far as it goes. But can or should we go further? Yes. The command to love our neighbors is not risk free, otherwise it would not be genuine love. To love the stranger is to accept some exposure. Extending hospitality is a more positive way of stating this loving response.

An extensive historical and theological account of hospitality is beyond both the scope of this chapter and my expertise.[3] One salient feature, however, needs to be emphasized—namely, the important role hospitality plays in both Scripture and Christian teaching, especially in respect to the stranger. In the Old Testament, for example, Israel is enjoined to treat aliens and sojourners in its midst in a hospitable manner. In the New Testament, strangers are to be treated hospitably—for the stranger (whether welcomed or denied) may prove to be an angel, Jesus, or God (see Matt. 25:31–46).[4] Subsequent Christian teaching often framed the provision of hospitality as a moral obligation owed to one's neighbors.[5]

As Christine Pohl acknowledges, hospitality is largely neglected in contemporary Christian thought and practice.[6] This neglect is unfortunate, for it weakens the witness of the gospel to a world in which strangers are largely relegated to invisible corners of one's perceptions and concerns. Pohl contends that recovering hospitality as a vital Christian practice is needed not only to offer a robust witness to the world but also to strengthen the spiritual vitality

3. For an informative overview, see Pohl, *Making Room.*
4. See Pohl, *Making Room,* chap. 2.
5. See Pohl, *Making Room,* chap. 3.
6. See Pohl, *Making Room,* chap. 1.

of believers.[7] More succinctly, hospitality "provides a bridge which connects our theology with daily life and concerns."[8]

Pohl is correct in insisting that hospitality is a crucial practice that needs to be recovered. But before exploring what, in part, this recovery entails, a caveat is in order. Extending hospitality to strangers does not negate the need for prudence. As noted above, loving the stranger involves risk, but risk-taking is *not* synonymous with recklessness. There are different types of strangers that should be treated differently within differing contexts. Consequently, an initially *wary* hospitality is not incompatible with neighbor love. By "wary" I mean proceeding cautiously in light of neighbors about whom little is known. This does not denigrate the neighbor who is a stranger but is an appropriately loving response within the parameters of given circumstances. To use a crude analogy, it is encountering the stranger with a yellow rather than a green or red light. Yellow lights are indispensable for ordering traffic, and the moral life as well.

Hospitality and Nomadic Culture

Recovering hospitality as a Christian practice is a daunting challenge. The difficulty stems primarily from the nomadic character of the dominant, late-modern culture.[9] Some explanation is required. Traditional nomads traveled well-known trade routes, often following a seasonal pattern that determined where and for what length of time they sojourned. Unlike later pilgrims and travelers who needed hospices, public houses, or monasteries for lodging and refreshment, their need for hospitality was not great; hospitality was extended infrequently to fellow travelers or accepted occasionally from trading partners in villages or towns. Although traditional nomads were mobile, they were also communal and insular.

In contrast, late-modern nomads wander, both physically and imaginatively, aimlessly. With the advent of affordable transportation and information technologies, they can be virtually anywhere—and nowhere in particular. They value mobility that enables them to form temporary spaces, either materially or virtually, where they admit friends, colleagues, or strangers of their choosing. Even when in close proximity to strangers, they are far away with the aid of their communication and information devices. These fabricated spaces are intentionally temporary; there is no expectation that they will

7. See Pohl, *Making Room*, part 3.
8. Pohl, *Making Room*, 8.
9. For a more detailed account of late-modern nomads and nomadic culture, see relevant references in Waters, *Christian Moral Theology in the Emerging Technoculture*.

endure for an extended period of time. Late-modern nomads, then, are free-floating rather than grounded; they do not belong in a particular earthly place whose history and hopes for the future they share or are formed by. These neo-nomads are individualistic, using their mobility to construct a perceived autonomy, presumably liberating themselves from the encumbrance of enduring commitments and relationships. Consequently, late-modern nomads do not need or want hospitality extended by households or communities of strangers. Moreover, as the culture grows more nomadic, there will be no perceived reason for nomads to be hospitable to other nomads. All these nomads require is a banal cordiality that is best provided by a so-called hospitality industry.

To be clear, I am not offering a blanket condemnation of transportation and information technologies or the mobility they promote. I have no nostalgic longings for a return to some supposed pristine age that was probably much worse than we imagine it to be. Instead, my concern is that relatively recent technological developments have exacerbated troubling tendencies that were already latent in the modern era—namely, a propensity to simultaneously construct one's life as an artifact of the autonomous will and to render the stranger effectively invisible. To assert one's will has become the chief feature of one's identity, while making strangers invisible is one way to ease external constraints against the will. If strangers can be easily ignored, then—more broadly—the demands placed on us by neighbors can be more easily dismissed. My characterization of late moderns as nomads is a way of portraying these troubling tendencies, with a dash of hyperbole.

A chief weakness of late-modern nomadic culture is the perception that hospitality is extraneous: therefore the practice of offering and receiving hospitality has atrophied. All that is required is a cheerful and trite cordiality, a passing gesture or impersonal service centered on a function rather than on persons. But is anything important lost in failing to offer and receive hospitality? Yes. The teaching and practice of hospitality is central to the gospel, and it is a concept that deeply informs broader questions of social and political ordering. Through hospitality we learn important lessons about gratitude and attentiveness. We are grateful in accepting hospitality, and we must be attentive to the needs of neighbors, especially strangers, when offering hospitality. Hospitality, then, is not a burdensome duty but a way of life.[10] And when the hospitable life is diminished there are penalties to be paid. For example, historically the household has been the principal institution of hospitality.

10. See Pohl, *Making Room*, chap. 9.

One wonders whether the decline of household hospitality in late-modern nomadic culture is a symptom or a cause of the decline of the family.

How might we go about recovering hospitality as a way of life? There are three crucial concepts undergirding this recovery. First, following O'Donovan, is a natural equality among neighbors. All human beings are created equal in the eyes of their creator. This ontological principle is an essential component of a just social and political order. In its absence, such evils as slavery and racism could be justified as reflecting a natural inequality. Such a belief, however, is contrary to Christian moral teaching, in which slavery and racism are seen as unnatural results of sin. To be clear, such ontological equality does not negate the need for certain functional limitations or inequalities. Refugees, for instance, are not treated as citizens sharing equal legal rights, but they are not therefore inferior beings. The first step to attending to the needs of a stranger is to simply recognize an equality of being that transcends all other distinctions that may serve, rightly or wrongly, to divide.

Second, there are social structures of affinity in which associations are formed and maintained, the "intimate affinity of the family, the wider affinity of the local community, and the wider affinities which create our national and cultural homes, affinities of language, tradition, culture, and law."[11] People are drawn to one another, and over time they develop patterns of interactions, institutions, and practices that become customary and are taken for granted. Traditionally, they have become a people sharing remembrances and hopes, common objects of love.[12] Christian teaching has largely commended these affinities, but with an important caveat: our affinities should not serve to make us insular. The identity and support derived from familiar affinities is not a barrier to protect us from change or from outsiders. Such a perversion of affinity would deaden our perception of the work of the Holy Spirit and promote xenophobia in defiance of the command to love our neighbors, many of whom are strangers. Affirming affinity simply recognizes that we do not encounter strangers as blank slates but as individuals grounded in particular associations and communities. This is why, in part, strangers must learn from each other in order to be mutually attentive to their respective needs and good. The stranger, one not sharing our affinities, is then, by default, not only a potential threat but also the "neighbour whom we are to love."[13]

Third, there is reciprocity that "permits each community in its own integrity to interact in fellowship with other human beings, thus establishing the

11. O'Donovan, *Desire of the Nations*, 262.
12. See O'Donovan, *Common Objects of Love*. See also Augustine, *City of God* 19.
13. O'Donovan, *Desire of the Nations*, 268.

communication of a universal humanity, not as an integrated super-home but as a network of meetings and mutual acknowledgments."[14] It must be emphasized that a universal humanity is not an amalgamation of identical or generic individuals, nor should it be ruled by a universal empire or single world government. Uniformity virtually precludes human flourishing because it destroys the very possibility of singular or unique expressions of humanity. The reciprocity that is a prerequisite for community presupposes an equality that is expressed in pluriform, as opposed to uniform, ways. Universal humanity is not a family or household writ large but more akin to a meeting in which differences must be disclosed and negotiated. Consequently, humans require strangers if they are to flourish, for ultimately reciprocity and fellowship require difference. It is worth quoting O'Donovan at length in this regard: "No community should ever be allowed to think of itself as universal. All communities . . . should have to serve the end of equal, reciprocal relations between their own members and the members of other communities. One could put it this way: it is essential to our humanity that there should always be foreigners, human beings from another community who have an alternative way of organizing the task and privilege of being human, so that our imaginations are refreshed and our sense of cultural possibilities renewed." The imperial strategy of treating all foreigners or strangers as enemies until they are incorporated into homogeneous spheres of affinity is "simply a creation of xenophobia." Rather, to recognize and prudently welcome the stranger as a neighbor is to also offer the "distinctive friendship of hospitality" as a basic form of human communication.[15]

In contrast to the prevalent banal cordiality of late-modern nomadic culture, I am proposing a more settled hospitality. This requires recovering a stronger sense of mutual and timely belonging associated with enduring places as opposed to temporary spaces that are created in response to fleeting objectives. Households in particular need to be strengthened, for historically they have been prime providers of hospitality. Moreover, strong households will not be havens in a heartless world, offering seclusion in which families may hide, but places where strangers are welcomed and treated hospitably by familial residents.

This proposal does not assume an end to mobility, for strangers cannot be encountered if no one is on the move. But the mobility envisioned is more akin to pilgrimage than nomadic wandering. Pilgrims do migrate, but not

14. O'Donovan, *Desire of the Nations*, 262.
15. O'Donovan, *Desire of the Nations*, 268.

aimlessly. Instead, as Saint Augustine recognized,[16] since Christians know this world is not ultimately their home, they belong wherever God calls them to be to exercise their callings and vocations for however short or lengthy period of time might be required. Pilgrims do settle down for a while in particular places.

Most importantly, I am proposing that strangers should be treated with a presumptive charity. This is merely stating the obvious in respect to neighbor love. Such charity requires unselfing to discern the good and needs of this neighbor who is unfamiliar to us and to respond accordingly. To love the neighbor, to be hospitable to the stranger, requires that one's attention be redirected, at least in part, away from the self. As mentioned earlier in this chapter, how strangers should be treated must also take into account specific circumstances and be governed by prudent judgments. Such caution, however, does not preclude the possibility that strangers, in response to the charitable hospitality they are offered, may become friends.[17] Yet even if this does not happen, even if some strangers refuse the hospitality offered, becoming indifferent or hostile, they nonetheless remain neighbors and should be treated as such. These are also acts based on a presumptive charity that does not negate the needs of hospitality in a world populated predominantly by strangers with inimitable goods and specific needs. However, strangers, especially over time, can prove to be trustworthy or untrustworthy, grateful recipients and prodigious givers of care or insensitive individuals who are inimical to one's wellbeing. I turn now to a novel to portray some of the ambiguities of loving strangers.

In *Good to a Fault*, Marina Endicott writes, "Clara Purdy had been drifting for some time in a state of mild despair, forty-three and nothing to show for it." Clara is "angry with herself for this sadness." She has plenty of money and no pressing financial burdens; she lives comfortably in the bungalow she inherited from her mother. Clara has worked in an insurance firm for twenty years, has no children, and got out of a "short, stupid marriage." "Instead of the heavy work of being with people, she gardened, read books on spirituality, and kept the house trim."[18]

Clara's life is about to change. She is going to be doing some heavy work. One day she crashes into another car that ran a red light. Clara is OK, but the occupants of the other car are not. No one in the Gage family—Lorraine and

---

16. See Augustine, *City of God* 18–19.

17. Matt Ridley argues that exchange plays a more central role in reinforcing an innate trust among individuals. I do not dispute this claim because I assume that although exchange and charity are acts prompted by differing motivations, they are not thereby incompatible. See Ridley, *Rational Optimist*, chap. 3.

18. Endicott, *Good to a Fault*, 4.

Clayton; their three young children Darlene, Trevor, and Pearce (an infant); and grandmother Pell—is obviously injured, but they are homeless, and they live in the car that Clara totaled. Everyone is taken to the hospital as a precaution. The doctors discover that Lorraine has lymphoma and will probably die despite the aggressive therapies deployed during a prolonged hospital stay.

Clara is not at fault for the accident, but she nonetheless feels terrible. Like it or not, she was involved in turning the life of the Gage family into a mess. She feels a need to help these strangers. But what should she do? Clara is an Anglican. She admits to her priest, "'I see what they need. . . . But I am unwilling to help.' But that was not it, she was not unwilling—she was somehow stupidly ashamed of wanting to help."[19] Clara explains the plight of the Gage family, babbling most of the time. She does not want them to go to a shelter, but neither does she want them in her house—or maybe she does.

Later that day she prepares her house to receive the Gage family, changing the sheets in the spare bedrooms, washing and folding towels, rearranging some furniture, and buying groceries. "She was surprised at herself, and again thought that she was doing the right thing—but maybe a foolish thing."[20] Yet these strangers need a place to live while Lorraine is in the hospital, or until Clayton finds a job and a place of their own. Their stay does not turn out as expected. After a few days Clayton steals the old car left by Clara's mother, as well as some other items, and leaves for parts unknown. Clara now has a brood of houseguests who are incapable of caring for themselves.

Clara quickly learns the hard work of being a mother. She is helped by her next-door neighbor, Mrs. Zenko, a holy woman who provides a high chair and endless batches of cookies, soup, and pierogies. Clara buys a bunk bed for the older children and a crib for the baby. She also buys clothes, diapers, and a lot more food. She keeps the children clean, reads them books, enrolls them in school, takes them to visit their mother, cares for them when they're sick, and even removes head lice. Members of her extended family and Lorraine's brother help her out. Eventually Clara quits her job to devote herself full time to caring for these strangers. But they are no longer strangers. She is starting to think of these children as her own, especially Pearce. Yet she also prays that "Lorraine's cancer would be healed, as far as she could reach to God, knowing that it would be no use."[21]

Lorraine, however, recovers. After many weeks of therapy, the cancer is in remission. Much to everyone's surprise, Lorraine is cured. And much to

19. Endicott, *Good to a Fault*, 18.
20. Endicott, *Good to a Fault*, 21.
21. Endicott, *Good to a Fault*, 13.

everyone's astonishment, Clayton returns. Lorraine is discharged from the hospital and wants her children back. She tells Clara how grateful she is for all she has done for her family, but the tone of voice sounds phony. Clara tries to stall, and Lorraine turns on her, accusing her of class snobbery and prejudice. The insult stings because it is partly true. Lorraine and Clayton take their children, insisting that Clara have no further contact with any of them.

Clara is devastated. She is angered by Lorraine's ingratitude. After all the time and money Clara has spent, after having her life turned upside down for these strangers, how could Lorraine be so ungrateful, curtly dismissing her as an insufferable snob? More importantly, Clara believes she is a better mother than Lorraine, better at caring for the children and providing them with opportunities they will now be forced to forgo. After all, there is more, much more, than biology in being a good mother. Lorraine's marriage to a loser like Clayton, Clara thinks, tells you everything you need to know about her lack of judgment and poor character.

Lorraine is, of course, overjoyed to have her children back. She missed them terribly while she was hospitalized. She also knows that she owes Clara a debt that can never be repaid. Clara was a frequent visitor while Lorraine was hospitalized, helping her get through some tough and dispiriting days. Without Clara, the children would have been either confined to a shelter or divided up among foster homes because Clayton, as usual, proved undependable in an emergency. Such a happy outcome was due, in large measure, to the help of this stranger. But this did not entitle Clara to lord it over Lorraine with her presumed social and moral superiority or to think of herself as a better mother. Lorraine will do anything to keep her family together—even if it requires attacking the overbearing Good Samaritan.

The children are bewildered. They are thrilled that their mother is alive and they are back with her. Yet they also miss Clara and would like to spend some time with her. Why can't such important people in their lives get along? But they remain silent, fearing their mother will think them selfish or disloyal. They become the young, tiny stoics of this story.

In many ways, this is a story about strangers at their best and at their worst. Clara did indeed turn her life upside down for strangers she was under no obligation to help. She offered hope to what she thought was a dying woman, extended the protection and comfort of her home to children who in turn thrived. She personified charity and xenophilia. And, to their credit, Lorraine and her children responded as they should: with gratitude, not only to Clara but to the health care workers, strangers who devoted themselves to Lorraine's care. They did not make the mistake of refusing charity; instead, they gratefully accepted the help they needed. The initial trust shared among these strangers deepened—at least for a while.

Eventually, the trust shatters. Clara is angered by Lorraine's ingratitude and hostility, hurt by her reverse, crude working-class snobbery, and deeply saddened by the injustice that she will no longer be the mother—the better mother, she believes—of three children she has grown to love as her own. Lorraine can no longer trust Clara because of Clara's clumsy attempt to buy away the affection of Lorraine's children and the blatant bigotry she shows by assuming she is better in every way because of her upbringing, money, and education. Trust can be broken, particularly when respective self-interests collide.

In many respects, *Good to a Fault* is also a love story—a story about loving strangers. Like all forms of love, there is risk. Loving a stranger may warm one's heart or break it. Receiving charity from a stranger may prove to be a godsend or thinly disguised manipulation. Yet, like all other forms of love, without this risk xenophilia is shallow, even empty. In this story, a gesture seemingly designed by our perceived inferiors or betters is used to preserve a gulf in which riskless prejudice keeps us safe. This is a story, *perhaps*, that suggests it is worth taking the risk of turning one's life upside down to love strangers even though it may all end in heartbreak. And, *perhaps*, it is also a story that commends the acceptance of charity even when the charity is not driven by the purest of motives. For, in both instances, the only alternative is to maintain a safe distance from any and all strangers. But a life safe from strangers is not necessarily a good life.

I would be remiss if I implied that this story ends on an entirely bleak note. Eventually, contact between Clara and the Gage family is restored. They spend some time together, primarily for the sake of the children, but the adults are not friends. The trust they now share has been repaired but not restored. How could it be otherwise? For this is a love story involving imperfect people, strangers bound together by bonds of imperfection. And in these bonds, in the risk of loving strangers, we discover an important thread in the fabric of daily, ordinary living—namely, that we depend on and are often at the mercy of people we barely know or may not know at all.

In so many ways, strangers bless us with a casual indifference or hurt us with apathy. Trust, then, is warranted in a world populated predominantly by strangers, but such trust never guarantees safety.

CHAPTER 10

Citizens

C itizens are unique, even peculiar neighbors. In some ways they share certain characteristics with other kinds of neighbors encountered in preceding chapters, while in other ways they are quite unlike them. For example, fellow citizens are associated with one another whether they like it or not. Unless we are immigrants, we do not choose our fellow citizens. In this respect, fellow citizens are similar to family members (other than spouses), for we do not choose with whom we share family ties. Yet, unlike in a family, no intimacy is expected among citizens and most of our fellow citizens are strangers we never meet. Citizens share common activities such as voting in elections and paying taxes, but no collegiality is needed like that required in the workplace.

Citizenship is derived from a distinctly political association. It is an association that one is born or immigrates into, and certain expectations of loyalty, obedience, and respect for authority are explicitly or implicitly imposed on citizens with or without their immediate consent. Moreover, citizens are bound together by the dictates of governing that are enforced to a large extent by coercion or its threat. Citizens, for instance, are not free to pick and choose which laws they will obey and are punished when they choose to ignore or disobey a law. For a political association to exist over time, the cooperation of citizens is required, but citizens often compete with one another for political power. In short, citizens share a relationship that is necessary for their flourishing, even survival, but one fraught with challenges and contradictions.

What exactly, then, is a citizen, and—more importantly—a good citizen? Before answering this question, we must first examine, briefly, the social and political contexts in which people express themselves and encounter each other as citizens.

Civil Society and the State

Citizenship is neither a primary nor a foundational relationship. We are not citizens first and foremost: citizenship is not the identity from which all our other relationships are derived. Rather, it is as citizens that we pursue common actions designed to protect such primary and foundational relationships as families and other communicative associations. When this ordering is ignored or reversed it distorts social ordering, thereby effectively diminishing human flourishing. We are loyal citizens because we are first loyal family members, friends, and associates. Or, to use a more heavily freighted theological category, the ordering of neighbor love is centered on intimacy and only peripherally on the threat of coercion. Attempts to move citizenship to the center disclose a menacing consequence of disordered love.

The proper subordination of citizenship to other forms of human association should not be surprising, for it corresponds to some crucial political precepts that inform Christian moral and social teaching. The state, for instance, is the principal expression of political association.[1] But the state is not prior to or foundational to the associations that its citizens form and maintain. A state does not need to first exist and then grant permission to its citizens in order for them to form families, friendships, and churches or engage in commerce. Rather, the state derives its legitimacy to govern from its role as a cooperative enterprise designed to protect and support its citizens through the rule of law, and at times through the use of force. In short, the state serves civil society, and when that ordering is reversed, human flourishing is diminished.

Nothing I have written in the preceding two paragraphs should be construed as being anarchist or anti-political, or even as accepting the state grudgingly as a necessary evil. To the contrary, political association as embodied in the state is a positive good and a necessary prerequisite for human flourishing. Without the rule of law humans fall into Thomas Hobbes's notorious state of nature, in which life is "solitary, mean, nasty, brutish, and short."[2] The challenge is establishing and maintaining states that best promote the flourishing of their citizens. This is a difficult challenge because it requires some clarity about what constitutes the good of political association. Where should such an inquiry begin?

1. At least in modern political philosophy.
2. Hobbes, *Leviathan*, 84.

One possible starting point is political authority. What exactly is a state authorized to do in governing the citizens and civil society within its jurisdiction? Offering a comprehensive answer to this question is beyond the scope of this chapter and my expertise, but a few observations on authority may be briefly noted. A state has the authority to enact and enforce legislation. Ideally, laws are designed to protect citizens from harm and to enable peaceful interactions within civil society. To achieve these ends, the state is also authorized to use coercion when required. This may be as simple as issuing a parking ticket or as dire as using lethal force against violent criminals or enemies. The state also has the authority to regulate the commercial activities, education, health care, and workplaces of its citizens.

The authority of the state, however, requires the consent and support of the citizens it governs if it is to effectively protect and promote their flourishing. If laws, for example, are widely perceived as unjust, they may also be widely ignored or disobeyed. If unwarranted coercion is used routinely to prevent citizens from assembling or associating, the state itself may be held in contempt or seen as an enemy of the people. If regulations prove overly intrusive, it is likely that ways will be found to get around them. If a state abuses its political authority it may become ineffectual or, at the other extreme, use increasingly violent methods to enforce compliance. In either instance, the wellbeing of citizens, as well as of civil society, is diminished.

Political authority is best exercised as emblematic of the citizens that compose and are governed by a particular state. When citizens become so alienated from a state that they no longer see it taking their interests into account, the authority of a state to govern is called into question. More troubling are certain strands of late-modern political theory that reject the notion of authority altogether. In such instances, raw power fills the void, "justifying" tyranny of the few over the many or of the many over the few. Ideally, political authority is a limiting precept representing and promoting the values and aspirations of the citizens whom the authorities govern. Authority cannot (or should not) be invoked to justify, for instance, a tyrannical or totalitarian state.

The type of regime best corresponding to this ideal of limited authority is a limited state. What makes for a properly limited state, however, may not be as obvious as it seems. The state that governs least is not necessarily a properly limited state.[3] A well-ordered state avoids two extremes. On the one hand, it avoids doing too much, encroaching on the private affairs of its citizens and on the associations composing civil society in ways for which it

---

3. Cf. Helmut Thielicke's account of the "minimal state," especially in contrast to totalitarian regimes. See Thielicke, *Theological Ethics*, vol. 2, parts 1–2.

is neither authorized nor competent. States commonly attempt to remedy perceived social problems through intrusive legislation, policies, and programs. Yet the state is often ill-equipped to deal effectively with many of the issues it attempts to address, and by restricting more effective, market-based solutions and private initiatives, it effectively weakens civil society and the freedom to associate. In this case, the public is, unfortunately, subsumed into and disfigured by the political. In the most extreme form, this type of state regards citizens as individuals serving the state, and ideally the communicative and commercial associations composing civil society are eviscerated or eliminated. A tactic of totalitarian regimes is to isolate individuals until their only common interest is the state.

On the other hand, a well-ordered state avoids doing too little and effectively failing to protect and promote the wellbeing of the citizens it governs. The threat of state-sanctioned coercion is sometimes required to promote the good of civil society. The state fails, for instance, when it does not provide adequate policing, thereby subjecting citizens to extensive crime. Or the state does too little when it fails to support the education of its citizens. How a state best honors its limited authority in protecting and promoting the wellbeing of its citizens and civil society is highly contentious. Difficult questions abound: What kind of policing is most effective at preventing and responding to criminal conduct, especially in ways that prove just? Are citizens best served by educational systems in which state-funded and state-regulated schools have a virtual monopoly, or, following the Swedish model, should parents be issued vouchers to send their children to state, nonprofit, or for-profit schools of their choosing? My point here is not to recommend specific ways of conducting policing or education, or to suggest policy solutions for any other particular issues; it is simply to emphasize that when the state ignores or fails to adequately address such issues through political channels, private action, or some combination of the two, it fails to assert its rightful authority. And it is individual citizens and the communicative associations of civil society that suffer the ill consequences of such political reticence. Failing to act dishonors the limited authority of the state, because it is through limitation that the state is free to act in ways that protect and promote the flourishing of its citizens.

To summarize, civil society is foundational and prior to the state. Consequently, the state should promote a robust civil society in which citizens benefit through their formation and participation in various communicative associations. The authority, and therefore the power, of the state is rightfully limited. Such limitation works both to restrict the state's intrusion into the private lives of its citizens and to prompt the state to undertake certain actions that protect and promote the wellbeing of citizens. This balance between political restraint and initiative is best portrayed in a well-ordered relationship between civil society and the state. Although there will be cultural variations regarding this ordering, in general civil society is primarily a realm of exchange and communication, whereas the state is a domain predicated on coercion. Although the two realms overlap, their respective tasks and forms of association are nonetheless distinct, and care should be taken not to confuse or conflate the two. This is why *citizen* and *consumer* are neither interchangeable nor adequate as sole descriptors of a person's life; it is not as citizens but as consumers that we shop, and it is not as consumers but as citizens that we exercise our civil rights. Each individual necessarily has many identities—such as Christian, child, parent, spouse, friend, worker, and patient—in addition to consumer and citizen. Human flourishing is due, in part, to these multiple identities, and social and political ordering should honor and support this multiplicity. Although the identity of citizen is important, it is properly limited, and selected implications of this limitation are visited below.

Civil Citizens

Given the preceding discussion of the relationship between civil society and the state, we may now ask, What is a citizen? This is a difficult question to answer. Aristotle, for instance, contends that humans are by nature political and that their life together in the *polis* (city) is the highest form of human association. "A city," he writes, "is a society of people joining together with their families and their children to live agreeably for the sake of having their lives as happy and as independent as possible."[4] The *polis* has many and various associations promoting civic friendship. A similar theme would later be propounded by Augustine in his characterization of a commonwealth as a people bound together by common objects of love.[5] Yet a city does not exist to enable people simply to reside together but to live together as they ought. Law, then, and not the will of the people, both rulers and ruled, is the supreme power of a rightly ordered state. Aristotle concludes that a citizen is one who both governs and is governed; hence the supremacy of law. A cursory reading of this conclusion implies political equality. This deduction is not wrong, for Aristotle insists that good governance requires a relationship among equals, so presumably citizens are also equal.

4. Aristotle, *Politics* 3.9.
5. See Augustine, *City of God* 19.

Citizens are equal, but Aristotle also asserts that not all people are equal, and therefore not everyone is a citizen. Women and slaves are not citizens because they are not equal to free men. The very young and old are not full citizens because they are not effective at governing. Mere residence in the city does not bestow citizenship. Moreover, the vast majority of people are incompetent to govern, and should therefore submit to the rule of sagacious and virtuous leaders. Citizenship is restricted to a small cadre of male elites who have the intelligence, education, and moral rectitude to govern wisely. Aristotle is no proto-democrat propounding universal suffrage. Indeed, he condemns democracy as the corrupt rule of the mob.

Moreover, many traditional Western regimes have been kingdoms in which the rule of the monarch was often absolute over his or her subjects, and empires often presided over expansive territories and colonies populated by people with few or no rights resembling those associated with citizenship. Even late-modern states that extend citizenship to nearly everyone within their jurisdiction as a birthright (as well as to approved immigrants) often, perhaps routinely, fail to achieve Aristotle's goal of civic friendship. As Helmut Thielicke notes, some zealous citizens are driven to impose their respective "ideological tyrannies" on their fellow citizens, effectively constricting their rights and freedom. More commonly, many individuals, as members of "mass society," grow increasingly alienated from or indifferent to political governance, and therefore pay little serious attention to their duties and responsibilities as citizens.[6]

Despite these difficulties, virtually every neighbor we encounter is or has been a citizen of some particular state.[7] Even displaced people and refugees are citizens of the countries they are fleeing. Although the identity of citizen varies in terms of the métier it represents, and in terms of the relative power it confers, the category cannot simply be ignored. How should we love neighbors who are also our fellow citizens? Answering this question forces us back to the prior question that prompted this inquiry: Who is a citizen? Since I can no longer avoid this question, I offer the following, admittedly minimalist, definition that I believe accords with the laws and practices of many contemporary nation-states, at least those whose roots can be traced to a broadly construed Western tradition of political thought and practice. A citizen is an individual who is born into a particular political community and, by birthright, enjoys the full range of political rights and responsibilities enumerated by the laws

6. See Thielicke, *Theological Ethics*, 2:257–64. Cf. Grant, *Philosophy in the Mass Age*, esp. chap. 8.

7. This is why stateless people prove to be both politically and morally tragic. See Arendt, *Origins of Totalitarianism*, chap. 9.

and constitutions of that community.[8] A citizen may also be an individual who is legally admitted to a political community and, upon admission, is granted specified political rights and responsibilities which—although extensive—may not be as full as those afforded to native-born citizens.[9] It should also be noted that there are people governed by nation-states who are not citizens and have a more restricted range of political rights and protections.[10]

The vast majority of people are politically associated with fellow citizens not of their choosing. There is no reason to assume that citizens will necessarily like each other. The bonds of this association are not predicated on reciprocal fondness or unanimity of beliefs or opinions. Nonetheless citizens are bound to each other, as Augustine recognized, by common objects of love. Citizens may share, for instance, a love of country or a desire for freedom or justice. Yet they may also disagree strenuously about how these loves and desires may be best expressed practically through laws, policies, and political convictions that are frequently divergent rather than convergent. At their best, political debates and contests are not unlike lovers' quarrels—they are passionate and animated but ultimately do not destroy the lovers' bonds.

How is a healthy tension maintained between common loves and equally common disagreement? In this respect a *good* citizen practices civil virtue while avoiding uncivil vice.[11] Civil virtue is grounded in Augustine's teaching that it is out of the one, many. All human beings share a common origin and are therefore ontologically associated, or—in biblical terms—all are kin because of their shared lineage back to the first parents, Adam and Eve. Humans are bound to each other not only by artificial political ties but also by blood. At the very least this means that political opponents cannot, or should not, be treated as anything other than fellow human beings entitled to moral and humane treatment. Regardless of how heated their rhetoric may become or how enflamed their passions, regardless of how stubborn and disagreeable certain individuals may prove to be, citizens are nevertheless members of a shared, though unchosen, political association, and they are therefore bound together. Yet if political bonds are irreparably broken as a result of divisive conflict, all parties ultimately suffer. The good citizen recognizes that attentive,

8. Not all rights of citizenship are operable at the moment of birth. The right to vote, for instance, is restricted to those who reach a specified age.

9. In the United States, for example, a naturalized citizen cannot be elected to or otherwise hold the office of president.

10. In the United States, for example, a legal or resident alien has the right to work but not the right to vote. An undocumented immigrant may be working and paying taxes but does not have a right to residency and can be deported. Citizens living in protectorates, such as Puerto Rico and Guam, have the right to vote in local elections but not in federal elections.

11. See Gregory, *Politics and the Order of Love.*

unselfed listening, toleration, respectful persuasion, and even compromise[12] are not signs of weakness but of civil virtue—pluriform and at times contending expressions of a common good.

Uncivil vice is derived from a quasi-metaphysical belief that the world is best characterized by a pervasive diversity. According to this outlook, this is especially true in human affairs: human beings do not share a common origin but have multiple origins, as reflected by our various and differing cultures. These cultural expressions of an underlying diversity often prove insular and irreconcilable; from out of the many, many. Yet this pervasive diversity does not prevent attempts to impose a singular political will of one group over others. Politics, on this view, is not so much a lovers' quarrel but a mortal combat to be won or lost. Effectively, citizens view one another as potential allies or enemies in a war in which the principal weapon is silencing opponents. Moreover, this silencing is not limited to elections or political offices and institutions but extends to the entire culture in which the privacy and freedom of civil society are displaced by a totalizing politics.[13] As Martin Luther feared, rather than an executioner the state becomes a shepherd, trying to rule the minds and souls of its citizens.[14] This is a dangerous transition, especially when linked to the premise of the many becoming one—for then, ultimately, power settles which among the many prevails. In contrast, starting with the premise of the one expressed in pluriform ways, there is a stronger motivation to appeal to persuasion than to coercion. The politics of diversity is dedicated to shaping a citizenry that speaks with a single voice, a goal achieved by canceling any voices that do not fit the prescribed narrative. Ironically, citizens shaped in a "diverse" politics are far more monochromatic than those who argue for pluriform expressions of a common good. Ultimately, the vice of diversity fashions vicious citizens who grow increasingly intolerant of contending opinions. In short, a pluriform political order in which inclusion is achieved through choice is preferable to a diverse one in which inclusion is achieved through fiat.

The preceding discussion is admittedly limited to states in which the rule of law and protection of political rights are honored, however tenuously. I have said nothing about what good citizens should do when they face (real, rather than merely rhetorical) tyrants and dictators. Under these circumstances,

---

12. There should be no compromise with evil, however—and this requires good citizens to resist their fellow citizens who have become complicit with evil. Doing so requires careful discernment and appeal to an objective good rather than to subjective reactions to circumstances that individuals might judge to be personally troubling or undesirable. See Thielicke, *Theological Ethics*, vol. 2, chap. 20.

13. See O'Donovan, *Ways of Judgment*, chap. 9.

14. See Thielicke, *Theological Ethics*, 2:369.

resistance of varying kinds takes on a more central role, one with which I, mercifully, have no firsthand experience. But I do live in a political associa-tion in which civil virtue is still practiced and uncivil vice resisted, contrary to what the media routinely reports. I think it is important not to take this condition for granted but to support and strengthen it at every opportunity, for it expresses a love of neighbor. In short, I am urging that good citizens model civility in their speech and actions, in the ways they treat their fellow citizens.

To be clear, I do not have in mind a syrupy civility of good feelings and platitudinous rhetoric. An overly courteous citizen is not necessarily a good citizen. Rather, civility is a way of living together with fellow citizens in which our many political quarrels are not with enemies but with kin, however stub-born and disagreeable they might be. Without civility, politics degenerates into rhetorical civil war or worse, and neither the victors nor the conquered flourish.

Good citizens also acknowledge and respect that their fellow citizens, like themselves, have multiple rather than singular identities. Such acknowledg-ment and respect may be understood as patriotic neighbor love, a love of one's own. As mentioned previously, citizens are also spouses, parents, family members, workers, volunteers—in short, neighbors. The patriot loves her country, and necessarily, then, she must also love the people who inhabit it. This is a formidable necessity, incorporating a variety of people representing a nearly incomprehensible range of differences. And to love one's own is to also respect their variances stemming from their multiple identities. Politics is the art of associating different people. These differences, however, are nei-ther endless nor definitive. The apparent differences are ultimately pluriform expressions of commonalities that bind humans together in ways resembling kinship. Consequently, humans "organize themselves politically according to certain essential commonalities found within or abstracted from an absolute chaos of differences."[15]

Herein lies the fundamental tension of citizenship. On the one hand, overemphasizing the essential commonalities among citizens diminishes the respective differences and multiple identities or renders them problematic. Loose ties of kinship are artificially tightened into strong familial bonds; love of country is corrupted into a love of family. And families, by necessity, exclude more than they include. Consequently, those who cannot embrace what is held in common or are perceived as lying outside it are treated with suspicion or as enemies. More troublingly, as Arendt contends, "we begin to play God" to solve the problem of differences. "Instead of engendering

15. Arendt, *Promise of Politics*, 93.

a human being, we try to create *man* in our own image."[16] Citizens are fabricated artifacts of the state to which they owe their predominate, if not exclusive, love and loyalty.

On the other hand, accentuating differences to the detriment of commonalities diminishes citizenship to a tool for satisfying individual desires. Citizens assert political rights to construct preferred lifestyles that purportedly satisfy their most treasured desires. To achieve this end, temporary alliances are formed to channel political power and silence opposition. The state and civil society are simply constructs of the individuals they serve, and they can be shaped and reshaped by those with sufficient power to assert their will over the will of others. Since all relationships are willful acts, kinship, especially familial kinship, are derided, for there is no nature that might guide how humans should govern their social and political ordering. Politics is reduced to a deadly game of nihilistic maneuvering. Citizens, then, selectively give to and withhold from the state their love and loyalty, in accordance with the degree to which particular regimes enable or prevent the satisfaction of their most cherished desires.

This tension is even more intense for the good *Christian* citizen. Christians are pilgrims or sojourners. This status is derived from their simultaneous participation in what may be characterized as two cities. As described by Saint Augustine, there is the heavenly city (or city of God) and the earthly city (or city of man). The heavenly city is the final destination or home that Christians should desire. In the meantime, they sojourn in a world that they should love as God's good creation. Consequently, Christians are never entirely at ease or at home in the world, because this is not where they eventually belong. They will always be a bit restless. Yet this restlessness should not prompt Christians to despise the world. Rather, it is in the world that they love and serve their neighbors. But loving the world and the neighbors inhabiting it is always partial or limited, because only God should be fully and unconditionally loved. This effectively requires Christians to withhold any predominate love and loyalty from various identities or relationships, including those of citizenship and kinship, in the earthly city.

A patriotic love of country affirms it as a place for sojourning—a transitory but not an ultimate home. The patriot loves his country by keeping it in its proper place in the ordering of his loves. He treats it neither as an idol, conferring upon it a counterfeit divinity, nor as an object of derision, approaching it with smug indifference or callous repudiation. Such a properly ordered love of country in turn liberates the patriot to properly love her

16. Arendt, *Promise of Politics*, 94 (emphasis original).

fellow citizens as kin sharing particular political ties, rather than as fellow religionists devoted to the welfare of the state or as potential allies or enemies in unending political battles. This is not simply offering Goldilocks counsel (find the happy middle between extremes). Rather, it encapsulates the life of the good Christian citizen as one of pilgrimage, a life of continual and simultaneous affirmation and resistance. The state is to be affirmed as a necessary political association tasked with promoting human flourishing, yet any unwarranted intrusions of the state that disrupt the privacy of households and the interactions of civil society must be resisted as sinful manifestations of disordered desire. Likewise, efforts to effectively reduce the state to little more than minimal policing must also be resisted. Coupling affirmation and negation is the prerequisite of freedom, for it is only when we are free to negate, to say no, that we are also free to affirm, to say yes. This is a principle the good Christian citizen, the good pilgrim, may embrace, because the "meaning of politics is freedom."[17]

How do we prepare ourselves to be faithful sojourners? Perhaps we can gain some helpful clues by turning our attention to the mundane. Regarding the state with either complete confidence or disdain should be resisted, because in both instances, citizens are reduced to bloodless abstractions. In the first instance, citizens are little more than political resources to be used and discarded as needed, while in the latter instance citizens are voracious consumers with little time for politics. Both conceptions are falsehoods directing attention away from the conditions that actually promote human flourishing. To treat citizens as real, flesh-and-blood people requires attending to one's own and one another's physical, emotional, material, and spiritual wellbeing. It requires an attentive, unselfed love of neighbor in which we care for one another through ordinary, daily acts that address the necessities of finite and mortal creatures. Focusing on the mundane is a way of resisting a disordered politics in order to serve rather than ignore our neighbors.

In her reflections on Augustine, Jean Bethke Elshtain contends that the good bishop of Hippo simultaneously affirmed and negated all attempts at political ordering. He sketches a "complex moral map that offers space for loyalty and love and care, as well as a chastened form of civic virtue." But he is a "thorn in the side of those who would cure the universe once and for all," while also tormenting "cynics who disdain any project of human community, or justice, or possibility." Augustine tries to capture a wisdom that comes from "experiencing fully the ambivalence and ambiguity that is the human condition. This is what Augustine called our business 'within the common

---

17. Arendt, *Promise of Politics*, 108.

mortal life,' and any politics that disdains this business, this caring for the quotidian, is a dangerous or misguided or misplaced politics."[18] The good citizen, the good Christian citizen, will therefore resist the state when it tries to do too little or too much, to keep it in its rightful place. The mundane is a helpful lodestar for locating this place.

Yet inevitably the demands of the state will be in conflict with the needs of neighbors, especially those nearest and dearest to us. The two loves of country and neighbor can pull us apart, and individuals will need to negotiate this tension directly. Does attending to the mundane shape us in ways that may help us make wise choices under such extraordinary pressure?

To help answer this question, however incomplete my reply proves to be, I turn to an unlikely source. Toward the end of World War II, a large number of young Japanese men "volunteered" to be kamikaze pilots. They were primarily university students drafted into the military and "encouraged" to volunteer so their families would avoid the shame of their cowardice. Despite the initial fear of many of the men, most eventually accepted their final duty to die for the emperor with emotions ranging from equanimity to nationalistic fervor.

A disproportionate number of kamikaze pilots were Christians. Since political and military leaders were suspicious of their faith, Christians were frequently singled out to test their loyalty to Japan and the emperor. This suspicion in part stemmed from the fact that Japanese Christians not only tended to be highly educated and prosperous but were also predominantly political liberals and were among the principal founders of the reformist Social Democratic Party. Their military training and indoctrination, often accompanied by harsh discipline, pressured these pilots to forsake their religious and political beliefs in favor of an absolute loyalty to the emperor and the war he was waging against Japan's enemies.

Many, perhaps most, of the Christian pilots were torn between their faith and love of country, but the tension was not usually resolved by choosing one or the other. The issue was *not* one of choosing whether to be a Christian or a patriot (with the understanding that the two were mutually exclusive). Many pilots believed they were caught in an inevitable flow of history and that they must resist, often clandestinely, the new imperial Japan that had become corrupted by greed and militaristic values. They believed they had a patriotic duty to destroy this new cult of the emperor in order to recover the old, real Japan for the good of their neighbors—which made fulfilling this duty an act of neighbor love, and therefore also an act of faith. They would serve their country, their fellow Japanese people, but

18. See Elshtain, *Augustine and the Limits of Politics*, 91.

not the emperor. This resolve is perhaps reflected, in part, in how the Christian pilots spent their last night before their suicide missions. In contrast to the non-Christian pilots, many of whom sang martial songs or drank heavily, the Christian pilots usually gathered to sing hymns, in defiance of thought-control policies.

A poignant example of resolving this tension is found in the letters and diary entries of Hayashi Ichizo.[19] Ichizo was part of a highly educated and devout Christian family. His father was a member of the faculty at the University of Tokyo. Ichizo was the eldest son and had two older sisters and a younger brother. His father died when he was two years old, and his mother, Hayashi Matsue, struggled financially to support herself and her four children. Although a convert to Christianity because of her husband, she remained devout after his death. Matsue and her children were actively involved in their church, and the "Bible united the family spiritually, keeping the children close to their mother."[20] As was customary, the family sent a national flag to Ichizo shortly after his military induction, and his mother and sisters wrote biblical passages on the flag. The religious beliefs of the family members also shaped their political sensibilities. Matsue opposed the war. When, for instance, she and her daughter were in Kudan, where the Yasukuni National Shrine is located, Matsue refused to accompany her daughter on a visit to the shrine. "Her refusal to go up to the shrine was clearly an act of protest against the war and the state ideology."[21]

Ichizo's faith, love for his mother, and patriotism are tightly interwoven. In a diary entry, he admits that whenever he thinks of his mother, he "cannot help but cry." He recalls how difficult it was for her to raise the family, and how loving and talented she was. There is nothing he can do to "ease her pain," but there is the consolation that they worship the same God, and that "God takes care of everything." He hopes that "our country will overcome this crisis and prosper," but in the meantime he cannot "bear the thought of our nation being stampeded by the dirty enemy." He does not fear his impending death, but he expresses no genuine wish to die for the emperor.[22] Rather, his death will have meaning because he dies to protect his family and neighbors. In a letter to his mother, Ichizo explains how his faith, love, and duty are woven together. He reminds her that in his baptism he died in Christ, and so both of them must now trust God. He also informs her that he reads the Bible every day: "When I am reading the Bible, I feel I am next to you. I

19. See Ohnuki-Tierney, *Kamikaze Diaries*, chap. 5.
20. Ohnuki-Tierney, *Kamikaze Diaries*, 165.
21. Ohnuki-Tierney, *Kamikaze Diaries*, 166.
22. See Ohnuki-Tierney, *Kamikaze Diaries*, 170.

shall bring the Bible and the book of hymns on my plane and sortie."[23] But he reminds her that he is a man, and all "men born in Japan are destined to die fighting for the country."[24]

Ichizo's death is not one he has chosen; it was forced on him by circumstances beyond his control. Yet he is at peace knowing that he has remained faithful to his God, his mother, his family, and his fellow Japanese. On the day before his one and only mission, he sings some hymns with his friends. Ichizo is a peace-loving Christian. He regrets, for instance, the abuses committed by Japanese soldiers in China, and he knows that the imperial strategies of absolute devotion and conquest are wrong. And yet, he remains to the end a patriot who wants to protect his country.

Hayashi Ichizo illustrates the tension that often exists between faith and citizenship, or in Augustine's imagery, between the overlapping heavenly and earthly cities. As Christians, we live in both cities, so the tension is inevitable. For Ichizo, the tension is never entirely resolved, but he neither embraces an easy resolution by choosing one city over the other nor becomes paralyzed by a crippling indecisiveness. He acts as a Christian patriot, denying neither love nor duty.

Fortunately, many, if not most, of us do not face this tension with such stark clarity. But we nonetheless face it, albeit in less intense ways. Scripture is right in insisting that we cannot serve two masters, but in serving God we are required to serve our neighbors, many of whom are our fellow citizens.

Where did Ichizo find the strength of character to face this tension between love and duty? Admittedly, I cannot answer this question with much precision or certainty. I do not have any firsthand knowledge of him, and all I have are a few excerpts from his diaries and letters with some commentary from an editor. Nonetheless, I will hazard a conjecture. On numerous occasions, Ichizo mentions such mundane activities as household chores, playing and fighting with siblings and friends, running errands, and caring for members of the church and community. There is a tone of fond remembrance for these simple acts, which at the time were tedious and despised. Over time the mundane became formative for Ichizo. In learning to care for family and friends, he perhaps gained some valuable lessons about how to care for fellow citizens.

To be clear, I am not asserting that mastering household chores and the like is directly transferable to the duties of citizenship that may require great personal sacrifice. But I am suggesting that undertaking ordinary activities

23. Ohnuki-Tierney, *Kamikaze Diaries*, 173.
24. Ohnuki-Tierney, *Kamikaze Diaries*, 173.

that seem devoid of any greater purpose may in fact serve us in facing the tensions inherent in being a citizen, including in those times requiring extraordinary acts of courage and discernment. For loving our neighbors who may happen to be our fellow citizens often requires performing unwanted but necessary duties, a condition that is not entirely remote from the households and neighborhoods of daily living.

Part Three

EVERYDAY
ACTIVITIES

CHAPTER 11

Work

Work is probably the most common human activity. Almost everyone works. Even God works. The created order in which we live is divine handiwork, and Christ himself is a work of salvation. We often think of work as being confined to a job, performing an activity for which we are paid. This assumption is too limited. We work to maintain our homes; we work hard to be good parents, good students, good neighbors. Taking care of people in need, such as aging relatives, is laborious. We often work strenuously in pursuing our recreation; think of cyclists on an early weekend morning. As late moderns we often refer to ourselves as works in progress. Even worship involves working, for liturgy literally means a public work. Work is inescapable.

Work is also important—very important. Work is the predominant means by which we provide for ourselves and our loved ones and participate in civil society. Without work people do not flourish. Think of the discouragement accompanying unemployment, underemployment, or having nothing to do. If the loss or lack of work persists for an extended period of time, it can damage one's physical, emotional, and spiritual health. For many people work is fulfilling because it provides their lives with a tangible sense of purpose and direction. Blessed indeed are those individuals who love their work.

Not everyone, however, is so fortunate. For some, work is unwanted toil required to put food on the table and a roof over one's head. There is nothing necessarily rewarding or fulfilling about work, for it often involves repetitious, mind-numbing, or backbreaking labor. Think of people who rightfully despise their jobs. And work undertaken for family, friends, and communities may prove fruitless if it is greeted with indifference or ingratitude. When work proves either wearying or pointless, it eats away at the soul. Cursed indeed are those individuals who hate their work or find it to be futile.

To be clear, there is nothing praiseworthy about work that is an act of wasted time and pointless action. But this does not mean that work is irredeemable, and even if work proves highly gratifying in and of itself, that gratification alone is not sufficient. We do not work for the purpose of working. Rather, we work as a way of loving God and neighbor. In both instances we keep work in its proper place as a means by linking it directly to the need for rest and leisure. Work should never be endless.

Yet we cannot simply leap from work to leisure, for there are many other ordinary activities that require our work (and for most of these we will never be paid or receive any financial reward). This chapter initiates an exploration of a selection of mundane activities requiring our effort, our acts of love. After this exploration, we will venture into the territory of rest and leisure. But first, back to work.

Work and the Mundane

Even if our work is highly rewarding, it still has its dull moments. For example, I enjoy being a seminary professor, but I do not have much enthusiasm for attending meetings and writing reports. Additionally, much of the work I do maintaining my household or attending to bodily needs often seems bothersome. Even cooking, which I enjoy a great deal, entails disagreeable chores of preparation and cleanup. To be honest, when I think about my work, I must admit that a lot, perhaps most, of it is rather dull. I spend much of my working time doing commonplace things. Why? I think it has something to do with the nature of work, and in the remainder of this section I explore, briefly, several aspects of work to see whether my hunch is correct.

Work is necessary. We work because we must. Humans cannot exist for long if they refuse to work. This is the case because we are embodied creatures, and bodies demand a great deal of attention. As Hannah Arendt insists, "There is no doubt that, as the natural process of life is located in the body, there is no more immediately life-bound activity than laboring."[1] Humans, for instance, must expend time and effort to procure food and clothing, maintain shelter, tend to the physical and emotional needs of loved ones, and undertake voluntary tasks for the sake of their community. Accomplishing these tasks is

---

1. Arendt, *Human Condition*, 110. Arendt draws a distinction between labor and work. Labor is effort required to maintain embodied existence, whereas work creates a lasting object. Cleaning the bathroom is labor; writing a book is work. I find this distinction unclear and do not presuppose it in this chapter. Rather, I use *work* and *labor* as synonymous terms.

frequently time-consuming, laborious, and uninteresting. Technologies have greatly eased and somewhat disguised the demands of time and effort, but they haven't eliminated them. Indeed, much of the money we earn is used to pay for the services we require, and learning how to properly use and maintain these technologies requires further expenditures of money and time. Meeting the needs of embodied life necessarily requires our labor.

Work is often monotonous and boring. The work of maintaining embodied creatures requires actions that must be repeated over and over again. Meals must be prepared, clothes must be washed, houses must be cleaned, bushes must be trimmed, and the list goes on and on. Even if people are paid to take on this work, this doesn't make the requisite labor any less tedious for those performing the tasks. Our jobs are also not free of tedium. Teachers grade stacks of papers and physicians peer down endless throats. I can attest that grading papers is often boring, and I assume that after a while the sight of another throat does not evoke much excitement for a doctor. Specialized education or training does not guarantee that work is free of tedium.

Work is often drudgery. The work attending to natural necessity is often physically or intellectually exhausting. It is not easy to plant and harvest a crop. Constructing a building or a road requires energy that saps one's strength. Delivering goods to stores or customers on time is demanding. The hours required for preparing a business plan or designing a website are tiresome. Those on the front lines of maintaining public safety must contend with the stress and accountability that accompany such responsibilities, and their work sometimes puts their own lives at risk. And we should be mindful that this drudgery is frequently endured to protect or enhance the welfare of others. Work, regardless how rewarding it may prove to be, takes its toll and imposes its risks.

Despite the monotony and toil that are inherent in work, work remains a crucial feature of human identity and an essential means of human flourishing. Consequently, most work is never devoid of dignity and is at least somewhat ennobling.[2] For, ideally, *work is an act of love.* Work expresses the love of God. The Bible enjoins humans to be the stewards of God's good creation. Such stewardship is not an act of preserving nature. The first stewards were gardeners. Humans must work to transform the earth into a more hospitable habitat in which they fulfill their calling to multiply and fill the earth. As Arendt argues, the world is a human artifact, a home that people build and

2. There are, of course, exceptions. Slave labor is an obvious example. It could also be argued that degrading activities should not be regarded as "work" but as some other form or type of action.

maintain over time.[3] The earth and its resources enable humans to attend to their manifold needs as embodied creatures. God does not place humans in an environment in which physical and mental effort is not required, but in a realm of necessity that requires them to work in order to both survive and thrive. But God has also provided all that is needed for humans to accomplish their stewardship. In this respect, work is a response of gratitude.

Work is a way of loving oneself. Self-love, when properly ordered, is not synonymous with selfishness. Most basically, through work a person provides for herself without needlessly becoming a burden on others. But this does not mean that the self is ideally self-sufficient. To be oneself is to serve and depend on others. Indeed, genuinely loving oneself can never be separated from loving others, because these others contribute to one's sense of self. We become ourselves in the company of others, sometimes being the center of attention and other times not. For example, when I am sick it is appropriate that I receive care, and in the moment of receiving care it is appropriate that I am at the center of my caregiver's attention; on the other hand, when I am a caregiver I should not be concerned about the attention I am receiving (or not receiving) from the recipient of my care. Consequently, a well-ordered self-love is always relational. I love myself in relation to God. That relationship is weakened if I fail to perform the works of worship, prayer, discipleship, and ministry, or if I fail to receive God's mercy, grace, and forgiveness. I also love myself in relation to my neighbors. This relationship is expressed through work that is productive or caring. For instance, I love my neighbors by producing goods or providing services they need; their consumption in turn helps me meet my material needs.[4] Caring for our neighbors through simple acts of kindness and voluntary activities in the community also reflects a regard for their wellbeing. Indeed, I cannot truly love myself in isolation, if all I have to love is myself.

Work is a way of loving one's neighbor. Adam Smith contends that work is self-interested.[5] There is no reason to deny the truth of his observation, but it is only half the story. Work is also interested in the wellbeing of the neighbor. The neighbor benefits from our labor. This is certainly true in the marketplace where neighbors benefit from our work in exchanging goods and services. It is also true in the household and other communicative associations. Everyone in the family benefits when the dishes are cleaned; boys and girls on

---

3. See Arendt, *Human Condition*, 136–39.

4. This mutual dependence underlies much of Adam Smith's work. See *The Theory of Moral Sentiments* and *An Inquiry into the Nature and Causes of the Wealth of Nations*.

5. See Smith, *Wealth of Nations*, 25–27.

a Little League Baseball team are coached by a volunteer; worshipers enjoy the floral arrangement placed by a parishioner for Sunday morning worship.

Work is almost always a work of love, be it obvious or not, for work almost always benefits someone else: a neighbor known or unknown. In the remainder of this chapter, I examine how work overlaps and is both similar and different to exchange and communication.

Work and Exchange

The survival of individuals and communities is predicated on work. Each day, at a bare minimum, food and shelter are required. The provision of each of these may be understood as work or labor. Such work is more efficient and effective when individuals cooperate. For instance, individuals hunting as a pack obtain more game; a large number of laborers construct a house more quickly. Survival is enhanced when individuals work together. Additionally, the wellbeing of people and communities is improved when individuals concentrate on a limited number of tasks. Life would be dismal (and probably short) if every individual had to plant, cultivate, and harvest a crop, prepare meals, construct equipment for cooking and eating, construct and maintain a house and its furnishings, and make clothing. It is doubtful whether there would be enough time for such an individual to become skillful in any one of these chores, much less in all of them. Everyone is better off when each makes a needed item or two that can then be swapped. For example, I might trade some of my vegetables for a shirt. In short, much of our work is geared toward exchange.

The two great insights of Adam Smith and David Ricardo are, respectively, the specialization of labor and the comparative advantage of trade.[6] Smith argued that, for an individual, making one item that can be traded is vastly more productive than making a few different items for one's own use. Additionally, rather than trying to barter with these items, it is easier and more efficient to be paid a wage that is used to purchase a variety of needed items. For example, I am paid to be a theologian, and I use my pay to buy food and clothing. Ricardo built on this principle of specialization and applied it to international trade. A nation should not strive to be self-sufficient in meeting all the wants and needs of its population. Rather, it should make only the items it is adept at producing and that are needed by other countries that are not adept at producing them. For instance, Scotland can easily produce large

---

6. See Smith, *Wealth of Nations*, book 1; and Ricardo, *On the Principles of Political Economy*, chap. 7.

quantities of wool, but is not a good place for vineyards and wineries. Portugal, on the other hand, has excellent vineyards and wineries but is not a favorable locale for herds of sheep. Scotland should specialize in wool and Portugal in wine; they can then trade with each other. Both countries use their respective advantages to obtain what they need through exchange. Exchange improves the material wellbeing of individuals, households, communities, and nations.

Much of our work, then, is oriented toward production and consumption. We produce goods and services that are purchased by others, and we, in turn, consume goods and services that are produced by them. Consequently, much of our work depends on markets in which exchanges take place. There is no reason to deny that markets are competitive. There is also no reason to deny that such competition presents both promise and peril in respect to employment.

First, the peril. In market economies, most jobs are never guaranteed. This is partly due to the so-called natural business cycle of periodic booms and busts. New jobs are created and filled when the economy is strong and growing, but unemployment increases dramatically during a recession. The introduction of new technologies also proves disruptive. Workers manufacturing and selling typewriters, for instance, lose their jobs in favor of those making and selling computers. Certain sectors are highly competitive, requiring workers to put in long hours at less pay to keep their jobs. In global markets some jobs may disappear because of the competitive advantages of trade. Most of the clothing worn by Americans, for example, is imported from other countries where labor is cheaper. Most jobs in market-based economies should never be taken for granted, for when markets are working correctly, they promote what may be described as "creative destruction."[7]

Now, the promise. Markets are efficient mechanisms for matching supply with demand. There are always producers searching for new and better ways to meet the demands for goods and services. Since markets are ideally competitive, consumers benefit from lower prices. With increased deregulation over that past few decades, a burgeoning global middle class has emerged. Many people now enjoy higher levels of discretionary income than they have before because the cost of meeting basic needs, such as the need for food, has dropped dramatically. This rise in purchasing power has stemmed in large part from the expansion of and increased participation in markets in which virtually all workers are simultaneously producers and consumers. The promise of jobs generated by expanding markets is that it is now easier to promote the material wellbeing of more people. Despite periodic setbacks, over time

---

7. See Schumpeter, *Capitalism, Socialism and Democracy*, chap. 7. See also Waters, *Just Capitalism*, chap. 3.

markets have enabled human flourishing by providing people with a greater range of opportunities for work and trade.

Additionally, the work created in competitive markets helps many people become affluent. I am cognizant that for some people, including some Christians, affluence is not held in high regard. They assume (mistakenly, I think) that affluence is necessarily gained at the expense of others—that one person's riches must cause ill fortune for another. Somehow, exchange is regarded as, fundamentally, a zero-sum game rather than as a win-win activity. I have no desire to refute this assertion or to defend affluence as a good; I have done that elsewhere.[8] Rather, I am using affluence both to lift up work as an important means of promoting human flourishing and also to demarcate its limits.

Affluence enables human flourishing when it is used to promote the material wellbeing of individuals and their social and political associations. Affluence indicates the availability of increased discretionary income and financial resources that can provide greater comfort and leisure as well as an expanded consumption of goods and services. To oversimplify, affluence can satisfy more wants in addition to needs, which presumably enriches the lives of individuals and families, and—more expansively—civil society. When one's time and income are devoted almost exclusively to supplying necessities such as shelter, food, and health care, then human flourishing is, in most instances, diminished.

I am *not* arguing that affluent people are inherently happier than the less affluent. There are many examples of affluent people who are unhappy and of impoverished communities whose members are flourishing. Rather, I am arguing that affluence helps improve the material wellbeing of people, thereby providing a foundation for its beneficiaries to flourish more broadly, so long as it is used properly. In this respect, affluence serves as a warning—namely, that it is not a proper end in itself but a means to enable human flourishing. The purpose of seeking affluence is not to become affluent but to support and assist a life that is judged to be good in a full and complete sense. Improving material wellbeing is important, but it is not sufficient in itself. Although human flourishing is not divorced from an economy of exchange, it occurs more substantially in an economy of communication.

Work and Communication

As noted previously, human flourishing occurs predominantly in communicative associations. Unlike political associations or market-based associations,

8. See Waters, *Just Capitalism*, chap. 4.

which are predicated, respectively, on coercion and exchange, communicative associations are based on communicating the goods of God's created order. Communicative associations are not unrelated to the state or markets; indeed, they require the support of both in order to thrive. But their ability to promote human flourishing is threatened when either the state or markets intrude too deeply into the ordering of their private affairs. The family, for instance, is neither a state writ small nor a tiny marketplace, but a unique form of association whose members are intimately related to one another. And its members do not flourish through either authoritarian rule or managerial control.

Why does human flourishing occur predominantly in communicative associations? Because, at least in part, they respond most fully and directly to the social nature of human beings. Political and commercial associations are needed but artificial, since neither is based on familiarity. One can be a citizen or a consumer without knowing or fully trusting fellow citizens or consumers. This is not the case with many of the communicative associations, both voluntary and involuntary, that compose civil society. Unlike the state or the market, communicative associations provide enduring places where people belong. And these places are filled with other people with whom to belong: we belong with one another. Human flourishing occurs in these places because they are neither coercive nor competitive but mutual.[9]

Such mutuality is simultaneously limiting and liberating. It is limiting because communicative associations are not inclusive. Not just anyone, for example, may be admitted to a family. This restriction also liberates family members to forge the bonds of being spouses, parents, and offspring over time. To be genuinely free, we must have both the capacity and the opportunity to say yes to this and no to that. I can be free to be a husband only by saying no to being single.

In this respect, it is through communicative associations that we most fully exercise our callings and vocations, because it is within these social contexts that we most directly encounter our "freedom of obedience" and "freedom in limitation."[10] According to Karl Barth, God calls us to pursue a particular way of life that God has chosen for us to follow, and we in turn must choose whether or not to obey this summons. Our freedom, then, is limited by these divine and human choices. It is only in choosing to be obedient, however, that a person is truly free, for disobedience enslaves one to rebelling against God. God does not issue general or generic callings but a particular calling

---

9. At least, they are not coercive in comparison to the coercion encountered in political life or competitive in comparison to the competition encountered within the marketplace.

10. See Barth, *Church Dogmatics* III/4, 595.

issued to a particular person. "God does not want anything and everything" but "always wants this and that."[11] Additionally, fulfilling these callings most often requires enduring fellowship or relationship with others. For instance, I am not called to be a father to daughters in general but to be *the* father of *my* daughter in particular, and it is a lifelong vocation—although one that changes over time as my daughter grows older or other applicable circumstances change.[12]

To be clear, pursuing our callings and vocations does not negate what was discussed previously. We are called to be workers and professionals. These too are important and particular callings, but they are lodged with an exchange economy and are oriented principally toward material wellbeing. Such callings and vocations, then, are necessary but not sufficient, for their contribution to promoting human flourishing is supportive and indirect. We need our daily bread to live, but we do not live by bread alone. It is within communicative economies that we live beyond our daily bread, where our flourishing occurs more directly because of the congeniality of this economy to *koinōnia*. Consequently, our nonremunerative vocations are more expansive and overarching, demanding priority over remunerative vocations. My callings as a husband and father, for example, are more important than my vocation as a theologian. Consequently, my potential flourishing is more intense in my home than in my seminary campus. This is why, in part, the vocations associated with communication rather than exchange often prove more satisfying, more difficult, and less precise.

The classic novel *Silas Marner* illustrates this vocational priority, and how it promotes human flourishing when ordered properly and diminishes it when disordered. Silas Marner is a weaver. As a young man he is a respected member of his profession, church, and community. He happily enjoys the company of a close friend and a fiancée, though he suffers occasional "fits" (probably epilepsy) that render him unconscious. The elder deacon of the church becomes seriously ill and, since he is a childless widower, church members take turns watching over him. During Silas's watch, a bag of money hidden by the deacon disappears. A quick search of the house reveals Silas's knife in the drawer where the money was kept. Silas remembers that he had recently used the knife to cut a leather strap for his friend, but he tells no one. He insists he is innocent, but the church members draw lots that determine he is guilty. Within the next few months, his wedding is called off and his former

11. Barth, *Church Dogmatics* III/4, 595.
12. An exception is foster parents, whose relationship with children is temporary. See Meilaender, *Limits of Love*, chap. 1.

fiancée marries his friend. Silas is embittered by the injustice he has suffered and his subsequent abandonment by everyone he knows, including God. He quietly leaves the community.

Silas moves to the village of Raveloe, where he throws himself into his work. He avoids most social contacts with the villagers, other than what is required to conduct his business as a weaver. The one time he reaches out to someone, it ends badly, for he treats an ill woman with herbs, and that gives him a reputation as a conjurer—an untrustworthy man best avoided. Silas becomes even more embittered and withdrawn. Since he lives simply, he accumulates a modest fortune. Each evening he enjoys counting his money and then returning the coins to their hiding place under some bricks in the floor. His treasure has become a solace, filling the void of lost friends, wife, and church. Silas assumes that he does not need anyone else, for others will inevitably disappoint him: he has effectively become a reclusive miser. Yet Silas loses the comfort of his wealth. One evening while he is away from his house, a thief steals the money. Silas is enraged by what he believes to be still another betrayal, and he rushes off to a nearby inn hoping to find the constable. A search party is quickly formed, but it fails to find either the thief or the money.

A few weeks later, a snowstorm lingers over the village. That evening a woman and her young child struggle to walk through the drifts, keeping warm as best they can. Unfortunately, the woman is an opium addict, and she grows increasingly drowsy. After a while her daughter cannot rouse her and wanders off, searching for shelter. The young girl enters Silas's house and heads toward the fireplace and its warm fire, lies down, and goes to sleep. Silas does not see her because he is in the midst of one of his fits. When he comes to, he finds the child, realizes she has come in from the cold, and discovers her mother—dead in a nearby drift. Silas takes the child to the squire's home in order to fetch a doctor. The doctor and the squire's son go to the woman to confirm her death. The son recognizes the woman as his wife, whom he had foolishly and secretly married. He knows he is the father of the child but says nothing, fearing that revealing the truth might jeopardize his impending marriage to a more suitable woman.

Much to everyone's surprise, Silas decides to keep the child and raise her as his daughter. Silas names the girl after his mother, Hepzibah, though the name is quickly abbreviated to Eppie. Over the ensuing years they enjoy a happy household. One day a nearby pond is drained and Silas's stolen money is discovered, along with the remains of the thief. Eppie, now a young woman, is engaged to a young man from a working-class family.

Shortly thereafter the story takes an interesting turn. Eppie's biological father and his wife are childless. He tells his wife about his previous marriage, and she agrees to adopt Eppie, despite the many years that have passed by. They present their offer to Eppie and Silas, promising her a better life than Silas—even with his restored fortune—could ever hope to provide, and the prospect of marriage to a man of a better class. Eppie refuses the offer, insisting that she will always regard Silas as her father, and that she loves her fiancé and cannot imagine marrying anyone else. The point of the story is clear: the source of Silas's and Eppie's happiness is not their financial state but their relationship as father and daughter, and Eppie presumes that this priority will also prove to be true in her future marriage. Quite literally, money cannot buy happiness.

We may be tempted to dismiss this story as perhaps charming but overly sentimental, a farfetched tale of humble virtue vanquishing opulent vice. But a bit more context is needed. Nowhere in the story is money, even wealth, dismissed as inherently evil. When Silas's stolen money is recovered, he admits that it will help improve his and Eppie's lives. Material wellbeing is not unrelated to one's happiness. But Silas also realizes that it is the love shared between him and Eppie that has enabled their flourishing, an understanding that gains greater strength after his modest fortune is regained. The mistake is believing that affluence *alone* is synonymous with flourishing, or that wealth can purchase one's happiness. Material wellbeing helps us enjoy life, but material prosperity in itself is not the good life. We flourish through communicating rather than exchanging. This is what Saint Paul alludes to as the abundant life: a life that is abundant in both embodied and spiritual wellbeing.

Additionally, Silas's new role as a father pulls him into the community. Neighbors provide him with clothing, toys, and other necessities for raising Eppie, and he is "blessed" with a profusion of free advice on how to be a good parent. Silas and Eppie become frequent churchgoers. The once embittered recluse and miser becomes a treasured member of the community, increasingly reconciled to the misfortunes of his past. A lonely existence centered on a festering sullenness slowly gives way to a healing grace. Silas cannot flourish in perpetual isolation and loneliness. He needs the company and fellowship of others.

After Eppie's unexpected, and one might surmise disruptive, arrival, Silas spends his time differently. He does not spend virtually all his time working as a weaver. He must also use his time working as a parent. There are the countless chores that must now be accomplished to raise a child and maintain a home (work that has no financial reward or inherent interest). There is no mention in the story of the joys of cooking, cleaning, and washing day in and day out. But the story does presuppose a tidy household rather than a filthy and messy one. Tending to Eppie's physical needs alone isn't enough to cause her to flourish, but neither could she have flourished if Silas had ignored or neglected the mundane tasks of being a father and keeping a tidy home. Silas's time is now much more dispersed than it used to be, for he has a much more diverse range of work that he must perform. Ironically, it is also in taking on a wider range of work that Silas learns the value of rest or leisure. Sunday is a kind of Sabbath for Silas and Eppie. Silas stays away from his loom, and after church he and Eppie spend the day resting, doing little more than taking a leisurely walk.

Work requires rest or leisure in order to be effective or fulfilling. This is true in both the economies of exchange and of communication. To labor continuously is ultimately pointless, for work itself becomes its own purpose; one works in order to work. But this means there are never any fruits of one's labor to enjoy. Work becomes a tree choked by fruit that merely withers and rots. The same is true in communication. Communicating the goods of creation requires a rough and never-exacting reciprocity. Except in cases of providing care at the beginning and end of life, sharing depends on an underlying give-and-take. Members of a household, for instance, may trade chores or cover for each other as needed. These reciprocal arrangements are informal, with no monetary value, and are not enforced through the threat of coercion.[13] A household is not a contractual but a covenantal association. And when some do all the work for others in a household, the covenant is violated and its members do not flourish. When Silas Marner is a reclusive miser, he works for no other reason than to collect more coins—and when they are stolen, he falls into despair at the loss of this semblance of meaning. His life grows smaller, collapsing in on itself, for he fails to take those risks of loving God and neighbor that alone nourish the soul.

Without work, human flourishing is diminished because the physical needs of embodied creatures are not fully met. But without leisure, work is rendered ineffectual. Rest is the *telos* of work, and the two cannot be separated without damaging oneself and others. We work and we rest not only for our own sakes but in obedience to the command to love God and neighbor. It is in and through work and rest that we love ourselves, our families, our friends, and our neighbors. Activity must be followed by being still for a time, otherwise we forget the purposes for which we work. Work and rest are two sides of the same coin. In this chapter I have concentrated on work, and I will address leisure and rest later on. But we have some other things to cover first.

---

13. This does not exclude, for example, a daughter purchasing the labor of a sibling to complete a disagreeable chore, or parents withholding privileges when their children fail to complete assigned tasks.

CHAPTER 12

Housework and Homework

When I was a boy, household chores were my nemesis. I hated them. Cleaning my room, raking leaves, and washing the car were a terrible waste of time and energy that could be better spent playing baseball or just hanging out with the neighborhood kids. Chores were pointless and unending. No matter how well I might do them, my room would always be messy again, there would be more leaves to rake, and the car would attract more dirt. To this day I cannot think of a positive adjective to describe chores other than perhaps "done."

Yet chores are important. Why? Because they remind us that we are embodied beings who require a great deal of physical care and maintenance. Much of this upkeep is repetitious and dull—painfully dull. This important message, however, is being lost in late-modern cultures that place little, if any, value on the ordinary or mundane. It is presumed that we are better off when we are free from tending to what may be called the secondary needs of embodied existence as opposed to the primary pleasures. As late moderns we may enjoy pampering ourselves at a spa or working out at the gym, but the secondary needs requiring disagreeable and time-consuming labor are best avoided as much as possible. The primary pleasures are energizing and rewarding, whereas the secondary needs are monotonous and dull.

This bifurcation is a result, in part, of the love-hate relationship many late moderns have with being embodied. We love our bodies because of the pleasures derived from the senses. Hence the time and money spent keeping our bodies healthy and attractive. We also loathe our bodies because, despite our best efforts, they age and eventually fail us. Hence the widespread neglect of physical health.

Bodies also limit what we can do. Most significantly, bodies impose severe constraints on mobility. As embodied creatures we can only move so fast from here to there, and we cannot be in two places at once. Much of our technology is designed to help us overcome our limited mobility. IT, for example, can transport us instantly to real and imaginary destinations, so long as we are happy with virtual or digital realities. With the aid of software and social media we can project ourselves simultaneously at various locales throughout the web in both real and virtual time.

Consequently, there is a growing preference for space over place.[1] *Space* may be understood as a temporary milieu that is used to achieve an immediate objective. Sometimes the space is physical—a conference room in a hotel to conduct a meeting. But increasingly the space is virtual—a teleconference to conduct a meeting. In both instances the spaces are abandoned once the objective has been accomplished, and such temporary spaces characterize how late moderns overcome the constraints against their mobility in getting things done. Spaces are routinely constructed and deconstructed as needs arise with little thought or desire for permanence. A so-called space requiring maintenance is of little value. We go to work but never leave the house.

In contrast, *place* may be understood as an enduring milieu that is often indifferent to the objectives of its occupants. Place is always a physical location, suggesting durability over a relatively lengthy period of time. These durable locales may be natural, such as a mountain, or constructed, such as a building. Unlike temporary space, the significance or value of place is not derived from its utility. Rather, people bestow meaning and value on a place over time. Place becomes a landmark demarcating important events in the lives of individuals or associations. Unlike space, place commonly evokes care, even affection from those who find it important.

The mobility that space offers helps us achieve certain worthwhile goals such as managing business and commercial ventures. Late moderns, then, tend to be nomadic—not nomads in the traditional sense of communities traveling well-established trade routes on a cyclical basis. Instead, late-modern nomads travel quickly, either physically or imaginatively, in response to emerging opportunities. Place, then, is a liability best avoided. But if humans are to flourish, is space an adequate substitute that can displace place entirely? No. Human flourishing requires physical places where embodied humans congregate to collectively undertake certain tasks and establish relationships over time. It is difficult to imagine, for instance, a town existing without any permanent residents, or a family whose members are always at remote

---

1. See Waters, *Christian Moral Theology in the Emerging Technoculture*, 161–73.

locations. People require places where they belong together. The mobility afforded by space needs to be counterbalanced by the constraints of place.

Since place is physical, it requires maintenance, which brings us back to those pesky chores. In the next section, on *housework*, I explore the necessity of place more deeply. In short, I contend that embodied beings require physical locales where they belong with others over extended periods of time. These physical places must be maintained if they are to promote human flourishing, and I use the house as my primary example of such a place. But a house alone will not do. We must also speak of home, and here the focus shifts from the physical structure to the people living inside it. In this section, on *homework*, I argue that humans are also spiritual beings occupying physical places. Consequently, we may speak about the need for a spirituality of place, which I do by employing Albert Borgmann's concept of focal things and practices.[2] Consequently, housework should also promote the homework or homemaking of its residents.

Housework

Human beings require places in which to flourish. We need a place or places where we can live out our mutual belonging with others. This is especially true in respect to families or other intimate associations. Intimacy requires physical proximity. As embodied beings, humans require mutual, physical presence. A "conversation" is more than words and voice. There are facial expressions, gestures, body movements, other sensory inputs that are needed in getting to know each other. Faces, even familiar ones, on a screen are cold facsimiles, lifelike replicas.

A conversation is an exchange, but it is also communication. Returning to Iris Murdoch, we cannot be attentive to the good of the other if the other is not present. Texting, emailing, and video conferencing may help to maintain a relationship when necessity dictates distance, but they do not assist intimacy. The limits of technologically mediated communication are exposed when we require the physical care of others. When I am sick, for instance, a text message from a family member or caregiver is of little use. I need someone to help me attend to bodily needs; I need a caregiver who is physically present. Space can perhaps preserve but not promote intimacy, and thereby human flourishing more broadly. For space subtly reinforces the mistaken belief that we do not really need each other, except temporarily and preferably at a distance. But, as argued in previous chapters, without friends and family,

2. See Borgmann, *Technology and the Character of Contemporary Life.*

without communicative associations of neighbors, humans are diminished both as individuals and as communities. Some of the more conspicuous imagery of the COVID-19 pandemic was of the (un)social distancing and masks, because whenever people ventured out in public, they presented themselves to one another as potential sources of contagion best avoided. That kind of suspicion is not a promising foundation for a robust civil society as an expression of neighbor love.

Places identify and track one's being and life over time. As embodied creatures, humans are also temporal beings. They have a past, present, and future that are inescapably linked to physical locales. Every person is from somewhere, is somewhere presently, and is heading somewhere, even if the destination is unknown. Without time and place in mind, personal identity becomes a jumble. To illustrate, when I was younger strangers would frequently ask me where I was from or even where I was heading. I am no longer asked these questions. Instead, I am usually asked what I do. Answering this question requires no reference to place or time because I can perform my work (what I do) almost anywhere and anytime.

Being untethered to place and time is, of course, an illusion promulgated by late-modern nomadic elites. The hitch is that embodied beings cannot really shake off their dependence on place and time, a reality apparently discounted by the lockdown dictates during the COVID-19 outbreak that urged people to work remotely—a luxury unavailable to much of the labor force. The comfortably sequestered were often unmindful of their dependence on workers who produced and brought both necessities and luxuries to their doorsteps, goods and services derived from real places and in real time. Humans do not flourish by adopting the fantasy that they have overcome the fetters of place and time. On the contrary, they flourish when they live within the timely boundaries of past, present, and future that are demarcated by particular places.

Two important caveats are in order. First, place is not absolutely determinative of personal identity. Individuals evolve over time, overcoming, for instance, an unpromising origin while striving to achieve a more promising future. One's place in life can, and often should, change over time. Without this acknowledgment it is easy to fall into the false and prejudicial trap that assumes place of origin is destiny: "'Nazareth! Can anything good come from there?' Nathanael asked" (John 1:46). My emphasis on place is simply to remind us that humans are temporal and finite creatures despite any efforts to disguise this basic, given condition. Second, mobility is not inherently bad. To be locked in place does not promote human flourishing. This is why restricting travel and imposing curfews are among the favorite tools for asserting authoritarian control. Moreover, mobility is a key ingredient of

Christian faith and practice. Christians are commanded to travel the world and proclaim the gospel, a command reflecting their status as pilgrims. Yet, unlike late-modern nomads, pilgrims do not wander endlessly but are headed somewhere. And during their pilgrimage, they often stop and stay in place for a while. My criticism of mobility again serves as a reminder that humans, as embodied creatures, are not and cannot be perpetually on the move.

With these caveats in mind, we may return to examining the necessity of place. Place provides parameters within or against which identity is formed and expressed over time. Place is formative as a physical locale that identifies where one has been and where one is currently located. Formative and identifying places may include expansive mountain ranges or coastlines; city landmarks; and, most commonly, residential buildings—that is, houses.[3] These places help us identify where we once belonged and where we belong now. To ignore the formative significance of place is to open the door to vain attempts to somehow transcend bodily limitations. Embodied creatures, however, must be in place for periods of time in order to flourish. They can neither work nor rest if all the while they are striving for the impossible goal of always being on the move.

Yet place is unassuming and delicate, easily ignored and easily neglected. The mountain range or coastline becomes a mere background devoid of beauty or grandeur; the city landmark becomes an ugly relic and object of derision; a house is simply a building in which to relax, eat a meal, and take a snooze. But to ignore the significance of place is to effectively strip life of any direction, for failing to coordinate place and the passage of time disorients human creatures from the very physical substances that preserve and enrich their individual and social lives. A timeless, nomadic life that maligns the limitation of place is preferred over a life of pilgrimage that blesses whatever place one may be in for a time. The timeless, nomadic life ultimately diminishes, rather than promotes, human flourishing.

To undertake the preservation of place, then, is also an act of upholding human wellbeing. Conserving mountain ranges and coastlines, ensuring that city landmarks are neat and tidy, and keeping houses clean and in good repair all contribute to human flourishing, for these are, in differing ways, acts of unselfing. In losing oneself in the beauty of a sunset over a mountain or shoreline, in reflecting on the heritage of landmarks that have stood through the generations, in taking care that houses are safe and comfortable abodes, we take aim at the fat relentless ego by putting it in its proper place—at

---

3. I am using *houses* as shorthand for all the various kinds of structures, buildings, and physical units in which people reside.

the periphery rather than the center. In contrast to the nomad, whose only center is the ego, the pilgrim recognizes that we are created to love God and neighbor and to be in fellowship in those places where humans congregate as the embodied creatures they were created to be. Nomads wander to enrich themselves, whereas pilgrims move to serve their neighbors.

Humans encounter the necessity of place most directly in the household—or, more precisely, in the structure in which the household is located. A house should be a safe and comfortable place to live. This does not occur on its own, and that brings us back to those bothersome chores. There are countless tasks required to keep a place in good repair, and almost all of them are repetitive and uninteresting.[4] Yet, if they are neglected, a house falls into disrepair, diminishing the wellbeing of its inhabitants, perhaps even endangering them. This is one way in which attending to the mundane is an act of neighbor love.

To be clear, this does not make the mundane any less boring, but it does disclose its importance. We spend time on the ordinary because this is how, to a large extent, we come to know the good of others and to care for them. If we fail to maintain those places where people belong together, they will not flourish. Consequently, it is in and through the mundane that we express, in part, the love of neighbors with whom we share common places over time.

Homework

Families, and people in general, tend to thrive when they live together in a house over an extended period of time. Although the arrangement is not permanent (nothing in a finite creation is permanent), it has the feel of permanence or at least endurance, and that provides a sense of home. Home and house are closely related, but they are not synonymous. *Home* is more fixated on a particular association of people living together in a shared place. In many instances, homes are held together by bonds of kinship, marriage, or other covenants. The nexus of home and house acknowledges that embodied humans are also spiritual beings who live in physical locales. As houses require work to keep them in good repair, so too do homes need work to enable human flourishing. If the preceding section is understood as the materiality of spiritual wellbeing, this section focuses on the spirituality of place.

It may seem absurd to talk about spirituality since immaterial spirit transcends material place. In this respect, virtual space would presumably have

---

4. I have met individuals who enjoy doing household chores. I do not question their enthusiasm, but I must confess that I do not understand or share it.

more in common with spirit. These assumptions, however, fail to recognize that the material or physical necessarily mediates the spirituality of embodied creatures. Humans are not bifurcated beings, with parallel physical and spiritual lives. To the contrary, the physical and spiritual are integrated; we are embodied souls and ensouled bodies. Consequently, we are both origins and objects of spirituality. As origins, we seek self-transcendence; at the same time, we are also objects of God's love that is transcendent and incarnate. Moreover, spirituality is not confined to what we do in solitude; it also has to do with what we do in the company of others. The home, then, offers some revealing insights into a spirituality of place, given its close relationship to a physical house: the house enables the communicative interactions of the home.

The work of the philosopher Albert Borgmann helps to identify this important relationship between house and home.[5] In a late-modern nomadic culture, goods and services are reduced to commodities that are easily consumed, disposable devices well-suited for mobile and autonomous individuals. Such commodification encourages shoddy work. Devices are designed to be used for a short period of time and then discarded and replaced rather than maintained and repaired. This preference in turn drives a ravenous consumption of commodities and the ubiquitous presence of devices that alter the patterns of daily life, especially within the household. Late-modern nomads, for instance, tend to graze rather than dine. Increased mobility changes where, when, and how meals are prepared and eaten. They are frequently eaten on the run, in a fast-food restaurant, or on the coffee table, in front of the television, rather than at the dining room table at regular hours throughout the day. Food is a commodity to be consumed quickly rather than an occasion for leisurely conversation with friends or family. The introduction of other devices has also changed household living patterns. With central heating, for instance, a family need not gather around the living room hearth as the only source of heat but can be scattered throughout various rooms.

In response to these commodifying tendencies, Borgmann argues that the best "counterforce . . . is the dedication to focal things and practices."[6] What are focal things and practices? Defined succinctly, "Generally, a focal thing is concrete and of a commanding presence. A focal practice is the decided, regular, and normally communal devotion to a focal thing."[7] A focal thing is not a commodity to be consumed but an objective reality that shapes the

---

5. The following summary of Borgmann is adapted from Waters, *This Mortal Flesh*, 41–45. For a more extensive overview of Borgmann's work, see Waters, *Christian Moral Theology in the Emerging Technoculture*, chap. 4.

6. Borgmann, "Reply to My Critics," 356.

7. Borgmann, *Power Failure*, 22.

values and behavior of those whose attention is seized by its presence. A focal practice consists of acts that express the convictions and behaviors that are formed by those devoted to the focal thing. Although a focal thing commands the attention of its devotees, it is not self-sufficient but requires the care and attentiveness of practitioners. Focal things and practices embody a transcendent and immediate presence to which adherents conform their character and virtues.

Borgmann uses family dining to illustrate the formative power of focal things and practices. "The great meal of the day, be it at noon or in the evening, is a focal event par excellence. It gathers the scattered family around the table."[8] Those gathered at the table are not present only to eat food. The meal is a focal point of activity, drawing the family together through common traditions and practices. Ingredients are carefully chosen and prepared following beloved recipes. The table is properly set, and later the tableware is carefully cleaned and stored. Family members adjust their schedules to be present at the prescribed time and are attentive to the conversation and the people conversing around the table. Moreover, the meal links the family to a larger network of social relationships. When guests are present, there are rules of hospitality to follow, and the meal itself should inspire thanksgiving for the efforts of farmers, cooks, dishwashers, and crafters who make the meal possible.

As a focal activity, such a meal is the "enactment of generosity and gratitude, the affirmation of mutual and perhaps religious obligations," a far cry from the "social and cultural anonymity of a fast-food outlet."[9] Most importantly, the meal reinforces the fact that those formed by the fellowship of the table are finite and temporal creatures. They depend on bountiful harvests, and unlike the easy and incessant consumption of packaged commodities, the communal meal is bracketed by time; it has a designated beginning, middle, and end.

Focal practices require time and attention. Lots of time and attention. Maintaining a house where homework may occur requires fixing things when they break and cleaning things when they get dirty—often unnoticed touches of loving care. To reiterate, this is mostly achieved through ordinary and routine effort. In the case of the family meal, dishes must be washed, dough kneaded, a table set just so, hospitality extended, conversation encouraged. Admittedly, these are little things, mundane deeds. But they matter. They make a difference. Compare a carefully prepared meal with one in which the

8. Borgmann, *Technology and the Character of Contemporary Life*, 204.
9. Borgmann, *Technology and the Character of Contemporary Life*, 205.

dishes are not quite clean, the food is not up to par, the place settings are haphazard, and no one says a word. Cumulatively, focal practices maintaining a house improve the wellbeing of the home. Housework supports homework.

This close relationship between house and home should not be surprising given the status of humans as simultaneously embodied souls and ensouled bodies. Body and soul are inseparable. To neglect one is to neglect the other, and—conversely—tending to one is tending to the other. Tending to the embodied needs of humans is foundational to any spirituality. This is why properly caring for place is not unrelated to soul craft. Housework is also homework. The significance of housework, however, is easily overlooked because it is so commonplace that we are rarely mindful of it. Yet habitats form their inhabitants, and inhabitants must in turn maintain and attend to their habitats. The two are related: the quality of house and home are intertwined, and both are focal things requiring the requisite practices, the necessary work.

Anne Tyler's *A Spool of Blue Thread* is a story about a family, the Whit-shanks. They are not a notable collection of human beings. "There was nothing remarkable about the Whitshanks. None of them was famous. None of them could claim exceptional intelligence. And in looks, they were no more than average."[10] Yet neither are they bad people; they are just easily overlooked because they are "not remarkable in any way whatsoever."[11] Red is a contractor, easygoing and generally even-tempered. He is a steady husband and father. Red has been married to Abby for a long time. She was a social worker but is now retired, and she is eccentric. Her eccentricities amuse Red, and she was often a source of embarrassment to her four children when they were young. The children—Amanda, Jeannie, Denny, and Stem—are now adults with lives and families of their own.

Tyler's story is also about a house. Junior Whitshank, Red's father and also a contractor, built a house for a customer. He fell in love with that house and eventually persuaded the owner to sell it to him. Since 1936 it has been the Whitshank family home, and it is a fitting abode. "It was not a grand house, of the sort that you might expect a man like Junior to covet. It was more, let's say, a *family* house. A house you might see pictured on a thousand-piece jigsaw puzzle, plain-faced and comfortable, with the Stars and Stripes, perhaps, flying out front and a lemonade stand at the curb."[12] Yet Junior built the house with loving devotion, minding the features and details. The house was immaculate. When the house became Red's, he cared for it with the same

10. Tyler, *Spool of Blue Thread*, 71.
11. Tyler, *Spool of Blue Thread*, 74.
12. Tyler, *Spool of Blue Thread*, 54 (emphasis original).

devotion. There are no squeaky hinges, every window opens easily, and repairs are accomplished quickly and efficiently.

It is impossible to comprehend the story of the Whitshanks without taking into account the parallel story of their house. Over time, the house has taken on the "comfortably shabby air of a place whose inhabitants had long ago stopped seeing it."[13] Despite their blindness, it is in this place where the Whitshanks learn and conduct the focal practices of homemaking. Since they are an average family, they have their share of accomplishments to celebrate: graduations, new jobs, grandchildren. And since they are mediocre, they also have their sins to confront: bickering, jealousies, even a fistfight between the brothers.

It is in this place, this house, where the Whitshanks accuse and console, resent and support, blame and forgive one another. It all takes work: long, hard, and persistent work; ordinary, yet crucial and indispensable, work. Over time, one outcome is that the place and its inhabitants take on a symbiotic quality; house and home mirror and depend on each other. "'Houses need humans,' Red said. '*You* all should know that. Oh sure, humans cause wear and tear—scuffed floors and stopped-up toilets—but that's nothing compared to what happens when a house is left on its own. It's like the heart goes out of it. It sags, it slumps, it starts to lean toward the ground.'"[14] The same could be said when people are left on their own.

Lest the reader think that this is merely a sentimental tale about a house and its family, there is a bittersweet tone. As Red and Abby grow old, it becomes increasingly difficult for them to care for the house and each other. Abby is particularly troubling, since she will occasionally wander off for hours at a time. Denny and Stem and his family move in to help care for their parents and the house. Despite their best efforts, during one her wandering episodes, Abby bolts in front of a speeding car and is killed. Understandably, the family, especially Red, is devastated. Red misses Abby, most starkly at night. Even when he is asleep, he knows she is gone.

Friends and family console Red as best they can. He receives a lot of advice—some good, some bad, most banal. For Red it is the effort that counts, and he takes some comfort in that. He slowly heals, but never fully. His healing does not mean he reverts to the man he used to be. He has changed, not necessarily for better or for worse, but he is different. With Abby's death, how could it be otherwise? Yet the bond they shared is manifested in his new behavior. Red becomes more like Abby. His daughters notice: "Yes, last night I

13. Tyler, *Spool of Blue Thread*, 4.
14. Tyler, *Spool of Blue Thread*, 91 (emphasis original).

had this peculiar moment when I was saying goodbye to him. He asked, 'Don't you want to take some leftovers with you?' *Mom's* thing to ask! 'It'll save you from cooking supper,' he said, 'one of the nights this week.' Oh, Lord, isn't it strange how life sort of . . . closes up again over a death."[15] Perhaps in that closing up we find a sampling of the peace that passes understanding.

But Abby's death is not the only one the Whitshanks must deal with. Red is finding it difficult, nearly impossible, to run a business and take care of himself and the house. His children rise to the occasion in myriad ways. Stem quietly takes over running the business. The others take turns running errands, doing repairs, and keeping Red company. Everything is under control—sort of. So the family is shocked when Red announces that he will sell the house and move into an apartment. The children make no effort to dissuade him; they are relieved. It will be easier. It will be better for everyone. Red, at least, believes this to be true.

Selling a house and moving to an apartment—"downsizing," as they say—should be easy. It's not. Red quickly finds an apartment, an older one that was built to be sturdy. The apartment is small, and he will need only a few pieces of furniture and kitchenware. The rest is divided among his children, sold, given to the Salvation Army, or tossed. There are literally decades of stored items, some infused with memories or sentiment, but most lacking any meaning. The children are perplexed as they sort through the clutter. One of the daughters says, "It makes you wonder why we bother accumulating, when we know from earliest childhood how it's all going to end."[16] Perhaps. Yet if habitats reflect their inhabitants, then clearly the house has been a fitting place for the Whitshanks, for all of their lives became cluttered over time.

The housing market is slow, and Red is dismayed when he learns that the house may be vacant for a while. He complains to his real estate agent: "In four to six months it will go to seed. . . . You know it's not good for a house to sit empty. It will molder; it will get all forlorn; it will break my heart."[17] His children assure him that they will visit the house frequently and keep it from moldering. He is grateful, but not entirely convinced. Moving day arrives. Red is moving slowly. He doesn't want to leave, but he knows he must. Leaving this house will be another loss, another kind of death. Abby and this house are the two loves of Red's life. Now both will be gone.

Red's grief is understandable, even palpable. To lose that which one loves creates a cold void that cannot be filled, only eased over like scar tissue. It

15. Tyler, *Spool of Blue Thread*, 283 (emphasis original).
16. Tyler, *Spool of Blue Thread*, 283.
17. Tyler, *Spool of Blue Thread*, 277.

is right to offer Red our sympathy. But the sympathy offered should be accompanied by a warning. Although it is good to love, for we were created by love and for love, be careful about the ordering of your loves. A beloved spouse and place are worthy of devotion—but not ultimately. Our highest love is rightfully directed to God alone. It is right to grieve the loss of our lesser loves, but that does not mean that the origin and destiny of Love itself has been lost. To believe otherwise is to commit idolatry, or at least bad faith. We know that Red has two loves, but the story reveals nothing about whether there is a third, higher love. There are scant references to religion in this story about a family and a house. Stem's family are devoted churchgoers, a habit the rest of the Whitshanks find annoying. Some attention is paid to religious symbols, music, and allusions at Abby's funeral that the family members find bewildering (other than Stem's family). This should not imply that, had Red been an overtly godly man, his pain would necessarily have been removed or lessened. But it does suggest that an ultimate Love remains a horizon, a destination when lesser loves leave or fail us. In the end, Red is floundering because he has nowhere left to go.

Despite this warning, Red's two loves are good. Loving people and places—people who grow old and places that prove impermanent—are ways in and through which finite and mortal humans love their neighbors. They love particular people in particular places. And they form and are formed by these particularities over time. Yet all such loves come to an end, because they are not eternal. Nonetheless, it is right to mourn the loss of people and places, beloved spouses and houses. For what we give to and receive from others goes a long way in shaping who we are, and such giving and receiving is done by being in place with them. Consequently, to grieve is to also be grateful for what we have received. Perhaps Red will bring his gratitude for his two lost loves with him into his new apartment, knowing he could not have been the man he was and is without them.

I am now old and I still dislike doing chores. In my more sensible moments, however, I do not complain. I realize they are important despite the drudgery and boredom. My housework is part of my homework—and an essential part at that.

CHAPTER 13

Manners

Are good manners important? Admittedly this seems to be an old-fashioned question, one perhaps best consigned to a bygone era. What was once generally regarded as coarse language or rude behavior is now socially acceptable. Cursing, for instance, is employed routinely in public discourse, and disrespectful behavior is unexceptional. Discourtesy is tolerated as self-expression. Still, this *is* an important question, and I will spend this chapter explaining why my answer to it is a resounding yes.

But first, what are manners? They range from conventions and informal expectations for how members of a household or workplace treat (or should treat) each other to formal rules of etiquette governing conduct among superiors and inferiors, such as in the military. In both cases, the rules are not inflexible and can be waived or changed as necessity requires. For example, the harried coworker up against a deadline is forgiven for missing the customary morning coffee break, and a badly wounded soldier need not salute an officer.

Roger Scruton contends that manners assist us in navigating various social settings that would otherwise prove awkward. The chief value of manners is that they codify behavior within these settings. In this respect, manners are simultaneously self- and other-regarding. One learns table manners, for instance, to avoid splattering "food and drink on one's face and clothes," as well as to take care "not to offend or alienate one's neighbours."[1] Simply put, manners "steer a course through varied disasters, to achieve an 'optimal solution' to varied aims."[2] Manners vary a great deal among differing social

1. Scruton, *Aesthetics of Architecture*, 210.
2. Scruton, *Aesthetics of Architecture*, 210.

settings and cultures, but the need for manners is universal. Consequently, these codes must be learned and adapted to changing circumstances. A person needs to "understand and use certain conventions" for "creating settled expectations, against the background of which the true freedom of social intercourse may develop. But someone who remains punctiliously ruled by those conventions," demonstrating a lack of humor and grace, "to do what is appropriate in those circumstances where convention denies its helps, such a person is, socially speaking, a disaster."[3]

What are good manners? Succinctly, they are habitual patterns of speech and conduct that, as Scruton insists, help us avoid disasters stemming from innate proclivities toward regarding oneself at the expense of others. Manners are not natural and must be learned. Contrary to popular notions, mastering manners is not an enterprise of self-improvement but a community practice. Manners guide behavior within varying contexts that simultaneously enable civil relations and preserve the privacy and freedom of individuals within these interactions. Good manners respect both the privacy and the mutual dependence of the parties involved in exchanging or communicating.

To be sure, manners can be abused. For instance, manners may be used to keep oppressed people "in their place"—as when those in power insist that certain types of people, because of their race, gender, or status, should know to refrain from speaking until they are spoken to. This kind of appeal to manners effectively perpetuates unjust discrimination. Or manners may be used to assert or maintain control by humiliating those who violate or do not know certain rules of etiquette. Or, worse, manners may be used as a menacing barrier to keep the "wrong" people out of one's social network.

Some may contend that the abuses of etiquette are so prevalent and egregious that the very notion of etiquette itself should be jettisoned. Manners, they might say, inevitably exclude because strangers or outsiders do not know the rules and customs and will be unfairly scorned because of their gaffes. Consequently, etiquette is inherently rude and should be condemned and ignored.[4] But this would be a mistake. The problem is *not* manners per se but the ways in which they are learned and subsequently used and abused. Returning to Scruton, the conventions and rules governing manners are flexible, and a well-mannered person will have an aptitude for applying this flexibility in response to particular persons and circumstances. Without this aptitude, no set of so-called good manners will avoid social disasters. Admittedly, participating in any group requires that one learn its customs and

3. Scruton, *Aesthetics of Architecture*, 211.
4. See Martin, *Miss Manners' Guide*, 31.

rules. Nonetheless, the first rule of etiquette is to not embarrass those who do not know the rules.[5]

Any group establishes formal or informal codes regulating speech and conduct. These codes will prove to be bad or good over time. Bad ones preclude the possibility of human flourishing because they help habituate behaviors that are uncivil and at times immoral. Good manners are not guaranteed to cultivate civil and moral people, but they at least offer the possibility of helping to build a foundation that promotes human flourishing. What makes good manners good? The question requires the following two-part answer.

Gracefully Interacting

Mastering good manners requires many personal and social attributes that, through practice, are habituated over time. There are two crucial ones: attentiveness and respect. To be attentive is to acknowledge the other as other and not as a projection of oneself. We can know the good of the other only by being attentive to her as a fellow human being. Manners help focus such attentiveness. Attentiveness demonstrates respect for the other as someone eliciting behavior that is engaging and graceful rather than manipulative or degrading. To treat a person one has encountered in a well-mannered way is to take a small step toward loving this neighbor. The polite person is striving to be unselfed and forbearing. This does not mean that the polite person ignores or indulges the poor or immoral behavior of the other. To the contrary, the habituation of good manners contributes to a strength of character that is able to resist and challenge bad, even evil, sentiments and actions. But it is able to do so properly. The well-mannered person remembers that, regardless of how objectionable the beliefs and actions of ill-mannered people might be, these people are not objects to be despised but human creatures created in the image and likeness of God. As such, they must be treated with the requisite respect.

In contrast, ill-mannered people are inattentive to their neighbors. This inattention may stem from ignorance. It may not occur to someone that other people should be treated with the courtesy and respect that is due a neighbor also bearing the *imago Dei*. To such a person, the other is simply there making no (or at best cursory) requests or demands for our attention. Hence other people are easily ignored.

Inattention may also stem from willful exclusion. Neighbors who may potentially help further one's interests are treated with feigned respect, often

5. See Martin, *Miss Manners' Guide*, 32.

expressed through the perilous rhetoric of flattery.[6] Meanwhile, neighbors lacking a fitting social or moral status are apt to be curtly dismissed as not worthy of time and attention. In either case, the resulting behavior is rude because it is profoundly self-absorbed or self-righteous: My interest or my cause is all that matters, and anyone getting in the way should be pushed aside. Or my beliefs and convictions are morally superior, and anyone who does not share them should be publicly shamed or even canceled. Such rudeness is not merely irritating but perilous, for it effectively reduces neighbors to either pawns to be used or fools unworthy of respect. More troublingly, such rudeness decays neighbor love, because the self is so inflated by it that it becomes the only object capable of capturing one's attention and affection.

Good manners are also useful. They not only help us avoid social disasters but also enable exchange and communication, two kinds of interactions that are foundational to human flourishing. How etiquette promotes human flourishing is best illustrated by looking at a series of commonplace relationships.

Before proceeding, however, a brief digression: In visiting these relationships and their respective codes of etiquette, I draw on the wisdom of Judith Martin, also known as Miss Manners. Martin is a journalist who writes a column on etiquette.[7] In response to letters sent by readers, she offers advice on what constitutes courteous behavior in almost any conceivable social setting. Her prose is direct, succinct, at times playful, usually humorous, and always polite. Yet why would I turn to her if I am purportedly writing a serious book about ethics? Her critics dismiss her as an elitist snob, and her expertise is uncredentialed (as far as I know there is no degree or certification in etiquette studies). Her authoritative discourse on manners is entirely self-asserted. Yet underlying her jocular rhetoric is a realist and hard-nosed analysis of the crucial, daily social interactions underpinning civil society. She is a wise and practical social critic. Two book endorsements capture her abilities rather well, affirming Martin as a "philosopher cleverly and charmingly disguised as an etiquette columnist" who has "helped transform etiquette from the realm of society matrons to a tool for everyday life." I make no apology for turning to Martin as a source of wisdom on the importance of manners. We may now move on to the illustrative relationships referenced above.

Youth and elders. "We are all born charming, frank and spontaneous and must be civilized before we are fit to participate in society."[8] Any Christian who believes in the fall and human depravity should not be shocked by this

---

6. On the dangers of flattery, see John of Salisbury, *Policraticus*, book 3, esp. chap. 4: "The Flatterer, the Toady, and the Cajoler, Than Whom None Is More Pernicious."

7. She is also the author of many books.

8. Martin, *Miss Manners' Guide*, 75.

statement. Moreover, we are born into a fallen world, a harsh place in which to be a child, especially in grades K–8: the most "hostile and humiliating" social environments imaginable.[9] Children must learn how to be good and what it means to be good, and they learn from their elders: school teachers, coaches, adults in general, and—most importantly—their parents. Properly rearing and discipling children, however, does not include insulting and humiliating them. There is no justification for parents being rude to their children, particularly since instilling good manners is one of the principal goals of providing parental care.

But where do parents teach manners to their children? They do so in many places, both public and private, but the family dinner is the premier classroom for teaching and learning manners. "There are two social purposes to family dinner: the regular exchange of news and ideas, and the opportunity to teach small children not to eat like pigs. These are by no means mutually exclusive."[10] In this classroom children should be encouraged to listen and converse, to neither dominate nor remain aloof from conversation. Members of a family come to know each other, at least partly, through listening and talking. This table fellowship requires rules or customs ensuring that everyone has an opportunity to be heard and a duty to listen to what others are saying. Moreover, the fellowship of the table needs to be focused rather than diffuse. Other than the food, nothing should distract attention away from those at table.[11] To what extent a collection of individuals sitting in the same room munching food while staring at screens can be called a family dinner is highly suspect.

The need for manners is especially pertinent when there are dinner guests. Particular care should be taken to engage them in table fellowship that might seem stilted in comparison to other family meals, for there may be little or no shared experiences to draw upon, making attempts at conversation awkward. Nonetheless, charity demands that we listen attentively to and converse graciously with this neighbor we are commanded to love despite the lack of familiarity. Additionally, the very awkwardness of entertaining a dinner guest reminds us that the etiquette governing the relationship with those with whom we are familiar and those with whom we are not is not identical.

Friends and strangers. These are two different categories of people. We know or are coming to know a great deal about friends, their hopes and fears, their strengths and weaknesses—in short, who they are, warts and all.

9. Martin, *Miss Manners' Guide*, 80.
10. Martin, *Miss Manners' Guide*, 174.
11. This is one reason why Clement of Alexandria argues that meals should consist of simple rather than sumptuous food. Clement of Alexandria, *Tutor* 2.1. In chap. 15 of the present book, I take up the question of whether fine dining is more akin to gluttony or hospitality.

And we are comfortable with that knowledge. We know very little, or even nothing, about strangers. Our interactions with strangers are usually brief and utilitarian in nature. Strangers often provide services that require of us little knowledge of who they are as persons. And we are comfortable with that lack of knowledge.

Consequently, there are different codes of etiquette governing the relationship among friends and the relationship among strangers. For instance, one may tell a friend a secret that one would never entrust to a stranger.[12] However, the line separating how friends and strangers, respectively, should comport themselves is blurring. We live in cultures where instant and presumed familiarity is becoming the norm. First names (even nicknames), casual greetings, and chatter of questionable taste are often tossed about in an initial encounter with a stranger. Such presumed familiarity also diminishes friendship. The hard-earned trust and reciprocity that friends create over time, while retaining a necessary restraint, becomes a license to do and say anything one wants in the company of a friend, because the mystery of alterity is disregarded. The friend is not treated as an other.

I assume that relaxing the standards of etiquette is motivated by good intentions. Perhaps it is assumed that lack of formality and easy familiarity create more welcoming social environments. It is so much friendlier to greet someone barely known with "hi Ann" than with "good morning, Ms. Smith." Everyone is treated as a potential friend, requiring little if any formality. A good intention, however, does not always result in a good outcome. Presuming an instant and easy familiarity is one such intention that needs to be resisted. Why? There are many reasons, but two instances will suffice to illustrate.

First, an easy familiarity erodes the alterity and authority of strangers. To treat a stranger as if a deeper relationship can be fictitiously presumed is to exhibit disrespect for the other as other, because no attempt has been made to first learn the needs and good of the other. This is the opposite of unselfing, for the other is simply pulled into the orbit of oneself. To come to know the other as other requires social distance, and that distance may need to be kept wide to honor and preserve alterity. The well-mannered person respects the need for this distance through formality of both speech and conduct. The authority of strangers is also diminished by a casual disregard for the status of others. In light of the services that strangers provide and receive, formality is needed to sustain the efficacy of the service in question.

---

12. An exception might be when the stranger is providing a service, for instance as a doctor, psychologist, lawyer, or priest, or when one is compelled to reveal unprotected secrets, as when giving testimony under oath.

Providers and recipients of a service require mutual respect as determined by their respective roles.

Second, an easygoing familiarity cheapens friendship. Familiarity of the other is an outcome and not the starting point of a friendship. Being at ease in the company of a friend is a consequence of unselfing—of coming to know the needs and good of the other through deliberate attention over a period of time. Friendship is based on hard work and not casual contact. The misplaced friendliness practiced by many late moderns treats strangers as honorary friends, a lazy and disingenuous act reinforced by social media in which contact is transient, often trivial, and at times anonymous. It is difficult to believe that such "friends" would be willing to sacrifice their lives out of love for the other (see John 15:13). The informality of friendship reflects a depth of mutual trust and love that is not shared by strangers, who therefore require the greater formality of etiquette to help steer them clear of social disasters.

Workplace relationships. Briefly visiting two workplace relationships may serve to further illustrate the necessity of maintaining a distinction between friends and strangers, a distinction preserved, in part, by appropriate manners. Without this distinction, commerce and work would be inefficient and unpleasant. The relationship between sellers and shoppers is not one of familiarity; they are not friends.[13] Rather, it is a utilitarian relationship in which the supply of goods and services is matched with the demand of consumers—and matched, hopefully, in easy and efficient ways. Consequently, chatting up the customer, treating her as a pseudo friend, is a waste of time and potentially deceitful. Indifference and rudeness by either party also does little to help match buyer with seller.

The relationship between employers and employees is also not one of friendship or familiarity but one in which a fitting distance should be maintained. This distance is reflected in workplace etiquette that simultaneously protects the limited authority of employers and the autonomy of employees. These formal and informal rules of conduct are linked with respective duties. Employers have a duty to treat employees fairly, to pay them, and to maintain working conditions that are safe and nonhostile. Employees in turn have a duty to perform their work to the best of their ability, to be honest, and to treat their supervisors and fellow workers respectfully. When employers fail to exercise their authority, perhaps by treating their employees too casually, or when employees fail to honor this authority, perhaps by treating their

---

13. Granted, friendships between sellers and shoppers may develop over time, especially in small-business settings. Although such friendships may prove rewarding, they are not necessary for efficient and honest exchanges between buyers and sellers.

employers with contempt, the workplace becomes untenable or at least un-
bearable. The codes of etiquette derived from the respective duties of employers and employees help preserve this rightful exercise of authority, making the
workplace both productive and acceptable. And these manners have little to
do with friendship or familiarity. Consequently, the workplace teaches a valuable lesson: namely, that bosses and workers can, in obedience to the second
great commandment, love each other without necessarily liking each other.

Some might object that manners may make daily life a bit more enjoyable
on the surface—at least for those who have the luxury of time or social status to worry about such trifling matters—but they seem to have little impact
beyond that. What, if anything, does etiquette have to do with addressing the
big issues of the day, such as politics, poverty, injustice, and the like? Quite
a bit, I would argue.

Social Ordering

If manners were confined strictly to the interpersonal, they would nonetheless prove beneficial. Exchanging courtesies with one another in daily hap-
penstances is superior to treating one another rudely or worse. But manners
are not restricted to the interpersonal; they provide a foundation for broader
civil and political relations. This foundation tends to be either good and solid
or bad and unstable. Granted, etiquette can be misused to maintain unjust
relations, but that does not mean that codes of conduct should therefore be
discarded—in much the same way that a few bad cops do not justify disman-
tling an entire police force.[14] Without a basic framework of manners, civil and
political relations degenerate into assertions of unprincipled power. "Activities
as basic to the society as the classroom, the meeting and the athletic contest
cannot proceed unless everybody knows and agrees to obey the same specific etiquette rules that provide orderliness and fairness."[15] For Josiah Royce,
courtesy in particular displays a "loyal attitude towards all the causes that
are represented by . . . peaceful and reasonable dealings" with one another.
In short, courtesy is a "duty owed not so much to the individual to whom
you are courteous, as to humanity at large."[16]

Respect is a crucial rule. Respecting fellow citizens, as well as resident
and visiting aliens, is the essential first step toward orderly and fair relations.
Orderly and fair relations require cooperative action, and we cooperate with

14. Though patterns of misconduct should be investigated and their causes addressed in
order to maintain effective police forces and healthy communities.
15. Martin, *Miss Manners*, 4.
16. Royce, *Philosophy of Loyalty*, 155.

those we respect and who respect us in return. What inspires and perpetuates mutual respect? A recognition that each person has an innate dignity by virtue of being a human creature. In theological terms, every person bears the image of God and therefore has a divinely given dignity. Recognizing dignity is usually subtle and discreet, embedded in customs and conventions governing behavior. Governing, it should be added, more through habit than command. Good manners are ingrained in one's character. We are (or should) be polite to one another, for instance, not as a calculated gesture but because of the kind of people we are: people who embody common and binding rules of conduct. This is why etiquette, contrary to common misperceptions, is anti-elitist, because everyone is (or should be) subject to the same set of rules, and such equality is a crucial feature of civil comportment. A common etiquette "suggests that people making up their own rules and deciding which courtesies they want to observe, and which they don't, is exactly the problem that has been identified as incivility and lack of consideration."[17]

Manners, however, are not encased in customs and conventions as unalterable relics. Etiquette can, must, and does change over time. New insights regarding what constitutes human dignity lead to corresponding adjustments in how we treat one another. In this respect, paying attention to the necessity of evolving etiquette helps deflate prejudices. Since everyone is (or should be) aspiring to treat each other in accordance with a shared, innate dignity, prejudice—perhaps previously unrecognized or unjustly maintained—is exposed as a detriment. Consequently, customs and conventions must (or should) change accordingly. For example, previous codes that treated people of different races in discriminatory ways are no longer tolerated (or *should* no longer be tolerated). Admittedly, changing etiquette is a difficult and uncertain task. There is no guarantee that new insights into human nature are true or accurate; one risks promoting changes that prove to be retrograde rather than progressive. Moreover, as cultures recognize a greater range of pluriformity, what constitutes good manners will need to reflect a greater inclusivity without sacrificing commonality.

To be clear, I am *not* arguing that if everyone is polite and well-mannered all social and political problems will be solved and civil society will thrive. The problems and available solutions at hand are far too complex. But without a foundation of habitual mutual respect to build upon, the goals of achieving a just social and political order and a flourishing civil society will remain elusive—perhaps unattainable. Forming well-mannered people is not exciting, but the alternative is grim.

17. Martin, *Miss Manners*, 4.

As the emphasis on common etiquette declines or is attacked as an emblem of privilege, respect is replaced with indifference or, worse, contempt. Increasingly, people want to work, associate, and live in close proximity only with those who share their most cherished convictions. But this means we spend as much time avoiding the "wrong" people as interacting with the "right" ones. Moreover, the need to treat others politely and civilly tends to constrict us to only interacting with fellow members of our own group, and we effectively dismiss outsiders as individuals unworthy of respectful and polite treatment. Consequently, the lack of manners inflates prejudices. Any disagreeable statement or act of an outsider confirms our worst suspicions. Unselfing is effectively made superfluous, for we need not be attentive to the other since we have no intention of understanding their needs—and if indeed they possess a so-called good, it is not worth acknowledging. Rather than treating these strangers with a guarded trust and ostensible goodwill, our default positions are mistrust and ill will. We have exchanged a view of the other as one possessing inherent dignity for a view of the other as one constituting a means of either enhancing our own wellbeing or threatening it. When mutual respect and civility are jettisoned, the biblical command to love God and neighbor is corrupted into a practice of loving oneself and a few select neighbors.

A decline in manners is not a trivial matter of encountering more episodes of rude behavior that annoy the tender sensibilities of genteel people. Rather, ill-mannered people erode civility more broadly, and the cumulative effects of such erosion foster social and political consequences that diminish human flourishing. The decline, even ridicule, of etiquette is a symptom of a larger problem, indicating that power is coming to dictate behavior. A self-serving nihilism is privileged over an unselfed love of neighbor. Whenever nihilists are ascendant, it is always the poor and weak who suffer most. The primacy of self-enhancement is achieved at the expense of others, justifying the selective diminishment of and prejudice against convenient targets, targets often arbitrarily determined by race, gender, class, or religion. We look for what separates rather than what unites, and we are adept at finding what we search for. Ideological fiat masquerading as moral indignation becomes the dominant form of discourse in a divided society whose members do not want to understand each other. At least etiquette recognizes, albeit in a modest way, the equality and inherent dignity of every person, preserving a modicum of duty to try to identify the needs and good of the other.

Again, to be clear, I am *not* arguing that if every person were well-mannered all would be well. Yet the presence or absence of etiquette, its use and abuse, can offer some important clues about broader social and political issues and the state of civil society in dealing with them. To illustrate, I turn to the novel *The Remains of the Day* by Kazuo Ishiguro.

Ishiguro's story is about Mr. Stevens, an English butler. He performs his duties at Darlington Hall, the stately residence of his previous employer, Lord Darlington, throughout World War II and the turbulent decades preceding and following. The estate is now owned by Mr. Farraday, an American. Under Lord Darlington, Stevens supervised a large domestic staff to maintain the household, prepare lavish banquets, and serve the needs of frequent house-guests. Not much of a staff is now required, since many of the rooms in the large mansion are closed and Mr. Farraday does not plan to host many din-ners or guests. In many respects, the splendor of Darlington Hall is consigned to a bygone era. The story weaves back and forth between past and present, focusing on Stevens's difficulty in dealing with changes both professional and personal. For example, Stevens was comfortable with the highly formal rela-tionship he shared with Lord Darlington but is perplexed by the informality of Mr. Farraday, who enjoys banter—a skill that Stevens does not possess.

One thread remains constant throughout the story, however: answering the question, "What is a 'great' butler?"[18] Many popular butlers are flamboyant, performing their duties with self-aggrandizing flare. Their fame and careers are almost always short-lived. They fall victim to the vices of vanity and gos-sip, and their skills subsequently deteriorate because there is no substantial character to sustain them. To command the limelight for a while is not syn-onymous with being an excellent butler. In a word, *dignity* is what makes a butler great. Dignity is admittedly hard to define. It is more than competence, and it is not a trait someone is born with. Rather, it is "something one can strive for throughout one's career," procuring it "over many years of self-training and careful absorbing of experience."[19] This training and experience becomes the essential core of a butler's identity. "The great butlers are great by virtue of their professional role and inhabit it to the utmost; they will not be shaken out by external events, however surprising, alarming or vexing."[20] In short, a great butler is never off duty because duty is synonymous with who the butler is.

More often than not, a great butler works for an aristocratic household where skills and attention to detail are displayed to fullest effect. It is no dif-ferent with Stevens. He oversees staff to ensure that Darlington Hall is clean and in good repair, that the grounds are kept attractive, that guest rooms and

---

18. Ishiguro, *Remains of the Day*, 29.
19. Ishiguro, *Remains of the Day*, 33.
20. Ishiguro, *Remains of the Day*, 42–43.

kitchens are well supplied. The menus, wine lists, and entertainment at the frequent banquets hosted by Lord Darlington are planned in meticulous detail; the silverware and goblets are set at exactly the proper angle and precise spacing. The needs of guests, however important or trivial, are met promptly and efficiently; even the newspapers are ironed to make the pages smooth before they are delivered to the guest rooms. And all the while Stevens, as well as his staff, is polite and unflappable—even when guests are rude or thoughtless. Stevens is never off duty; he never reacts adversely to surprising, alarming, or vexing circumstances. He is a great butler.

Stevens's greatness is on full display one evening at an important banquet. Stevens is informed that his father, a member of staff who was himself a butler but is no longer at the top of his game because of his age, has become gravely ill. Stevens slips away for a few moments to visit his father. After the two exchange courteous greetings and sentiments, Stevens, at the urging of his father, insists that he must return to the banquet. Later that evening, when Stevens is informed that his father has died, his dignity prevents him from leaving the banquet where his professional duties are required. He is, after all, a great butler.

It is difficult to portray in the preceding paragraphs the richly textured behavior of Stevens, his staff, and Lord Darlington. All of them are courteous, well-mannered, exuding a habituated dignity that seemingly cannot be shaken. Without such apparent good manners, Darlington Hall could not be run in an efficient and hospitable manner. But the etiquette accompanying the dignity does not disclose fully the lives of the people performing their duties. Greatness is not as apparent as first meets the eye. A house guest, for instance, charmingly humiliates Stevens one evening, using etiquette to exclude the poorly educated butler from the select company of informed experts. Some strangers in a pub assume that the gracious Stevens is a gentleman, an error he does not correct. Customary manners often prevent staff members from being honest with one another.

More troubling, however, is how Lord Darlington uses the conventions of his aristocratic status to hide his political intrigues. The banquets recounted in the story occur before the outbreak of World War II. Most of the guests are Nazi sympathizers who want the harsh terms of the Treaty of Versailles revoked. Lord Darlington himself is not fond of Hitler and his thugs, but he believes that Germany is being unjustly punished. Lord Darlington is a good and decent man, motivated by a sense of fairness. The crude Nazis will not touch his dignity (or so he tells himself). Slowly, Lord Darlington is changed, despite appearing to remain a member of polite society. For example, Lord Darlington decides that Jews can no longer be employed as domestic staff because they make his guests uncomfortable. Stevens quietly acquiesces because his "Lordship has made his decision," and there is nothing to debate.[21] The propriety of authority trumps any moral judgment of right and wrong. The Nazis and their English toadies mock the well-mannered Lord Darlington, regarding him a useful fool, and after the war he is a disgraced and broken man. Stevens, in his turn, is left floundering, one moment insisting he was proud to serve such an honorable, albeit misguided, man, while at other times denying he was ever associated with Darlington Hall.

Yet one of the more disturbing lessons of this story is how an uncritical sense of dignity, and the code of etiquette accompanying it, may be used to preserve a comfortable but ultimately deadly fantasy. Lord Darlington and his polite band of aristocratic companions are incapable of any realism, of dealing with the thing as it is. This failing is exposed with great clarity when, at the closing banquet of a two-day conference on assisting Germany, various toasts are being offered. Mr. Lewis, a cheerful and well-connected American, stands. After a few introductory comments, he cuts to the chase. "You gentlemen here, forgive me, but you are just a bunch of naïve dreamers. And if you didn't insist on meddling in large affairs that affect the globe, you would actually be charming. Let's take our good host here. What is he? He is a gentleman. No one here, I trust, would care to disagree. A classic English gentleman. Decent, honest, well-meaning. But his lordship is *an amateur*."[22] Lewis goes on to insist that the world can no longer afford to be run by well-meaning but incompetent gentlemen dabbling in international affairs. Skilled professionals are needed to avoid disaster, and such professionals may not be gentlemen or even gentlemanly. Lewis raises his glass: "A toast, gentlemen. Let me make a toast. To professionalism."[23]

Lord Darlington ever so politely insults Lewis by suggesting that the only reason he is taking the time to reply is to spare Lewis the feeling of being ignored as "some soap-box eccentric." He goes on to insist that what Lewis decries as amateurism is what Lord Darlington calls honor. An honorable man is repulsed by professionalism, for it "appears to mean getting one's way by cheating and manipulation. It appears to mean serving the dictates of greed and advantage rather than those of goodness and the desire to see justice prevail in the world. If that is the 'professionalism' you refer to, sir, I don't care much for it and have no wish to acquire it."[24] Yet in stubbornly refusing any accommodation of an impertinent code of honor, bumbling

21. Ishiguro, *Remains of the Day*, 148.
22. Ishiguro, *Remains of the Day*, 102 (emphasis original).
23. Ishiguro, *Remains of the Day*, 102.
24. Ishiguro, *Remains of the Day*, 103.

gentlemen allowed the world to stumble into global war, and its aftermath of murderous totalitarian regimes.

The Remains of the Day is, in part, a cautionary tale about the limits and deceptions of dignity and honor in respect to personal character and sound judgment. When the attendant duties and etiquettes are stripped away from one's core being and reduced to performative practice, the resulting morality is a superficial justification for preserving a cherished but untruthful fiction that twists the real world into an illusion to be avoided. Manners become effectively an instrument of deceit and a tool for distracting attention from the person by fixating on the performance. But a mastery of skills and etiquette is not synonymous with a quality of character, a quality of soul. As Stevens demonstrates, a great butler is not necessarily a great person; Lord Darlington's honor is not necessarily synonymous with moral excellence. Appearance is not necessarily related to essence. We can learn how to be mannerly as if it were a manipulative technique rather than a reflection of one's being.

However, this does *not* mean that manners are unimportant. To the contrary, they provide an important foundation for habituating personal and civil virtues. Etiquette can certainly be, and frequently is, abused and misused. Yet in the absence of good manners, manners that are formative rather than performative, it is difficult to imagine how the habituation of personal and civil virtues can find any fertile soil in which to take root. Unfortunately, the habituation of vice does not require roots, only inattention. At the very least, the cultivation of etiquette supports personal, civil, and political relationships that exhibit (or should exhibit) genuine respect for one another as fellow human beings, each bearing the *imago Dei*. When such cultivation is neglected, we edge away from civilization and toward Hobbes's fateful state of nature. Manners are important, and we ignore learning, teaching, and embodying them at our peril.

CHAPTER 14

Appearance

As embodied creatures, humans spend most of their time on earth seeing and being seen.[1] We interact by presenting ourselves to others and perceiving their presentations to us in return. Our social natures are mediated through constructs. We take care how we are known by others, and their knowledge of us is largely based on how we appear. Appearance, then, is both necessary and universal, but it is not straightforward. What we see is often not what we get. Appearance both reveals and conceals. A smile may disclose a congenial personality while hiding a suffering soul. Appearance is simultaneously objective and subjective. The person I meet is real, but her presentation of herself and my reaction to what is presented are both interpretive. I encounter people who, consciously or not, construct and project their appearance, and I do the same. Although it is admittedly a stretch to characterize late moderns as living Facebook pages, the characterization is nonetheless disturbingly prescient.

It might be tempting to condemn or dismiss concern for physical appearance as a banal pastime, as little more than a distraction in trying to live a good life. Yet as Lord Henry, from Oscar Wilde's *The Picture of Dorian Gray*, insists, "To me, Beauty is the wonder of wonders. It is only shallow people

---

1. Concentrating on appearance admittedly privileges the sense of sight. I assume, however, that self-presentation occurs through a wider range of senses, including hearing, smell, and touch. My concentration on sight reflects dominant emphases in philosophy and theology as well as my own lack of ability and imagination to construct an account of appearance based predominantly on other modes of sensual presentation and perception. Such an account on my part would, I believe, prove shallow.

who do not judge by appearances. The true mystery of the world is the visible, not the invisible."[2] He may be on to something.

To a large extent, we know others by their appearance, how they present themselves to us. Likewise, we are known by others by how we appear to them, by how we present ourselves. It cannot be otherwise. Barbara Carnevali insists, "What we know about others and what others know about us are based essentially on appearances. None of us has direct access to the inner states of others—to their thoughts, desires, and emotions. None of us can present ourselves directly to others without resorting to a sensible mediation, to something that manifests itself to the senses and that can be sensibly expressed and perceived."[3] We must take people as they appear to be, for that is generally all that is available to us. Unlike God, we cannot see clearly the soul of another; we frequently cannot even delve deeply into our own souls.

Social bonds are created through public appearances. People mediate themselves to social worlds through material objects and ornaments. Carnevali uses the metaphor of a mask to describe this mediation.[4] A mask reveals how, ostensibly, we wish to be seen and assessed by others. A mask also hides features we, ostensibly, do not want to reveal, providing a modicum of self-protection. In this respect, masking coheres with the rules of etiquette examined in the previous chapter.[5] Etiquette simultaneously creates a civil space in which strangers may safely interact and preserves boundaries of privacy that should not be violated without good cause. Yet one appearance engaging with another appearance is an interpretive and subjective enterprise, rife with both understanding and misunderstanding. To return to the metaphor of the mask, what may appear welcoming to some may prove menacing to others, and neither response may reflect the intentions of the one behind the mask. Moreover, a person may, of necessity, require a variety of masks dictated by differing social contexts, so it is unclear whether the identity of the person behind the mask is many or one—whether there are multiple appearances corresponding to various identities or a singular identity with pluriform presentations. Either way, social interactions are never direct but always mediated through presentations and appearances.

Clothing is a primary instrument of such mediation. Our lives unfold over time within clothing.[6] Although we are born naked, most of our subsequent days are spent clothed. This is why some of our most delightful and shameful

2. Wilde, *Picture of Dorian Gray*, loc. 381, Kindle.
3. Carnevali, *Social Appearances*, 3.
4. See Carnevali, *Social Appearances*, 20.
5. See Carnevali, *Social Appearances*, 23.
6. I assume there are exceptions to this general rule, such as nudists and naked sleepers.

memories stand out in their defiance of this norm. Perhaps bathing provides a welcomed respite from the burden of clothing, a subliminal reminder or hint of baptism relieving us of our sins. But I digress. How we dress says a lot about how we wish to be seen (or not seen) and assessed by others. Some clothes demand to be seen, while others deflect attention. Clothing is not merely material we wrap around ourselves. Clothes are expressive and constitutive of who we are. As Shahidha Bari contends, clothes are "about desire and denial, the fever and fret with which we love and are loved."[7] Our presentations to one another are, especially to strangers, most often as clothed beings.

This does not mean, however, that our clothing is superficial, extraneous to the being of the wearer. On the contrary, to "engage thoughtfully with clothes is to acknowledge the nature of objects and our utter entanglements with them."[8] Even our interior lives, our souls, may be said to be clothed. Our appearing in the world, then, is not some explicit or implicit tactic designed to gain control over or protect ourselves from others. Rather, our appearing may actually be related to our being, and it is perhaps not unrelated to how the resurrected Jesus appeared to his disciples. Consequently, to "reflect on the way in which we are seen is also to pose questions about authenticity. How far are we able to present our inward selves with outward accuracy? Are there ever any moments that we make ourselves 'real' or 'true' to others?"[9]

Seeing ourselves is also a burden. Our clothes can be cruel, particularly as we grow older, accentuating physical decline. Clothing reminds us of how our bodies change in ways that we cannot control. But we also see the same vulnerability in other people.

The reader may object that I am assigning too much importance to clothing and metaphorical masks, or to appearance more broadly, because there is an internal human essence that renders external appearance ultimately unimportant. This objection assumes, however, that because appearance is ephemeral it is therefore unreal. But to the contrary, it is only in a constructed world that a person encounters other people; appearance is the reality of one's being, or at least the only ontological reality of one another that we can encounter. As Hannah Arendt contends, our lives are filled with various appearances that engage the senses. Consequently, being and appearance are interwoven and related. "In this world which we enter, appearing from a nowhere, and from which we disappear into a nowhere, *Being and Appearing coincide*."[10] Appearance presupposes a spectator and that which is observed. Nothing

7. Bari, *Dressed*, 5.
8. Bari, *Dressed*, 8.
9. Bari, *Dressed*, 13.
10. Arendt, *Life of the Mind*, 1:19 (emphasis original).

has its being in the singular. "Plurality is the law of the earth."[11] She goes on to elaborate: "Nothing perhaps is more surprising in this world of ours than the almost infinite diversity of its appearances, the sheer entertainment of its views, sounds, and smells, something that is hardly ever mentioned by the thinkers and philosophers."[12]

Every subject, then, is also an object, mutually encountered through the senses. This is worldly existence, and it is shared by all living creatures, who present themselves for a time—but only for a time. "To be alive means to live in a world that preceded one's own arrival and will survive one's own departure."[13] Finitude—that is, mortality—determines a creaturely experience of time, a passing appearance bracketed by the origin and end of eternity. Being alive literally drives one to construct his or her appearance in the world. This is why, in part, appearing requires both a constructed world and spectators, for one also plays with spectators in addition to being seen by them. In developing over time, a living being is an epiphany both to others and to itself. Although we come into the world from nowhere, we are adept at "[taking] part in the play of the world," again for a period of time.[14]

Any *sharp* division between one's inward life and outward life is misleading. Per Arendt, the soul is the "inside" of one's life.[15] Unlike the mind, the soul is not in dialogue with itself. It is conveyed through unconscious gestures. In contrast, the world of appearances is known only through thinking and reflection. We think about how best to present our emotions in the world. Raw anger, for instance, cannot be presented. The soul, then, encroaches on the body. The sensations of the soul are the feelings provided from the senses of bodily organs. Unlike the mind, the soul is thoroughly "body-bound."[16] Through appearances we present ourselves in ways that we want to be perceived. We choose what to reveal and what to hide. How we choose to appear affects the soul but never reveals it. If the soul is the essence of who one is, then our appearances in the world are always incomplete. We are never known completely by anyone but God. Because we self-present, we may deceive others or be misunderstood. We appear as we wish we were but not as we are.

Our social interactions, even our self-reflection, are necessarily ambiguous, fraught with uncertainty. To invoke Saint Paul's imagery, we appear in a world armed as poor reflections that are only partially known (see 1 Cor.

11. Arendt, *Life of the Mind*, 1:19.
12. Arendt, *Life of the Mind*, 1:20.
13. Arendt, *Life of the Mind*, 1:20.
14. Arendt, *Life of the Mind*, 1:22.
15. See Arendt, *Life of the Mind*, 1:30–31.
16. See Arendt, *Life of the Mind*, 1:32–33.

13:12). So where does this leave us? On the one hand, humans live out their lives with a fundamental insecurity when left to their own devices. Appearances guide but also mislead, and it is difficult to discern the difference except retrospectively. On the other hand, the souls of humans are protected from unwarranted scrutiny and the abuse of others. Appearances preserve the rightful opaqueness of the soul, except to its creator, to whom alone it is transparent. Unsurprisingly, our appearance as finite creatures in the world is both perilous and promising, conditions that require further investigation.

The Peril of Appearance

Appearance is perilous because it is ambiguous. We do not know with unambiguous certainty what we are dealing with when others appear in our world. We could be misled, threatened, taken advantage of, even injured. Or we may misread the other and react with unwarranted mistrust or prejudice. A person appearing to be a friend proves untrustworthy; a feared stranger turns out to be a Good Samaritan. How we present ourselves to others may prove delusional. We come to believe that the carefully constructed image we use to project our appearance in the world, designed to present ourselves in the most favorable light, is who we really are. But the deluded belief serves to prevent any truthful and sustained introspection. The person always helping others uses the appearance to ignore simmering resentment and jealousy; the apparently selfless person is actually, though perhaps unwittingly, self-absorbed.

The educated elites of the Greco-Roman world were aware of this peril and tried to devise moral safeguards for both the inward and outward dimensions of one's life. Philosophical introspection must be a brutally honest process, stripping away all pretense in order to properly care for the soul. The external world must also be seen as largely a realm of insubstantial shadows, a dark and foreboding world in which the enlightened must act accordingly. This is why classical education stressed knowing the true, the good, and the beautiful as an antidote to the pervasive falsity, evil, and ugliness of appearance.[17]

The suspicion of appearance, however, was not confined to abstract philosophical inquiry. Apparel, for instance, received significant attention since it was an obvious medium of self-presentation. How one dressed should reflect the quality of one's soul or character, as well as one's social standing. Modest attire reinforced temperance, while more ornate clothing reflected vanity. Apparel bringing undue attention to oneself was consonant with a character flaw, while trying to dress above one's means proved foolish when exposed.

---

17. See Murdoch, *Fire and the Sun*.

Historically, dress codes were imposed, usually unsuccessfully, to prevent the "lowly" from wearing the luxurious garments of their "betters."[18]

Early Christian leaders were also concerned about how their fellow believers appeared to one another and to their pagan neighbors. Saint Paul commends modest attire and urges affluent Christians to avoid ostentatious displays of wealth so as not to offend poorer Christians. Although Clement of Alexandria teaches Christians to dress in ways that would be inoffensive to their unbelieving neighbors, he also argues that appearance is ultimately unimportant because it is the soul and not the flesh that is beautiful. Unduly adorning the body hides this inherent beauty.[19] Tertullian goes further, contending that true beauty is always natural and never artificial. Salvation, then, is tightly linked with a modesty that accentuates one's natural beauty. Consequently, he strongly condemns cosmetics, for "whatever is *born* is the work of God. Whatever, then, is *plastered on* (that), is the devil's work."[20]

Admittedly, much classical pagan and early Christian literature was employed in a sexist manner to keep women in their place, one inferior to that enjoyed by men. For example, Athenian women (unlike their Spartan counterparts) were not permitted any substantive public appearance,[21] and Roman law, for a time, forbade women from wearing lavish attire.[22] Many of the early Christian dress codes were directed toward women because women were thought to have an "inherent" sensuousness and vanity[23]—although, to be fair, Tertullian enjoins men not to waste their time meticulously trimming their beards or removing body hair. To a significant extent, much of this literature on appearance was used to control the behavior of women and of those belonging to other socially subordinate groups.[24] Appearance was often used as a way of sequestering undesirables away from certain associations and activities, of protecting privileged groups from unwanted intrusions.

As late moderns, we may assume that the peril of appearance is far less pronounced now than it was in ancient times. We are aware that self-presentation is necessarily ambiguous, in terms of both how one presents oneself and how

---

18. For an overview of ancient dress, see Houston, *Ancient Greek, Roman and Byzantine Costume*.

19. See Clement of Alexandria, *The Tutor*.

20. Tertullian, *On the Apparel of Women* 2.5 (*ANF* 4:21).

21. See Arendt, *Human Condition*, chap. 5; and Elshtain, *Public Man, Private Woman*.

22. See Livy, *History of Rome* 34.1–8.

23. For a critical overview, see Upson-Saia, *Early Christian Dress*.

24. These efforts were not uniformly successful. For example, Roman statutes (the Oppian laws) prohibiting women from owning gold or wearing purple were overturned by the Senate largely in response to public protests initiated by women, and Christian ascetics often wore nondescript garments that blurred gender lines.

one is perceived. This ambiguity, however, is liberating—for one's appearance is now principally an exercise in self-expression rather than a means of controlling the behavior and social status of others. Moreover, this self-expression is frequently innocent and harmless, even playful. Only extremists, such as Antifa and Proud Boys, try to present themselves in menacing ways. Consequently, how people dress and comport themselves is far more subjective and relaxed, reflecting a decline in expectations and standards designed to control and exclude. On Sunday morning, the minister may be wearing liturgical garb or a business suit or may look like a hipster, as determined by personal taste and preference. Since we know that all social interaction consists of how we present ourselves and appear to one another, the so-called peril of appearance is reduced, if not effectively eliminated. Our attention should be fixed on the masks we wear and on enjoying the masks of others, since we can never see behind them anyway. Appearance is now a stage for expressing a widening range of unique personalities rather than a platform for controlling or excluding those who are not like us. Or so we are reassured.

The reassurance is misleading. The issue of appearance has changed over time, but peril remains in different guises. For instance, the more relaxed dress codes we now celebrate are frequently hypocritical, for rather than liberating they demarcate "in" and "out" groups. Designer jeans replete with holes and tears or celebrity-endorsed sneakers identify who is cool and who is a dullard, who has the wherewithal to appear cool and who does not. Moreover, expressing one's unique identity is an exercise in unconscious conformity. Identical goods and services are marketed to consumers seeking to express their unique identities, a superficial uniqueness disguising cookie-cutter conformity.

Appearance can be used to deceive as well as to express. A trustworthy persona may be presented to create an opportunity to defraud or otherwise harm another. Granted, this is not a new peril, but ubiquitous information and communication technologies dramatically increase the opportunities for wolves to appear in sheep's clothing. Identities are manufactured, discarded, and stolen, creating an alarming number of victims along the way. It is often difficult to know with much certainty who we are dealing with in an email, text message, or website. Even the visual "appearance" of the other may mask a fraudster or imposter.

Appearance is the preferred domain of narcissists. They present themselves to draw attention only to themselves. Somewhat like a black hole, the narcissist sucks everyone's "gaze" into his insatiable appetite to be noticed. And the favor of being perceived is never reciprocated, effectively leading to the death of alterity, for the other is at best a mirror. As narcissism spreads and gains acceptability as a mode of self-expression, the attempts to command attention grow more desperate, spectacular, outlandish. The consequences for society or any sense of community are withering, for there is nothing larger or beyond the self to attract common action. Yet it is never clear who the narcissist is, since the identity being expressed is constantly being constructed and deconstructed to gain the fickle attention that is craved.

There is the peril of prejudice and the injustice it inspires. Like it or not, we judge others by how they appear to us, and in many circumstances, we cannot know whether our judgments will prove right or wrong, just or unjust—especially when we encounter strangers. This is why profiling is a practice of, at best, limited value, and, at worst, a blatant disregard for the welfare of the profiled. Our snap judgments may prove highly inaccurate because they are, wittingly or unwittingly, embedded in prejudicial assumptions regarding race, gender, age, or even attire. The innocence and malice of others may be missed because our interpretive filters fail to read the appearance of others correctly. Moreover, such prejudicial profiling is not unidirectional, consisting of static sets of "profilers" and "profiled." To use a trivial example, the so-called casually dressed may harbor hurtful prejudices against the overdressed.

Most troublingly, appearance can become an idol. When this happens, rather than recognizing our appearance as that which *mediates* our identity to others, we come to think of our appearance as our dominant identity in its own right. Appearance is effectively perceived as substantive reality. This perception, however, is mistaken because it confers a presence that is illusional. The mask becomes the face. Or to employ an antiquated concept, the mask (the appearance) is a graven image, an idol. Idolatry is always perilous because it displaces truth with deception. The idol is thought to have an animating divine power when, in fact, it is inanimate and powerless.

When one's identity becomes an idol, both the presenter and the perceiver are caught up in a lie: namely, that the appearance is all there is. What lies behind the mask, if anything, is irrelevant. This disfigures unselfing into idolizing the illusional self. It is a deception that validates itself. The self is perceived to be simultaneously everything and nothing, because it has been lost in the image—an image referring to nothing but itself, an illusion validating an illusion. It is not wrong to worry about whether a society of people with masks but no faces is desirable, especially in an increasingly technological milieu in which presentation denigrates substance. Jacques Ellul is right in insisting that image humiliates truth.[25]

Appearance has its perils. But that is not the full story.

25. See Ellul, *Humiliation of the Word*.

Appearance and Promise

To reiterate, as human creatures we encounter one another by how we appear to one another. This is a fundamental reality of creaturely existence that need not be denied. Moreover, it is a multifaceted reality composed of simple, ordinary elements through which we come to know each other. "Appearance is everything that we express in the public sphere and offer to the perception of others through exchange and social communication: from the words we pronounce to the clothes we wear, from facial expressions and gestures that we draw in the air to the accessories with which we adorn ourselves, passing through all those minor features, more subliminally emitted and perceived, such as tics, bodily postures, smells, sounds, blushes, quick glances, and modulations of voice, which, more often than not, are all the more significant the more they are considered to be inconspicuous."[26] Appearance only becomes perilous when it is given the status of the exclusive or most important reality, when nothing is recognized behind or beyond the mask.

Ellul portrays this peril by equating reality with seeing and truth with hearing, the contrast between image and Word.[27] Through the image, we try to capture and manipulate reality in accordance with our desires. Seeing is an active, at times aggressive act of fabricating and projecting self-images in the world in which we appear. Yet the image slips easily into an idol, for it is regarded as real, but reality is not necessarily synonymous with truth. The images we present and perceive regularly deceive and mislead. In contrast, hearing is a passive and receptive act. The gospel is heard and received, not seen and grasped. Consequently, it is the Word that reveals truth, but this Word remains mysterious because it is not subject to our mastery and manipulation—unlike the idols, the graven images that we mistake for the Word. Late modernity has become a realm dominated by the image, by idols humiliating the Word, effectively removing it from the public world where people appear. It is not coincidental that the vast majority of popular technologies are visually oriented.

Ellul's account of our late-modern circumstances is grim. Too grim, because he goes too far, and also not far enough. Granted, the dominance of the image is troubling for all the reasons Ellul mentions, but idolatry is not inevitable. The image he decries is not as devoid of truth as he claims, for it still retains the mark of its creator, its divine likeness. Regardless of how distorted by sin the image presented and seen might become, there remains in it a residue of God's handiwork, of a creation spoken into existence through

26. Carnevali, *Social Appearances*, 34.
27. See Ellul, *Humiliation of the Word*, chap. 1.

the Word. By virtually ignoring any mention of the *imago Dei*, Ellul goes too far in his condemnation of the image, of appearance. Furthermore, by relegating the incarnation to a largely unfulfilled eschatological promise,[28] he takes away the means that God uses to affirm the *truth* of his creation as a visual and material reality. The incarnation is already the indwelling of the Word in created beings, in our lives, a truth to be received in response to its proclamation. Consequently, our appearance in the world is not simply an act of self-mastery but also one of obedience to Christ. By confining the incarnation to the future, Ellul does not go far enough.

The promise of appearance is that it can be a faithful and truthful witness to Christ, to the Word made flesh. In such a witness, the image becomes an icon. To be clear, it is *not* an icon in the popular sense of being a celebrity absorbing constant attention and adulation. Just the opposite. Properly understood, an icon redirects attention away from itself. An icon is both seen and seen through. When one's appearance is faithfully iconic, the truth of the Word made flesh is revealed through it, albeit to a limited extent. To use the terminology employed throughout this book, iconic appearance is the appearance of one who is an unselfed self. This is the biblically inspired paradox in which we find ourselves by losing ourselves. In Christ, we experience the grace of being unselfconscious—the foundation of true freedom. In being liberated from the anxiety of calculated self-presentation, a perilous enterprise that can fail miserably, we are at liberty to give witness to the source and end of life. When it is properly iconic, appearance is no longer an act of self-expression but one of obedience, of the obedience that is perfect freedom.

Another way to think about appearance as witness is in terms of fulfilling the two great commandments: to love God and to love neighbor. Too often we tend to restrict our understanding of love, regarding it as an inward state invisible to any external view. To whatever extent love may be said to appear in public, what is really at issue are secondary effects, and often ambiguous ones at that, rather than love itself. What we actually see are the antics of an infatuated young person or the outbursts of a jealous lover. Granted, and hence the need to take appearance seriously. Like it or not, we judge others by how we see them, and we are judged by others in the same way. Consequently, we should take care for how we appear to one another if we are at all concerned about embodying a faithful and truthful witness to Christ.

What does being attentive to a faithful and truthful appearance involve? Two examples will suffice. The first example is the appearance of piety. I know this is a word that has fallen out of favor, an unflattering word used to

---

28. See Ellul, *Humiliation of the Word*, chap. 2.

dismiss conventional thinking. Pity, for it is a good word that deserves better. Piety refers to a set of practices reflecting a person's objects of devotion. Piety is inescapable because it is not confined to conventional religion but is associated with any object to which ultimate importance is attached. To paraphrase Martin Luther, whatever our hearts cling to is functionally our God. Our so-called secular societies are swarming with pious devotees of this and that deity. An object of devotion may be career, pastime, hobby, or a variety of other interests, but all demand pious acts of devotion. And they show. Pious acts are revelatory. Compare the gourmet painstakingly preparing a sumptuous feast to the disinterested person casually popping a frozen dinner into the microwave oven. "Pious display" is not a derogatory characterization; it aptly expresses the core issue: the clinging of the heart.

It is no different in the life of a Christian. Piety is unavoidable even when it is unmindful. Simple acts disclose our most basic beliefs. What does how we pray say about what we think of God? Do we sit quietly with hands folded, or stand with outstretched arms? Do we pray loudly on a street corner or silently in a closet? More broadly, how is our faith shaped or misshaped in worship? Is worship a time directing our attention toward the judgment and grace of God or an entertaining spectacle? Does the sermon proclaim the gospel or does it showcase the rhetorical skills of the preacher? How these and similar questions are answered helps determine whether appearance is oriented more toward image and its peril of idolatry or more toward being iconic and the icon's promise of disclosing the incarnate Word. In this respect, piety displays the freedom of a self being shaped by obediently loving God. Self-presentation in the world also directs attention toward the transcendent origin and end of creation.

The second example is attire. Most people most often appear in public clothed rather than naked. This is a prevalent but often overlooked aspect of how we come to be known and to know others. How we dress says a lot about how we wish to be seen by others. Do we wear the latest fashion or dress down for comfort? Do we try to draw attention to ourselves, blend in, or be as nondescript as possible? Do we dress tastefully, to put other people at ease, or outrageously, to make others ill at ease? Whether it is conscious or not, how we are dressed makes a statement about who we are and how we regard others. We judge and are judged, in part, by what we see and how we look.

Since appearance is ambiguous, such judgments are notoriously vague even though they nonetheless create strong impressions. In reaction, one strategy is to take advantage of the situation. Present oneself in the most socially advantageous or dominant manner possible: dress for success. Project yourself as a leader and others will follow. Context, of course, dictates the required appearance. To be successful on Wall Street, for instance, requires an expensive suit that has never spent a day on the rack, while in Silicon Valley, chic designer jeans and a shirt whose collar has never been introduced to a necktie form the requisite uniform. An alternative strategy is to disregard appearance altogether. Don't play the game; ooze casual disdain. Dress however you want, in whatever way is most convenient, regardless of social context or of what others might think. That old T-shirt will do nicely when lounging at home, going to work, or sitting in church.

Both of these strategies fail. A strategically calculated appearance may gain some benefit initially, but over time it will be seen for what it is—a manipulative scheme. Once it is recognized for what it is, it can be met with other strategically calculated appearances, designed to counter or negate, that in turn prompt a new series of strategically calculated appearances. Ultimately, the world becomes cluttered with a lengthening series of appearances of appearances, digressions upon digressions, masks masking masks. The person disclosed and known through appearance is lost because there is effectively no self-presenting, at least no substantial self as perceived in her disclosure. Disregarding appearance fails because our disregarding itself becomes a kind of regarding and because, whether we like it or not, appearance matters. Others judge us in terms of our self-presentation; they cannot do otherwise. Furthermore, wanting to appear indifferent is not the same as actually being so; it is effectively a strategic ploy, a choice to disregard the judgments of others (which is, ironically, to *regard* their judgments as being of little worth). This projected indifference to others is bound to trigger various reactions, ranging from bewilderment to hostility. If social interaction is principally a process of presenting and appearing to one another, then indifference regarding the judgments of others is thoroughly antisocial.

The reader may be tempted to dismiss appearance as ultimately irrelevant to Christian ethics. Such things as acts of piety and how one dresses are too trivial to be taken seriously, even when we are focusing on ethics and everyday life. Surely it would be better to concentrate on larger questions—perhaps those of value, virtue, and character—rather than worry about how we appear to others. Don't be too quick to dismiss the "trivial," however, for it is often in the ordinary and overlooked aspects of how we appear to one another that we learn some of the most important lessons about who we and others might be, however imperfect that knowledge proves to be.

It is through appearance that we exhibit, most readily and (ideally) most unselfconsciously, a love of God and neighbor. Our physical stance, facial expressions, presentation of and participation in the liturgy indicate something about how we love God and how God loves us. The appearance of piety demonstrates, either wittingly or unwittingly, our understanding of that love, and of who plays the most significant role. When we worship, is the center-piece God or individual worshipers? Our apparently "trivial" pious acts go a long way in answering that question. And the "trivial" matter of how we dress also discloses how we love our neighbors. Do we regard them as a means to our success? Are we indifferent to them? For example, as a teacher, how I am dressed discloses something about how I regard my students. Granted, acts of piety and how we dress play a "small" role in the larger scheme of things. But that does not make them unimportant. Over time, small things contribute to how we perceive and respond to the bigger issues we encounter in life. If I always dress indifferently, there is a good chance that I am or will become an indifferent person who treats my neighbors accordingly.

We exhibit a love of God and neighbor by tending to our appearance, but we also, at the same time, exhibit a love of self. Not everything is appearance. There is something behind the mask requiring our care and attention. But this self-love should be properly ordered; we should be unselfed selves. This is not a clever contradiction but a truth that lies at the heart of the Christian moral life. Our self-presentation, our appearance in the world, is to be one of obedience to Christ, a truthful and faithful appearance bearing an iconic witness to Christ. Unselfing is required, for otherwise the presentation of the self is vain deception, empty self-flattery.

As Iris Murdoch contends, vanity is derived from fantasy—and fantasy prevents us from genuinely loving our neighbors and ourselves. Ideally, there is a real, unselfed self behind the mask. Murdoch goes on to suggest that it is through something like prayer that we imaginatively link the real, the true, and the beautiful.[29] Our appearances in the world manifest this linkage in revealing and concrete ways. If Murdoch is right, then properly tending to appearance is tending to the world, to our neighbors, and to ourselves; it is also, I would add, an obedient response to Christ. Oscar Wilde's character Lord Henry is right: "It is only shallow people who do not judge by appearance."[30] Appearance is often all that is readily at hand in the world. It is therefore too important to ignore or denigrate.

29. See Murdoch, "Ethics and the Imagination."
30. Wilde, *Picture of Dorian Gray*, loc. 381, Kindle.

CHAPTER 15

Eating

Eating is necessary. It is fundamental for survival. Food sustains our bodies, and if our bodies are not nourished, we die. Yet for humans, eating is about more than surviving. A meal may also be a time of fellowship or a festive occasion. Ideally, eating together builds social bonds promoting individual and communal wellbeing. Eating is also pleasurable and can be abused. We may eat too much or eat unhealthy diets, and we may eat in ways that promote social isolation rather than communication. When eating is abused or misused, human wellbeing is diminished.

I assume that the biological necessity of eating is evident, and I need not expend any more ink on this matter. Rather, I will concentrate on some of the social ills and goods associated with eating, on the contrast between eating badly and eating well. Before proceeding, however, I need to state a disclaimer and an admission.

The disclaimer: I cannot do justice to this topic in a single chapter. Delving into the ethics of eating or of food would require a hefty volume or two. For instance, the Bible is replete with stories of famine and feasting. In the Old Testament, it is lack of food that leads to Israel's Egyptian captivity, and the book of Esther unfolds in a series of banquets. Some of the most pivotal events recorded in the New Testament entail sharing loaves and fishes, and a final supper with friends. There are extensive collections of moral and theological literature on the sin of gluttony and the spiritual discipline of fasting. Pastoral theologians have addressed such health-related concerns as obesity and eating disorders. In the field of social ethics, issues such as hunger and malnutrition; access to nutritious food; justice for agricultural workers, consumers, farmers, and ranchers; humane treatment of animals; environmental sustainability; and the decline of rural communities and the values of agrarian life have received extensive attention. Many more items could be added to this list, and none are addressed in this chapter (well, perhaps aside from occasional allusions). This is not to say that these topics are unimportant. On the contrary, they are vital. But I leave it to authors with greater expertise to take them on.

My focus in this chapter is narrow. It is prompted by the question, How does eating communicate the goods of creation? More explicitly, How *should* eating be ordered to promote human flourishing beyond the necessity of surviving? Admittedly, eating is a commonplace activity, and that is exactly why it should attract our attention. As Margaret Visser writes, "The extent to which we take everyday objects for granted is the precise extent to which they govern and inform our lives"; ordinary things "embody our mostly unspoken assumptions, and they both order our culture and determine its direction."[1] Food is an ordinary thing, yet civilization is impossible unless food is taken for granted. How food is prepared and eaten, with whom it is shared, and the time allotted to dining reflect what is valued by those participating in this ordinary activity. "However humble it may be, a meal has a definite plot, the intention of which is to intrigue, stimulate, and satisfy."[2] How and with whom we eat is more important than why we eat. Answering this question suggests some links more broadly with the Christian moral life. In this respect, the daily, repetitive act of eating is not so unassuming as it might appear to be.

This leads to my admission: my interest in eating and the ethics enmeshed in everyday life grows out of personal experience. A few years ago, I took up cooking as a hobby, but I am now sufficiently proficient to split the task more evenly with my wife. I make no pretentious claim to being an amateur chef or a foodie, but I am handy around the kitchen and have learned to avoid injuring myself with the sharp instruments and complicated gadgets cluttering the drawers and cupboards. My cooking has taught me the importance of preparation and cleanup and the even greater importance of the fellowship of the table. A properly ordered meal involves much more than throwing a few ingredients together or opening a few cans. It takes attentiveness, hard work, practice, and occasionally some good luck.

Although my thinking is prompted by personal experience, the reader will be spared any detailed recounting of my misadventures and occasional victories in the kitchen.

---

1. Visser, *Much Depends On Dinner*, 11.
2. Visser, *Much Depends On Dinner*, 14.

Eating Badly

Iris Murdoch won the Booker Prize for her novel *The Sea, the Sea*. It is the ill-fated love story of Charles Arrowby. But it also includes some revealing digressions involving Charles's gastronomic habits and preferences. He believes that food should be prepared quickly and consumed slowly and that the one eating should avoid any intrusions, such as conversation. Eating and hunger are gifts, and every meal should be a treat. "I wonder if I shall ever write my *Charles Arrowby Four Minute Cookbook*," Charles muses. "The 'four minutes' of course refer to the active time of preparation."[3] Plain cooking is an art to be admired, and the true gourmet is a hedonist. "In food and drink, as in many (not all) other matters, simple joys are best, as any intelligent self-lover knows."[4]

A posh restaurant is a terrible place to eat, because it creates the ruse that "elaborate cooking is more 'creative' than simple cooking."[5] The menu inspires "guzzling large quantities of expensive, pretentious, often mediocre food," an activity that is "not only immoral, unhealthy and unaesthetic, but also unpleasurable."[6] Large dinner parties are even worse. Why waste a day preparing dishes for guests who are "usually so sozzled" that all they do is "toy" with the food?[7] Moreover, hospitality is nonexistent, for "amid much kissing, there is the appearance of intimacy where there is really none."[8] For Charles, a meal should be "eaten among friends who are unmoved by such 'social considerations', or of course *best of all alone*."[9]

Additionally, Charles's idea of simple cooking is, to employ the most charitable descriptive term possible, eccentric. An illustrative meal: "For dinner I had an egg poached in hot scrambled egg, then the coley braised with onions and lightly dusted with curry powder, and served with a little tomato ketchup and mustard. (Only a fool despises tomato ketchup.) Then a heavenly rice pudding."[10] Enough said about Charles's simple culinary pleasures.[11]

Murdoch offers a masterful display of eating badly. Meals are prepared carelessly, with little thought given to selecting dishes and ingredients other

3. Murdoch, *The Sea, the Sea*, 8.
4. Murdoch, *The Sea, the Sea*, 8.
5. Murdoch, *The Sea, the Sea*, 9.
6. Murdoch, *The Sea, the Sea*, 9.
7. Murdoch, *The Sea, the Sea*, 9.
8. Murdoch, *The Sea, the Sea*, 10.
9. Murdoch, *The Sea, the Sea*, 10 (emphasis added).
10. Murdoch, *The Sea, the Sea*, 53.
11. For a more elegant description of indulging the pleasures of eating, both in terms of recipes and of posh restaurants, see Barbery, *Gourmet Rhapsody*. It is a story in which a dying food critic recalls his most memorable meals. These occasions almost prompt a modicum of moral self-assessment.

than what lends itself to being put together quickly. Charles's insistence that his cooking produces superb, simple delights for the palate is delusional, for the results are unappetizing concoctions masquerading as recipes.[12] He doesn't care because he is ideally cooking only for himself and no one else. The consummate hedonist pays little heed to the taste of others around the table, and—better yet—eats at a table occupied only by himself. Restaurants and dinner parties are avoided because they shift the center of attention away from the self-indulgent hedonist. For Charles, eating at its best is an act designed to solidify social isolation. He is the only person who matters. Eating alone is the best way to eat.

Is the preceding paragraph unfair? After all, Charles's emphasis on simple food is in line with historic Christian teaching. Clement of Alexandria, for instance, commends a simple diet as an aid in regulating the body in accordance with religious and moral priorities. People do not live in order to eat; rather, they eat in order to live. The purpose of eating is not pleasure but health and strength, so eating simply is the best course to take.

The apparent similarities, however, are deceptive. Clement commends a simple diet as a way of resisting gluttony, since this sin leads to an ignoble life. Additionally, modest expectations regarding meals promote social interaction. Christians should eat what is given to them out of gratitude to their hosts. In both instances, a simple diet points to goods beyond eating—namely, self-control gained by controlling gluttonous hunger and communication gained by overcoming a finicky appetite. In contrast, Charles's simplicity draws attention to Charles himself, in particular to his grandiose declarations concerning excellent recipes and cooking. But his bravado is a feint hiding his meager talents and lack of taste as a cook. He is a self-indulgent hedonist without a care for communication, for as a proud hedonist he cooks only to please himself and no one else.

But isn't the preceding moral judgment unwarranted on the basis of Charles's banal culinary statements and practices? Do eating habits really disclose a person's character? Yes, to a limited extent, for how and what we eat says something about how we regard ourselves, especially in relation to others. As a young girl, Ruth Reichl loved to watch people loading up their shopping carts in the market, a pastime her mother found bewildering. "'I can look through the food,' I'd try to explain. 'Just by paying attention to

---

12. My uncharitable characterization of Charles's cooking may not be what Murdoch intended. "When a contemporary declared the recipes in *The Sea, the Sea* to be revolting, Murdoch replied, 'But this is what John and I eat all the time.'" "Iris Murdoch's Four Minute Feasts," *Bread & Oysters*, accessed December 10, 2020, http://breadandoysters.com/iris-murdochs-four -minute-feasts/.

what people buy you can tell an awful lot about them.'"[13] Reichl elaborates: "In time, I came to understand that for people who really love it, food is a lens through which to view the world. For us, the way that people cook and eat, how they set their tables, and the utensils that they use all tell a story. If you choose to pay attention, cooking is an important cultural artifact, an expression of time, place, and personality."[14]

It is not surprising that eating reveals, albeit partially, something about who we are, who we aspire to be, and how we regard others. Eating is a daily, highly routinized action, enmeshed in a series of related, often ritualized activities that are bound to be habitual and therefore formative. Our habits are not extraneous but parts of who we are. Reichl is right: what we pile into our shopping carts and what we do with the stuff when we get home says something, perhaps more than we can know, about the kind of people we are. These revelations may disclose an honest continuity or an unaware or mendacious discontinuity between words and deeds. The person who claims to be a good dinner host, for example, may prove to be ungracious, inept, or conniving. Granted, care must be taken not to jump to unwarranted judgments. There is certainly no reason to assume that every bad cook is also a bad person. But there is also no reason to ignore habits, good and bad, ours and those of others—and eating overflows with habitual behavior. In Murdoch's "love story," Charles is (again, to be charitable) a selfish bastard. He physically and emotionally harms everyone he "loves" because he considers only his own desires to the exclusion of the needs and good of the other. The other hardly exists except as an extension of his own feted ego and benighted imagination. This is not to say there is any direct cause-and-effect relationship. Charles is not vicious because he is a bad cook and host any more than an excellent cook and hostess would necessarily be virtuous. But in this story, Charles's eating mirrors his character. He is a consistent and thoroughgoing hedonist who "loves" or, better, "consumes" his neighbors accordingly.

Is there an antidote to eating badly? Thankfully, yes.

Eating Well

In contrast to eating badly, there is eating well. The first step is careful preparation. The most valuable lesson I learned when I started cooking was to mind the details. A meal is only as good as the time and care devoted to its planning. Try a new recipe, but make sure it is not far beyond your skill set

13. Reichl, "Introduction," loc. 42, Kindle.
14. Reichl, "Introduction," loc. 48, Kindle.

and experience. Double-check that you have the right ingredients in the correct proportions and the right tools to put the meal together. Stay focused. A missed ingredient or overcooking can prove ruinous. Presentation matters. Plated food should appear appetizing, creating a sense of anticipation for those about to eat.

Disclosure: my presentation skills are abysmal. I usually pray that the meal I have prepared tastes better than it looks. With time, however, I could expand the breadth of my focus and think about other things while chopping the onions or grating the cheese. This is not an opportunity to daydream or to otherwise allow my mind to wander; rather, it is an opportunity to be mindful of some of the broader ramifications of what I am doing. For example, although I might be alone in the kitchen, my cooking thoroughly depends on the work of countless people. There are farmers and ranchers, individuals who transport and sell ingredients, manufacturers of utensils and kitchen equipment—and more could be added to the list, including many of whom I am probably unaware. Eating is necessarily a shared activity, even when one dines alone. While preparing a meal, I try to recall my dependence on others, giving thanks for their work that makes it possible for me to put a meal on my table.

I have also discovered that careful preparation is not confined to the kitchen. The room where a meal is to be eaten and the company who will be sharing it require attention. That is, one must consider how the table is to be set and the seating arranged. This does not mean that every meal needs to be a formal occasion, but it should promote conversation and fellowship. At the very least, eating together is best when it is free from the noise of television, telephones, and other electronic gadgets. Nothing should distract from the people breaking bread together. A sidelight: I am now less concerned about whether I will like the meal I fix than about how it will be received by those for whom I am cooking. Unlike Charles Arrowby, I find eating alone to be the worst way to eat.

Far too little is said about the importance of cleanup. I have learned that eating is a messy business. Pots, pans, and dishes must be washed and put away, and leftovers must be properly stowed to be enjoyed another day. Unfortunately, one person—over and over again—often gets stuck with this chore. Those sharing a meal should also share in clearing away its aftermath. A kitchen strewn with the residue of a carefully prepared meal can be daunting when it is faced alone. An exception: dinner guests should not be expected to help clean up; this would imply that the chore is the price of dining.

Although eating is a common activity, it is also an act that helps direct the moral flow of daily living. Eating well, for instance, is not self-indulgent but oriented toward the welfare of the neighbor. As suggested above, preparing a meal is a modest exercise in unselfing. Food is selected and presented in ways that highlight the dinner guest over the cook. More broadly, the relationship among the producers, distributors, and consumers of food exhibits a love of neighbor. The fact that this relationship is maintained primarily through financial transactions does not diminish its moral significance. Without the ability to buy and sell food, the vast majority of people would starve. To provide and be rewarded for the physical and material wellbeing of others is at root motivated by concern for the needs of others. Recognizing the bond of shared human needs is a basic and common moral sentiment. Hunger and famine are rarely caused by a lack of food but by unavailable markets. Devising ways to ensure that all people have access to dependable markets, *and* the wherewithal to participate, is a way of helping them fulfill their petition to receive their daily bread. Without the presence of such exchange, communicating the goods of creation that a meal offers cannot occur.

Eating well, then, is a social practice and an exercise in communication. Preparing and eating a meal is not ordered toward the goal of seclusion. As Charles Arrowby demonstrates, when eating is corrupted into a lonely act, that same loneliness manifests itself in other facets of daily life. His incessant gastronomical gratification is mirrored in his destructive regard for and treatment of other people. They too are effectively reduced to items to be figuratively consumed rather than neighbors to be loved. When eating alone, Charles is not even in the slightest mindful of, much less grateful for, his dependence on others in concocting his eccentric meals. Such an unselfed attitude would only serve as an unwelcome distraction, for "eating is so pleasant one should even try to suppress thought."[15]

Christian moral teaching has consistently condemned gluttony because it recognizes that eating is pleasurable. A gluttonous attitude is not merely self-indulgent; it effectively renders other people invisible. Even at a shared table, the glutton makes no attempt to enable fellowship but is fixated on the food placed before him. Moreover, when food is in short supply (a prevalent condition throughout much of human history), gluttony literally endangers the welfare of others. Eating too much is being uncharitable to the hungry neighbor. Hence early Christian teaching promoting hospitality, expressing gratitude for the provision of food, and encouraging simple diets to suppress the selfish pleasure of overeating.

Today, talk about the sin of gluttony has been largely displaced by rhetoric concerning eating disorders and healthy diets. In some respects, this change

15. Murdoch, *The Sea, the Sea*, 7.

is to be welcomed. Eating well improves one's physical wellbeing, which in turn promotes human flourishing. If this worthwhile goal is best achieved through therapeutic interventions, professional guidance, and readily available nutritional information, so much the better. Condemning people for sinning may not be the best way of achieving worthwhile objectives.

Nonetheless, a largely unacknowledged moral component still casts its shadow on the enlightened dietary habits of late moderns. Eating is still often viewed implicitly as a matter of vice and virtue. Some eating disorders are viewed as medical or psychological problems plaguing individuals through no fault of their own and requiring therapeutic responses. But in many other instances, it is often assumed that unhealthy eating is caused by a lack of will-power. People enduring anorexia, for example, are blameless victims, whereas obese people are suffering the consequences of moral weakness. In contrast, slender people signal their moral virtue and strength of will by keeping to their healthy diets.

Such smugness is uncalled for, however, because it fails to recognize that obesity is at times a result of social and economic location. Some people simply live where healthy food or ingredients cannot be easily obtained, or they lack the financial resources to purchase them. A healthy diet is expensive, and more affordable options often promote weight gain and its related problems. Sadly, affluence is too often the prerequisite for eating well. Unlike in previous generations, when being slightly portly was a sign of social status, today being skinny frequently signals status.

The preceding foray into the morality of eating is meant to underscore that food often proves divisive, accentuating a number of social fault lines—a problem recognized by the early church and by subsequent Christian moral teaching. Whether the problem is meat sacrificed to idols, failing to share food with fellow worshipers, or hoarding scarce ingredients, eating can easily divide people and create strife. It ought not, however, since food is a basic good of creation that should be communicated among people, a precept also recognized by the early church and by ensuing Christian moral teaching and liturgical practice.

The rhythms of fasting and feasting are pronounced throughout the Bible and the church's liturgical calendar. The moral and symbolic import of food is central to Christian beliefs and practices—a status faintly preserved in, of all things, the potluck supper. This traditional role is well worth recovering in greater depth for renewing contemporary worship, ministry, and discipleship.[16] For instance, being theologically mindful of food is a step in

---

16. See Vanderslice, *We Will Feast*.

embracing our faith in Christ as an all-encompassing reality, in bridging the gap separating Sunday from the rest of the week, even in bringing the living and dead together through cherished recipes.[17] Eating serves as a reminder of the incarnation, in which the Word pervades the entire created order. "When we eat, we experience the delight of the created order, we experience sensory magnificence of our human bodies, we commune with one another, and, through this connection with all of creation, we commune with and delight in our Creator as well."[18] Moreover, it is also through meals that we extend hospitality to strangers, a powerful witness to Christ[19] and therefore a way of fulfilling the Great Commission. In short, eating is a reminder of God's presence in mundane human activities, and such participation, both human and divine, should bring and bind people together.

There is an artfulness to eating that needs greater recognition because, precisely in being such a commonplace activity, eating contributes disproportionally to human flourishing. But in order to appreciate and apply this contribution, care must be taken to keep eating an activity that, in addition to being necessary, is shared and playful, an act requiring attentiveness in order to promote communication. Idwal Jones's *High Bonnet: A Novel of Epicurean Adventures* offers some insight into this requisite attentiveness. It is a story about chefs and gourmet cooking in late-nineteenth-century France. The main characters are Gallois, a young chef, and his mentor, Francois. As a student, Gallois spends endless hours preparing sauces, vegetables, and legumes, in addition to performing other tedious chores. Finally, he is ushered into the head chef's office: "'Gallois,' [the head chef] said, 'you are accepted. And now a word or two for your benefit, young man. You have embarked upon an art that exacts of its devotees the utmost diligence, studious application, a large share of intellect, and the happiest co-ordination of eye and hand.'"[20] In two years (record time!) Gallois is awarded the high bonnet, a visible symbol that he has mastered the art of cooking.

The education and work of a chef is not easy, especially for one pursuing excellence. There are countless hours of repetitive and tedious tasks, endlessly searching for the right ingredients, and paying close attention to the details. There is a nearly religious devotion to cooking, at least for those who take it seriously. An old kitchen where "great chefs had plied their art with cumulative renown for many decades" is described as a "vast chancel,

---

17. See Vanderslice, *We Will Feast*, 20.
18. Vanderslice, *We Will Feast*, 16.
19. See Pohl, *Making Room*.
20. Jones, *High Bonnet*, 21.

the granite walls begrimed with smoke from ten thousand lordly feasts, the aisle a channel of blue haze through which the cooks and apprentices moved like sacristans and acolytes. From the ranges, charcoal gridirons, and rows of copper pots, burnished like altar vessels, incense lifted to the soot-hung louvre overhead."[21] From this religious devotion, the excellent chef strives to prepare the perfect meal, a feast delighting the senses. The emblem of success is a diner eating with "eyes half drooped, like a pigeon's in flight, allowing the *croustade* to splinter under her excellent teeth. She dabbled with lumps of bread and pushed them, dripping with sauce, into her mouth in absorption, as if listening to the orchestration of flavors echoing against the sounding board of her palate."[22]

Cooking also has its travails. Even the best chefs fail on occasion. Such failures are beneficial, for wise chefs learn from their mistakes. But wisdom is not synonymous with native skill, and the prodigy is most at risk, for too frequently "genius dares beyond its skill, or is overconfident," and when "genius fails, it fails mightily."[23] There are more conventional hazards associated with cooking. Chefs (and waiters), for instance, may become repulsed by the sight of food and grow weary of their customers. Bored and depressed chefs are not uncommon.

Yet cooking, especially when practiced as an art that entails more than cooking itself, is a pleasure. Gallois spends nearly two months traveling with some Gypsies. At the end of their difficult journey, he arranges a banquet at a small but excellent restaurant. He takes delight in the pleasure of his new friends. An intimate dinner with a friend is as important as—even better than—a banquet prepared for an aristocrat. The reader learns that, for the best chefs, eating is never an end in itself. It is, rather, an excuse to spend time with customers, friends, and loved ones, a means of transporting people beyond the confines of their immediate time and place. "The filaments of one's taste buds stretch into the past. Their ends are shaken by memories. And if there is fragrance, the past—even the forgotten parts of it—enfolds one instantly. A whiff of saffron, the smell of pastry in the oven, and one is a child again. The true pleasure in eating comes not from the gratification of the senses as in the awakening of a subliminal faculty."[24] In Jones's story, the chefs, when at their best, model unselfing.[25]

21. Jones, *High Bonnet*, 16.
22. Jones, *High Bonnet*, 12.
23. Jones, *High Bonnet*, 63.
24. Jones, *High Bonnet*, 94.
25. These themes also occur in other novels written by Jones. See esp. Jones, *Chef's Holiday*; and Jones, *The Vineyard*.

High Bonnet suggests an iconic role for eating or, more accurately, for the social interactions surrounding it. Anticipating, preparing, and sharing a meal cracks open a window to provide a more elaborate vista on the moral life. For instance, even hedonism requires self-discipline. Always being satisfied is boring, and boredom is hardly conducive to self-indulgent pleasure. Tino, the leader of the Gypsies Gallois travels with, eats sparsely throughout the trip. This is partly because food is not plentiful. But more importantly, it is in anticipation of the feast awaiting him when they reach their destination. "Tino was the true hedonist, aware that we cannot feast unless we are willing also to fast. No passion, no pleasure, no interest must be slacked at will. Indeed, to keep it sharp and alive, the wish to gratify it must often be denied, or else it becomes the foe of its own gratification."[26] To know and communicate the good of food entails knowing its absence, a lesson applicable to many, if not most, of the goods of creation. Restraint is cooked (forgive the pun) into the moral fabric of daily living.

The wisest chefs in this story display the value of modesty, a neglected virtue these days. Excellent chefs do not master the culinary arts in order to display their own talents and accomplishments. Those that do are striving to become celebrities rather than cooks. Celebrities have little to do with the natural necessity and social communication of eating, for they quickly rise and fall in accordance with the changing tastes (again, forgive the pun) of fickle consumers. True chefs are in for the long haul, disdaining popularity in preference for their calling to feed their clientele day in and day out. Wise chefs know the peril of self-aggrandizement as a vice corrupting the virtues of their calling.[27] In reference to a master chef: "He had toiled overlong since youth, being insatiable of fame—no bad thing in itself, if it procure a man happiness, and without oppression of his fellow human beings. But fame is not peace of mind, for ambition, vain and disturbing, is its mainspring."[28] In and through cooking and eating we learn something about working on behalf of and communicating with our neighbors. Ideally, cooking is a work of love, and, ideally, eating is the gift of fellowship.

I have devoted a chapter to cooking and eating not simply because I enjoy both. Rather, because they are ordinary activities that disclose some features that are central to Christian faith and practice. Fellowship (Gk. *koinōnia*) is at the heart of the Christian faith. The Christian life is one shared with others. Fellowship is often facilitated by a table, be it in the household, in a

26. Jones, *High Bonnet*, 122–23.
27. In several instances, "calling" is used in describing the work of a chef. See, e.g., Jones, *High Bonnet*, 67.
28. Jones, *High Bonnet*, 127.

public house, or in a Christian house of worship (i.e., by the Lord's Table). It is difficult to ignore a neighbor when one is breaking bread with her. The image of the hospitable table is neglected in contemporary society. For many people, sharing a meal around a table does not occur regularly. Some, like Charles Arrowby, simply prefer to eat alone, while others are forced to because of unwanted circumstances. Many eat on the run, barely pausing to grab something that can be eaten without stopping their other activities. Food has become a commodity to be easily acquired and consumed. Late moderns tend to graze rather than dine. On those rare occasions when they are forced to share a meal around a table, fellowship is not on their mind. Cooking and eating are reduced to useful tools to be used sparingly in accomplishing other goals: accommodating old, eccentric relatives, impressing the boss, closing a deal. Winston Churchill used dinners ruthlessly to achieve political and diplomatic goals.[29] Fellowship grows increasingly irrelevant. The link between eating and communicating is tattered.

Table fellowship is crucial, however—a fact recognized by the earliest Christians and by subsequent generations of believers. From the beginning, table fellowship has played an important role in the lives of Christians, and current attempts to recover this formative practice of hospitality are a welcome response to the indifference permeating contemporary culture. Sharing a meal with friends and guests around a table is too powerful a symbol and ritual of the faith to neglect. Indeed, the Eucharist, Holy Communion, is *the* center of Christian piety and sacramental life.

Fellowship, however, is not a natural derivative of eating. A meal must be organized toward achieving this end, and such ordering requires habituated behavior; it requires, at a minimum, table manners. As I argued in chapter 13, manners are important, and especially so at the dinner table. Recall Roger Scruton's dictum that manners help us avoid social disasters.[30] The dinner table is rife with potential disasters. Table manners, however, are not only precautionary; they also help reorient eating to bring it in line with more transcendent goals, such as fellowship. This reorientation is a crucial step in achieving the goal of fellowship, for eating depends on actions that are not inherently congenial to polite or civil behavior. Margaret Visser explains, "Violence, after all, is necessary if any organism is to ingest another. Animals are murdered to produce meat; vegetables are torn up, peeled, and chopped; most of what we eat is treated with fire; and chewing is designed remorselessly to finish what killing and cooking

29. See Stelzer, *Dinner with Churchill*.
30. See chap. 13.

began."[31] But a meal is, or should be, nonviolent. Table manners serve to solidify this transition from violent preparation to peaceful dining, which in turn encourages fellowship. Without an etiquette of the table, the good of human fellowship is attenuated, and—more broadly—no peaceful society can exist without manners and the moral behavior they help habituate. A meal binds together those sharing a table, and the bond is peaceful rather than violent or coercive.

Table fellowship has an anticipatory element. No meal is ever complete. Something is always missing: a favorite dish, the right ambience, a beloved friend or relative (perhaps even one who may never be at the table again). Every meal anticipates something larger than itself. A dinner prefigures a banquet, conversation strives for reunion with those lost. Dining, then, accentuates longing, unfulfilled desire. In this respect, ordinary table fellowship mirrors what occurs at the Lord's Table. The Eucharist celebrates both the presence and the absence of Christ.[32] In the bread and wine Christ is a real presence, communing with his disciples. Yet Christ is not fully present. The liturgy still cries out "*Maranatha!*" (Come, Lord!). The Eucharist anticipates a time beyond time when we will feast with Christ in the New Jerusalem. In the meantime, we wait. In the daily acts and rituals surrounding cooking and eating, we catch an iconic glimpse of this anticipation, this waiting. In the ordinary routine of breaking bread together we capture a glimmer of the extraordinary end awaiting creation. In the meantime, we wait.

So how do we wait faithfully? The mundane act of eating teaches an important lesson. Eating well entails minding the details. Choosing beloved recipes, carefully sorting through the ingredients, setting the table just right, allowing adequate time for cooking and preparation, leisurely lingering around the table to share food and conversation, cleaning up and readying the kitchen and dining room for another day, day after day. These are acts of love—love of God and of neighbor. They are also routine, unexciting acts repeated daily. But without them we eat badly. We miss the glimmer of the eschatological banquet, the destiny of eternal fellowship with the One who gives us the created goods that we partake of and communicate around a table. The iconic message of cooking and eating is that waiting faithfully entails the patience and skills to perform the daily, mundane acts of love that serve to prepare us for this fellowship. Living well, like eating well, is more an art of tending the details than a demonstration of creativity.

31. Visser, *Rituals of Dinner*, 3.
32. See Farrow, *Ascension and Ecclesia*.

To return to *High Bonnet*, in reference to his mentor, Francois, Gallois reflects, "Not originality but perfection is the lodestar of the virtuoso, who knows that a perfect work cannot be improved upon, and that it takes more skill and conscience to make a vibrant, living copy than to create a poor original."[33] Living well has little to do with poor originality and much to do with skillful, loving repetition. That is, I suggest, the iconic message of eating, of eating well.

33. Jones, *High Bonnet*, 128.

CHAPTER 16

Leisure

It is customary in the final chapter of a book for an author to tie some threads together, to bring the story to its end. I am following this custom, and leisure is the theme I am using to accomplish this goal. Leisure is a good way to conclude part 3, on everyday activities, which began with a chapter on work. The two go together like two sides of the same coin. We alternate between working and resting. More expansively, leisure is vital to our flourishing. When at leisure we enmesh ourselves in God's good creation, which in turn enables us to communicate its goods with one another.

Since we are finite creatures who live and move and have our being in a temporal creation, leisure is about *time*. Think of some of the prominent words and phrases we associate with leisure: downtime, my time, playtime, time to relax, recharge, rejuvenate, taking time for a hobby, taking a walk, taking a nap. It is *free time*, for leisure is also about *freedom*. We choose how to spend our leisure time. The range of our choices is not absolute, but it is less constrained in comparison to when we are working or on the job. When we are at leisure we are also at liberty.

What exactly is this freedom afforded by leisure? This is a good question. And in hazarding a provisional answer, I begin by describing briefly what leisure is not, in order to dispel some popular assumptions. Leisure is not time spent not working or laboring. If it were, then leisure would simply be killing time until time is spent doing something important. Leisure would be akin to a kind of holding pattern. Additionally, leisure is not about expending energy in alternative ways, such as on enjoyable activities (playing sports, for instance).[1]

Leisure is not a license to be selfish. Being at leisure does not mean doing anything we want, whenever we want, without regard for others. If that were the case, then leisure would be a loveless expenditure of time because it would be self-absorbed to an inordinate degree. The neighbor would be, at best, a means of enriching oneself without any thought of reciprocity or mutuality. The other would never be an object of love for the other's own sake; leisure would effectively negate the possibility of unselfing.

If leisure is not time spent aimlessly or selfishly, then what is it? To understand what leisure is (or what it should be) requires contrast—namely, contrasting it with work. Work is not aimless but teleologically oriented. We work to achieve some purpose. Neither is work selfish (though it is self-interested), for to achieve its purpose we must cooperate and work with others. Most importantly, work and leisure cannot sustain themselves independently for very long. The one requires the other. This interdependence is a core theological conviction. God works to bring creation into being and assigns humans to work as his caretakers. After six days, however, God rests. In keeping the Sabbath, humans emulate the divine pattern of working and resting, a routine that enables them to flourish by grounding their lives in the contours of God's good creation and orienting them toward its seventh day.

What is entailed in keeping the Sabbath? In being at rest or at leisure? Work and rest are intrinsically related but differ in basic orientation. Work is an active mode of being. We employ physical or mental effort to accomplish a purpose, to get something done. One works to build a fence or write a book. In contrast, leisure is a receptive mode of being. It is a contemplative orientation in which whatever benefit might be enjoyed is received effortlessly, as a gift or blessing. In work, the fence is built and the book is written; in leisure, the fence is beheld as one feature of a landscape and the book is read, its ideas contemplated.

For late moderns, only work is valued, because it is widely believed that anything worthwhile is the result of effort. Leisure may be seen and subsequently condemned as akin to laziness. In response to this fear, leisure is reduced either to an alternative form of work (exerting physical or mental effort, spending long hours in the gym or at the painting easel) or to a strategy for improving productivity (downtime to recharge so that one can then get back to work more efficiently than ever). These so-called breaks from work, however, are not leisure but its denial. As Josef Pieper has observed, a "break

---

1. Heintzman, *Leisure and Spirituality*, chap. 1.

in one's work, whether of an hour, a day, or a week, is still part of the world of work."[2] Leisure, rest itself, is corrupted into one more activity.

Genuine leisure "is a receptive attitude of mind, a contemplative attitude, and it is not only the occasion but also the capacity for steeping oneself in the whole of creation."[3] Furthermore, "Leisure is not the attitude of mind of those who actively intervene, but of those who are open to everything; not of those who grab and grab hold, but of those who leave the reins loose and who are free and easy themselves—almost like a man falling asleep, for one can only fall asleep by 'letting oneself go.'"[4] The point of leisure is to be enmeshed in reality as a whole, and it is in this receptive mode that we are most fully free, free from the tyranny of always having to act, to produce, to make something, anything. Humans are at leisure when they are at one with themselves. Far from idleness, leisure is the affirmation of their being and consenting to their status as finite creatures. Hence the necessity of ordering our desires, our loves, accordingly. It is in this ordering that the capacity for flourishing is opened and prioritized. We learn, for example, that grace teaches us that what is most important is received, not taken or earned. We can neither demand nor earn God's grace, God's blessing.

Since a blessing can only be given and received, celebration is the foundation of leisure. Celebrating is not working, for it expresses joy and gratitude for that which is received; the grace of benefaction encompassing giver and recipient. Worship, then, is the proper basis of celebration, because it has no utility and is an end in itself. We worship God because we are commanded to do so, and for no other reason. It is this end devoid of utility that gives meaning and direction to all prior activity. The active mode of life finds its completion in its receptive counterpart; six days of labor end in Sabbath rest. In this Sabbath, this rest, we worship, receiving the fruits of our prior labor. Without leisure, work becomes an idolatrous and dehumanizing routine of pointless effort. Without "real leisure," work is reduced to "naked toil and effort without hope."[5]

The relation between work and leisure is similar to that between exchange and communication—namely, it is one of support. Work makes leisure possible in much the same way that exchange makes communication possible. Consequently, exchange and work are aids to human flourishing, but not the modes of being in which humans flourish. Attending to material wellbeing through exchange and work is a crucial prerequisite of human flourishing,

2. Pieper, *Leisure the Basis of Culture*, 49.
3. Pieper, *Leisure the Basis of Culture*, 46–47.
4. Pieper, *Leisure the Basis of Culture*, 47.
5. Pieper, *Leisure the Basis of Culture*, 69.

but it is through communication and leisure that the end of flourishing as embodied souls and ensouled bodies is achieved. In short, we flourish in leisurely communicating the goods of a created order being drawn to its destiny in its creator and redeemer. The important role leisure plays in human flourishing can be seen by looking briefly at how work and play, and time and flourishing, are (or should be) related.

Work and Play

In chapter 11, I argued that work is the most common human activity. We work to get things done, to make things to sell, to earn a wage in order to buy things. Work is simply a necessary activity for embodied creatures, for it is through work that physical and material needs are met. The ways of meeting and reacting to this necessity are multifaceted. Work can be interesting and rewarding or dull and uneventful, creative or monotonous. Our work may provide a captivating venue for expressing our identity or it may be an alienating action far removed from who we are. Work may bring us joy or make us sullen. There is the labor of our hands and also of our minds. We spend a lot of time working, and the hours may seem to rush by all too quickly or drag on endlessly.

Regardless of the work we do and our reactions to its necessity, it is principally through work that we fulfill our respective callings and vocations.[6] In pursuing our callings—and everyone has multiple callings—we help meet the needs of one another, needs that often prove extraordinarily mundane and ordinary. We pursue the vocations of janitor and banker, farmer and nurse, teacher and student; we are called to a career and to create jobs for others, to clothe the naked and feed the hungry, to care for our children and our aging parents. Moreover, our vocational work is not restricted to remunerated labor. There are the equally important callings of being a spouse, parent, friend, citizen, and Christian. Since humans interact with one another in differing ways and associations, their vocational work is almost always diverse rather than singular, and it changes over time. For example, how I am and what I do as a teacher, husband, and father have not remained the same over the nearly half century that I have been in these roles. Since we humans are social creatures, we cannot flourish, especially over time, from generation to generation, without striving to fulfill our multiple callings and vocations.

It is within this striving that the formative power of the commonplace exerts itself most prominently. It is through the routinized and repetitive

6. See chap. 2.

patterns of ordinary relationships[7] and mundane activities[8] that we form basic habits that shape our interactions with and treatment of one another. We learn, for example, to habitually treat people with courtesy and respect, or to treat them rudely and indifferently. These habits, in turn, predispose us toward more formal practices for good or ill, preparing us for virtuous or vicious lives.[9] People habitually unselfed are well on their way to becoming temperate, while—conversely—selfish habits are preparatory for the vices of gluttony and vainglory. Virtues are crucial in pursuing our callings and vocations, for it is through virtuous conduct that we serve and assist one another. Consequently, preparatory habits and dispositions are equally important. For instance, a person cannot be prudent—doing the right thing for the right reasons—if he or she knows nothing of or disregards the trust, mutuality, and reciprocity pervading everyday life.

The virtuous work associated with one's callings and vocations, then, is a significant way of exhibiting the love of God and neighbor in practical ways, for virtue directs or orders the work of our hands and minds toward our flourishing *and* that of our neighbors. The wellbeing of the self and the neighbor is ultimately the same. But something is missing from my description. What prevents work, even the most virtuous work, from becoming burdensome, even oppressive, both for the worker and for the beneficiary of the work performed? If our obedience to the commands to love God and neighbor are at stake, isn't our virtuous work a very serious affair? Since the consequences of our failed work are potentially dire, isn't our most important work, that of resolute duty, largely devoid of pleasure?

The short answer is no. Work is *so* important that it should not be taken with undue seriousness. If we are to pursue faithfully our callings and vocations to love God and our neighbors, then our work must be playful, otherwise it becomes ineffective, even idolatrous, claiming a consuming importance it does not deserve. What is playful work, and why should we work playfully? In answering, we must start by revisiting the themes of chapter 3. There I argued that, historically, play has been an antidote to acedia because it draws us out from ourselves. We play with others, which requires give-and-take, reciprocity. Play is often competitive, but so long as the overriding goal is not to win at all costs, competing enables social interaction and cooperation. Most importantly, play aligns our lives properly to what is serious. That which is most serious (God) should be responded to playfully. Johan Huizinga contends,

7. See part 2.
8. See part 3.
9. See chap. 3.

"Play is a thing by itself. The play-concept as such is of a higher order than is seriousness. For seriousness seeks to exclude play, whereas play can very well include seriousness."[10]

I want to expand on what I wrote previously by suggesting that play promotes human flourishing because it both disorients and reorients. This apparent paradox is grounded in the gospel. Per John Webster, "Christian faith, and therefore Christian theology, emerges out of the shock of the gospel." In Christ, "all things are faced by the one who absolutely dislocates and no less absolutely reorders." Christian testimony to this reality is simultaneously perplexing and delightful.[11] Play is a means of disorienting by dispelling the mistaken assumption that a serious challenge or circumstance requires of us a reaction in-kind. This is a deadly response for finite creatures to make because we lack the inherent or natural capacities to deal with the extent of the moment. In being playful, we reorient ourselves to these moments in ways more fitting to our limited, creaturely aptitudes.

Take, for example, the story of creation and fall in Genesis. Adam and Eve's initial relationship with the creator is one of perpetual Sabbath—a practice, as described above, that does not exclude play.[12] In consequence of their disobedience, this easy relationship is broken, and the rift is exacerbated by their serious but foolish attempts to defend their actions. It is only through grace that the relationship is repaired, and the reception of such an unmerited gift inspires celebration, which is itself a playful response of gratitude. The *telos* of redemption anticipates a fellowship that is more light and joyful than heavy and serious, more akin to a playground than a courthouse.

Huizinga credits play with being foundational to any civilization.[13] Play undergirds formative and explanatory myths that in turn inspire imaginative reactions. For "myth knows no distinction between play and seriousness."[14] Play, then, is present in religious and sacramental acts and rituals. Through play, we enter the realms of beauty and the sacred. "Play consecrated to the Deity, the highest goal of man's endeavour—such was Plato's conception of religion."[15] It is in and through the playful realm of religious endeavor that we find our freedom, a freedom that liberates us from the oppressive burden of a constant striving to be serious, which ends inevitably in a vain and vicious

10. See Huizinga, *Homo Ludens*, 45.

11. See Webster, *Culture of Theology*, 43.

12. There is also no reason to assume that God's "serious" acts of creation were not performed playfully.

13. See Huizinga, *Homo Ludens*, chap. 1.

14. Huizinga, *Homo Ludens*, 129.

15. Huizinga, *Homo Ludens*, 27.

desire for glory. For without play we come to see ourselves as idols to be served. Hence the angry and unforgiving demands for an ill-defined justice devoid of joy, grace, and mercy. In such a disenchanted world, all that is effectively left is the serious task of controlling and manipulating without any thought of rest.

To remain playful in such deadly circumstances is to also remain faithful to the gospel, to the Word made flesh. For in play we are receptive, we are at leisure to be enmeshed in the wholeness of God's good and redeemed creation. In such leisure, we are "seized by the revelation of fate."[16] In coming to know our fate as finite and mortal creatures, to know the necessities of material existence is to also know the good that is latent within but also transcends the necessary. In this respect, play is a bridge between work and leisure, a bridge between surviving and flourishing. But as creatures, our lives are lived in time. How do we flourish as temporal beings in a timely manner?

Time and Flourishing

Oddly, late moderns find time perplexing. They expend inordinate effort trying to control, manage, even buy additional time. These efforts invariably disappoint. Time is both friend and foe. It is within time that humans live, move, and have their being. Our flourishing is timely. But time also works against us. Over time our desires must either shrink or be frustrated. Eventually we will literally be out of time. Our floundering is also timely.

This late-modern perplexity with time is due, partly, to a latent conceit of the now. It is assumed that if we can domesticate the present, we simultaneously create the future and redeem the past. Like most conceits, this one proves delusional. Time is one aspect of created order that will always successfully resist human dominion. The future already exists in the resurrection of Jesus from the dead. We do not create the future but prepare ourselves for its embrace; we await the *parousia*. We do not redeem the past by imposing on it the judgment of the "superior" knowledge and wisdom of the present. The now does not save the past or save us from the past by simply putting its presumed "inferiority" on display. Contrary to the conceit of the now, the past and future are already given and present to us. If we believe that all is in Christ, then past and future are not ours to either create or redeem. Again, Webster: "Jesus the risen one is our contemporary. He is alive and ascended; he sits at the right hand of God in the glory of the Father; he shares in the eternity of God. His existence, therefore, is not circumscribed or exhausted by his earthly manifestations in the days of his flesh, for that manifestation

---

16. Huizinga, *Homo Ludens*, 16.

is the presence in time of what he eternally is. And so his historical existence is surrounded by his pre-existence and his post-existence."[17] What has been and what shall be are implanted in what is.

What does this have to do with human flourishing? In recognizing that time (all time—past, present, and future) is oriented toward its appointed end in Christ, we are free to be embraced by this destiny; we are at leisure, receptive. But such freedom does not liberate us from the necessities of creaturely existence in the meantime, of attending to the physical, material, and affiliative wellbeing of embodied, finite, and mortal beings. We must still work to make our lives in and through time.

This interplay among time, work, and flourishing is a central theme in Wallace Stegner's *Angle of Repose*. The story is about Lyman Ward, a retired historian who is confined to a wheelchair following the surgical removal of his leg. Lyman requires help to accomplish such basic tasks as bathing, getting in and out of bed, housework, and the like. He lives in an old family home where, as a child, he lived with his grandparents. The story is also about them. Lyman is writing a book about his grandparents. His grandfather, Oliver Ward, was a competent engineer, a man who got things done without the luxury of many words. His footprints in the genealogical records are neither plentiful nor deep. Susan Ward, Lyman's grandmother, was an accomplished illustrator and writer. Her books, articles, letters, and pictures are strewn everywhere throughout the Wards' chronicle. Yet the sheer volume does not provide clarity. Pronounced ambiguities remain. Susan was a refined Eastern lady of her time, never entirely comfortable living in the West. It is not clear whether she was happy, or even in love, with her inarticulate husband.

The story, then, is also about time—Lyman's present and the past of his grandparents. Past and present flow back and forth. Lyman's simultaneous acceptance of and frustration with this fluidity is palpable. He is not happy with the now of his life. After twenty-five years of an ultimately failed marriage, he still does not know his ex-wife, and a wide gulf separates him from his son. Lyman sides with his grandparents, who had to make peace with time. "I believe in Time, as they did, and in the life chronological rather than in the life existential. We live in time and through it, we build our huts in its ruins, or used to, and we cannot afford all these abandonings."[18] Since Lyman also believes he has no future, or—more accurately—no future he wishes to endorse, he will fixate on the past, particularly by retelling his grandmother's life.

17. Webster, *Culture of Theology*, 87.
18. Stegner, *Angle of Repose*, 6.

In his retelling, Susan is admirable. She is a talented woman who writes and draws prodigiously, a loving mother watching out for her children and providing them a large measure of stability (despite the frequent relocations endemic to the career of an engineer), and an excellent hostess with a keen ability to attract and put at ease interesting collections of dinner guests. But Lyman does not hide her warts. Her marriage with Oliver is troubled. She is impatient with his lack of ambition and reticence to be a self-promoter, and she resents his inability to secure a reliable income. She worries about money constantly. The two repeat cycles of separation and reunion, and on at least one occasion Susan is tempted to be unfaithful. Susan resents living in the West and often treats the locals with snobbish disdain. In Lyman's retelling, his grandmother is a complex person, a mixture of good and bad, a sinner like everyone else. Over time she bestows and receives moments of grace and mercy, she remains loyal to those whom she loves and who love her in return, despite how awkward and unexpected these moments prove to be. She makes herself a life in the ruins of time.

Making one's life in time, however, is a tangible undertaking, accomplished in particular places. One of Susan's most pronounced shortcomings is her tendency to belittle where she is because she is seldom where she wants to be. *Angle of Repose* is a story about the West, a place that Susan barely tolerates. "Susan Ward came West not to join a new society but to endure it, not to build anything but to enjoy a temporary experience and make it yield whatever instruction it contained."[19] She copes by pretending that wherever she might find herself in this wasteland, it will have no claim upon her. Susan "made not the slightest concession to the places where she lived."[20] In her letters "back home" to her friend, Susan recounts her stays in shabby mining villages, describing them in demeaning rhetorical flourishes. The one "city" the family resides in for a while is curtly dismissed as a ramshackle collection of boring buildings and dull residents—hardly resembling a metropolis. San Francisco is the only place of any minimal interest, and they cannot afford to live there. Susan complains frequently to her friend about her present plight, and longs for the day when Oliver has established himself in his career and they will return to the East. It is a forlorn hope that dissipates into bitter resignation. Susan is stuck, and there is little she can do about it.

Lyman's retelling, however, discloses his own discomfort with time and place. He is no late modern. The problem is not the past's inferiority but its superiority. The present cannot redeem the past or even improve upon it.

19. Stegner, *Angle of Repose*, 77.
20. Stegner, *Angle of Repose*, 98.

The problem at hand is the current refusal to admit and draw upon ancestral wisdom as a source of strength and guidance. Lyman's son, Rodman, exemplifies the problem: "Rodman, like most sociologists and most of his generation, was born without the sense of history. To him it is only an aborted social science. The world has changed, Pop, he tells me. The past isn't going to teach us anything about what we've got ahead of us. Maybe it did once, or seemed to. It doesn't any more."[21] Lyman is living out his days in an era that has literally become displaced. His world is populated by inhabitants, especially the young, who have no idea where they have been or where they are headed, no trajectory or destiny, no tradition or eschatology. They have come from no place and there is nowhere to go, so they wander from moment to moment, trapped in the stultifying confines of the immediate. Lyman worries that being perpetually frozen in this immediacy will exact a heavy toll. "I wonder if ever again Americans can have that experience of returning to a home place so intimately known, profoundly felt, deeply loved, and absolutely submitted to? It is not quite true that you can't go home again. I have done it, coming back here. But it gets less likely. We have too many divorces, we have consumed too much transportation, we have lived too shallowly in too many places."[22]

The contemporary circumstances in which Lyman is stuck offer no charm and promise. Since there is effectively no past, there is no wisdom to help guide; and since there is effectively no future to anticipate, there is no hope that sustains. Unfortunately, Lyman is not the detached observer immune from the despair he describes. He remains uncertain whether he can escape the dispiriting consequences of an unwanted world that disparages time and place. He begins to question the real source of his own despondency. Why, for instance, is Lyman taking so much time to write about his grandparents? "Is it love and sympathy that makes me think myself capable of reconstructing these lives, or am I, Nemesis in a wheelchair, bent on proving something— perhaps that not even gentility and integrity are proof against the corrosions of human weakness, human treachery, human disappointment, human inability to forget?"[23] The questions are not rhetorical. They reveal that Lyman too is a man of his age, cut off from time and place. That in hiding away in an ancestral home and fixating on his grandmother, he too is biding his time, suspended in a familiar space until time runs out. And that time is expiring rapidly. "No life goes past so swiftly as an eventless one, no clock spins like

21. Stegner, *Angle of Repose*, 4.
22. Stegner, *Angle of Repose*, 303.
23. Stegner, *Angle of Repose*, 486.

a clock whose days are all alike. It is a law I take advantage of, and bless, but then I am not young, ambitious, and balked."[24]

Lyman's self-doubts cloud his perception. He is seemingly unable to see his dependence on others in any favorable light. Ada, his housekeeper of many years, faithfully cooks and cleans for him and comforts him without complaint. Her daughter, Shelly, is Lyman's competent secretary who treats her grumpy boss with good humor. Yet Lyman perceives these actions as reminders of his disability, his loss of independence that he resents. He cannot bring himself to acknowledge these "gifts" of kindness that tie people together in bonds of giving and receiving care. Nowhere in the story does Lyman offer any hint of gratitude for what others do on his behalf.

His self-doubts cloud his moral judgment as well. Ellen, his ex-wife, wants to see him. He is not disposed to grant her request. Too many bad memories. Ellen had no interest in being a professor's wife, even though his work provided them a comfortable living—or so he assumed. Shortly after Lyman's leg was amputated, Ellen left him for his surgeon. One evening her new flame disappeared while taking a walk. Months later his bones were found at the bottom of a ravine. Ellen has moved nearby to try to patch things up with Lyman. He is not inclined to forgive her. "I am a justice man, not a mercy man."[25] Yet he wonders what motivated her to abandon him. "Does a woman ever leave a man out of intolerable pity? Or because she fears what pity may do to her and him?"[26] Nonetheless, Ellen left him when he was helpless. She has earned his contempt.

But his contempt, his resolve to not forgive, is uncertain. Lyman and Ellen eventually meet at his house. He wants to show her that she is the one who is now helpless because she presumably needs him. While walking in the backyard, Lyman babbles on about his grandfather planting and tending the rose garden. As they talk, it emerges that when Lyman was a boy living with his grandparents, Oliver had spoken far more to his grandson than he ever did to Susan. Why? Lyman explains it to Ellen: "Because my grandfather was a man who couldn't forget. . . . Forget or forgive." Ellen assumes he was a "hard man."[27] Lyman insists that, to the contrary, his grandfather was soft, vulnerable, easily imposed upon by others. Consequently, he didn't expect much of people and rarely trusted anyone. Except for Susan, for a time. Lyman recounts the many sins Susan committed against Oliver, against the marriage, against their family, sins that destroyed the trust of her husband. These transgressions

24. Stegner, *Angle of Repose*, 438.
25. Stegner, *Angle of Repose*, 490.
26. Stegner, *Angle of Repose*, 491.
27. Stegner, *Angle of Repose*, 615.

effectively ended the marriage in 1890, but his grandparents stayed together for fifty more years—a half-century through which Susan endured a living death. Lyman loved his grandmother because she admitted her mistakes, repented, and put things right. She only came to appreciate her husband after it was too late. Lyman explains to Ellen, "But he never forgave her. . . . She broke something she couldn't mend. In all the years I lived with them I never saw them kiss, I never saw them put their arms around each other, I never saw them touch!"[28]

Lyman seems to be reliving his grandparents' marriage. Will he forgive Ellen? Will he find the spiritual strength and moral courage to prevent repeating another living death? The story ends with Lyman's haunting confession, "I lie wondering if I am man enough to be a bigger man than my grandfather."[29]

Stegner does not hint how Lyman answers his own question, and I have no desire to speculate. But I do submit that an affirmative answer would stem from a receptive mode of being. My submission seemingly defies common sense, since Lyman must actively choose to be a bigger man than his grandfather, so I must explain. Forgiveness occurs when we are at rest. Grace is the foundation of forgiveness, otherwise the spiral of vengeance cannot be broken. And that is what makes forgiving simultaneously wondrous and vexing. Vengeance is a logical response to being wronged—like for like—and is just when a wrong is righted. Forgiveness is unmerited, even gratuitous at times, because it is graceful, defying the law of like for like. It is loving rather than hating one's enemy. Forgiveness, then, is more akin to a gift given and received than a work constructed and earned. Forgiveness and its underlying grace is given and received when at leisure. Lyman must first be the recipient of grace before he can forgive Ellen.

Again, Stegner offers no clue about whether Lyman has the capacity to enter into rest, to be at leisure. It is an important question that is left unanswered. It is hard, perhaps impossible, to imagine how humans could flourish in the absence of grace and forgiveness. As social creatures and as sinners they would perpetually fail, betray, and hurt one another, building layers of distrust and countless plans of vengeance. And yet we don't, at least not always. Our daily lives are pervaded by a grace that is subtle and difficult to recognize unless you know where to look. Again, I submit (and, again, cautiously) that the most prevalent signs of this grace are found in the ordinary care we extend to and receive from one another.

Lyman should know this, but he doesn't. He is in this respect a poor narrator of his grandparents' story and his own. They are stories littered with

28. Stegner, *Angle of Repose*, 626.
29. Stegner, *Angle of Repose*, 632.

moments of grace that he fails to recognize because the practical, common-place acts of caring only serve to remind him of his diminished autonomy rather than serving as opportunities for expressing gratitude. In failing to be receptive, to be at leisure, Lyman's narrations are largely devoid of grace and thereby incomplete. If humans are to flourish, they must care for the ordinary as timely and elemental disclosures of grace. This is properly their angle of repose.

Time to tie a few loose ends together. I hope, dear reader, that you have taken away from your reading (for which I am most grateful) a better understanding of three sets of relationships. The first is that of work and leisure. Work is necessary, but we flourish when at leisure. That is not to denigrate work. Work is *required* to meet our needs as finite and temporal creatures, and if those needs are not met, we do not have time for leisure. But the priority must be maintained: work is a means for being at leisure. For us to flourish, the active mode of our being must give way to the receptive, day in and day out.

The second relationship is that between creation and Sabbath. Creation is a divine work that can be emulated but never replicated through human labor. We build a world as our suitable habitat. These creative efforts are responses to our callings and vocations as stewards of God's good creation. Many, perhaps most, of these efforts are common and mundane, but vital. We cannot flourish by ignoring the details of everyday life. Again, a proper priority must be maintained. Our callings and vocations are not ends in themselves but means: means of entering into Sabbath rest. Ours is a life of pilgrimage, tending lovingly to the places where we happen to be, but our destination, our destiny, is the eighth day of creation—eternal fellowship with our redeemer Lord.

The final relationship is between the extraordinary and ordinary. This is a vital relationship that needs to be salvaged. We live in an era in which the extraordinary has been cheapened into a tawdry simulacrum. Effectively proclaiming that everyone and everything they do is amazing is simply a polite way of saying that excellence, in its pluriform expressions, is to be despised. It is, effectively, to enshrine self-expression as the supreme expression of being human. This is, of course, banal pretense. At best, the resulting culture is one of mediocrity posing as accomplishment. At worst, it belittles those who, in being genuinely extraordinary, expose the ordinary as such. The truly extraordinary—such as creation, incarnation, and resurrection—need not be repeated and should not be diminished to a level that can be replicated as a cheap facsimile. As finite and mortal creatures, we best honor, serve, and utilize the extraordinary by concentrating on and caring for the mundane and commonplace. We flourish by caring for one another in the ordinary times and places of our creaturely existence. The task at hand is to be faithful pilgrims rather than to flatter ourselves as mediocre creators of our lives and fate.

Admittedly, the preceding paragraph was incendiary. It was meant to be, and explaining my intention requires a few more words. Turn the page, and I shall explain.

On the Good of Being Boring

Many of the earth's inhabitants live in late-modern cultures, or in cultures that have been at least significantly influenced by late modernism. We are fabricating a world saturated with excitement and pleasure, an endless array of experiential possibilities—a world congenial to a synthetic culture that is everywhere and nowhere in particular. Hence we imagine we are at liberty to make and remake ourselves at will, residual products of whatever ephemeral passions claim our attention. And we are constantly reassured through various media that our efforts will undoubtedly express our innate creativity, a creativity that is simultaneously existential and entertaining. We live in a culture in which everyone is or can be extraordinary. That, at least, is the spin.

This is not a good place to be, for it is actually a culture pervaded by cheap and banal amusements. The purportedly extraordinary residents of this culture resemble poorly made sequels to originals that few recall. Even the creativity that is championed as the principal liberative tool is reduced to a method for passing time, time passed in busywork and entertainment. Passing time by momentarily doing this and then that for a variety of trivial reasons effectively evades time for any real leisure. It is imperative to avoid leisure, for being in the receptive mode would belie the rationale of mastery and control that we use to make ourselves seem extraordinary. Our workmanship, however, is often shoddy.

Many residents grow uneasy, even belligerent, because despite their best creative efforts they remain unsatisfied and unhappy for reasons that evade their understanding. It is a culture of a pervading "sullenness that is both passive and aggressive, both indolent and resentful."[1] Rather than being at liberty, we—or, more accurately, many of us—are captive to the methods of self-expression that help ease the loss of time passing by. Consequently, late moderns tend to be ungrateful, for there is little to offer thanks for when leisurely receptivity is corrupted into an entitlement to be entertained or otherwise distracted on demand. This ingratitude helps form a culture that, despite its cheerful rhetoric, is tedious, humorless, devoid of playfulness, and deadly serious. For all the emphasis on the extraordinary and unique, we—at least some of us—have become adept at producing and consuming mediocre goods and services that make the time passing by less noticeable, more tolerable.

The good of being boring is an antidote to this corrosive sullenness. To be clear, being boring is *not* the same thing as being bored. To be bored admits a condition in which one is nearly debilitated by a prolonged lack of interest. The source of boredom may be uninteresting external stimuli, such as people or objects, which fail to capture attention. Or boredom may be a result of one's impatience or limited imaginative skills. In either case, boredom is not good because it negates both active and receptive modes of being that underlie human flourishing. Additionally, the good of being boring is *not* the same as being a bore. We have all encountered bores, individuals who impose themselves on others, dominating conversation or any other activity they choose to invade. They appear oblivious to anything or anyone beyond themselves. Nothing other than an inert audience and stage is of any interest. Bores diminish human flourishing by effectively ignoring the social nature of being human; they can do without alterity and reciprocity.

Being boring is good because it encapsulates the ability to be focused. The boring person stays with a task for as long as needed, regardless of how menial it might be, and can easily be at leisure when work reaches its end. The ideally boring person is attentive to others, attempting to discern their needs. Unlike the bored and bores, boring people know that their flourishing depends on their receptivity to the giftedness of life and on communicating this gift with others. Counterintuitively, it is boring people who are able to play, for they take delight and flourish in their mutuality with other human creatures, a serious state requiring their playful response. The faithful player remains focused on the other players, the game, the particular set of circumstances at hand.

The good of being boring is predominantly a matter of character. As I have mentioned throughout the preceding pages, character is formed through certain habits and virtues. To the reader's relief, I will not rehearse what I

---

1. Borgmann, *Crossing the Postmodern Divide*, 6–7; see also pp. 6–12.

have written but will instead highlight two features of being boring. The first is *loyalty*. To be attentive to the needs of the neighbor, to be focused on his or her good, is to also be loyal to the neighbor. Such loyalty, however, is not general or abstract but particular and concrete, and fitting to the relationship at hand. As part 2 (on everyday relationships) demonstrated, we encounter a wide range of neighbors who require an equally wide range of differing responses on our part. We do not interact with spouses in the same way we do with strangers, friends, or fellow citizens. Each of our callings requires requisite sets of vocational skills and virtues. And rightfully so, for we are loyal to particular people in particular ways. Minding particular people in particular ways, however, also aligns us within a common universality. In being attentive to this specific person we are bound together in a web of love with God and neighbor, the same love that is the origin and end of created order. Being loyal to neighbors, seeking their good, is, as previous chapters have exhibited, a complex undertaking, fraught with perplexing challenges and efforts. Yet regardless how imperfectly our loyalties are ordered and practiced, they nonetheless express a fundamental loyalty to love—God's foremost command to the creatures created in the divine image and likeness.[2]

The second feature is *tending*; taking care of one another. Humans, to repeat one more time, are social creatures. They cannot survive, much less flourish, without intricate networks of mutually beneficial relationships and actions. Most of these activities, as demonstrated in the chapters of part 3, are mundane and taken for granted: boring tasks and chores that almost never excite. Yet they are necessary, for when the ordinary is ignored human life becomes squalid, a breeding ground for the sullenness described above. Boring tasks and chores are best undertaken by people pursuing the good of being boring—people who know, often tacitly, the importance of such simple acts as cleaning, repairing, shopping, cooking, and on and on. This knowledge, in turn, is habituated into behaviors that are far from extraordinary but absolutely crucial if humans are to communicate and thereby flourish. This routine tending to each other's needs is almost never acknowledged, or even recognized. Yet to tend is at the heart of our overlapping callings and vocations. Pursuing them may provide some intangible emotional or spiritual benefit, but no calling or vocation can be practiced by ignoring the physical and material needs of embodied creatures. Undertaking the mundane acts that tend to these needs is loving one's neighbor, an extraordinary end accomplished through ordinary means.

---

2. For an extensive inquiry into the concept and ethics of loyalty, see Royce, *Philosophy of Loyalty*. See also Niebuhr, *Radical Monotheism*, 16–23.

In short, the good of being boring is synonymous with being steadfast. To be steadfast is to be resolute, dutiful. Being steadfast is manifested in our resolute loyalty to others with whom we are bound in our everyday relationships, and dutifully tending to their ordinary needs. Becoming steadfast is an exercise in unselfing. Unselfing is crucial to the Christian life, for it is only in becoming unselfed that we develop a capacity for genuine neighbor love. Becoming unselfed, however, does not mean misplacing oneself. Quite the contrary. One derived benefit of putting the "fat relentless ego"[3] on a diet is that we become more receptive to the gift of freedom. Remember, freedom requires a series of negations and affirmations. We must say no to this in order to say yes to that. Through these negations and affirmations—often in explicit or implicit response to our multiple callings—we focus our loyalty to the particular people with whom we are related through both choice and accident. We choose and are chosen by, for instance, our friends, but not our fellow citizens. In refining these loyalties, we also hone the skills for tending to their needs in fitting ways. What a friend needs from us is not identical with what anonymous citizens require. In becoming unselfed we are free to be fittingly loyal to our neighbors.

This freedom, however, is not a work we can create or earn. We receive it leisurely as a gift, and its reception prompts, or should prompt, a response of gratitude. We are grateful to be liberated from the tyranny of the fat relentless ego and hence free to be loyal to neighbors we are called and commanded to love. If gratitude is absent or is reduced to decorous display, we fail to recognize the gifted qualities of life, the unearned and unexpected gifts of grace and mercy. An orientation of gratitude withers, displaced by an egotistical expectation of entitlement. This displacement eats away at the prospect of human flourishing. Ungrateful people are fundamentally incapacitated from communicating with one another because playfulness is corrupted into sullenness. In short, it is as grateful and communicative people that humans flourish.

The good of being boring is at the core of Christian faith and practice. To be boring is to be unselfed—which is the basis for learning and habituating freedom and gratitude, for loyalty and tending to one's neighbors, for loving God and neighbor. We orient ourselves to receiving the gospel as gift, albeit with plenty of divine strings attached. Consequently, the good of being boring reminds us that the gospel, God's grace and mercy, is obtained only in the receptive mode. The origin and end of the Christian life is one of leisure. Ministry, service, and witness are not works, artifacts of our creative efforts, but free and grateful responses to what God gives us. Most often those

3. Murdoch, *Sovereignty of Good*, 51.

responses are manifested in the common relationships and mundane activities of everyday life. These are concrete ways of obeying the two great commandments. In communicating this love, we gain a glimpse of our destiny. Our end is identical with our beginning: God's gratuitous love. The love awaiting us is in part familiar, affirming our dependence on one another. Consequently, the love infused throughout the gospel is no abstraction but is tangibly known in how we treat one another, by what we do for one another. Charity is a focused love of the world—one that attends to its inhabitants.

This focus has important implications for the Christian moral life. In respect to the central virtues of faith, hope, and love, love is the greatest (1 Cor. 13:13). But that status does not denigrate faith and hope. To the contrary, they are inseparable and indispensable to any moral endeavor seeking to be faithful to created order and expressing hope in its eschatological end. The virtues of faith, hope, and love demarcate the parameters within which moral recognition, discernment, and action take place, emphasizing the purpose or end for which humans are created. "Human beings are created to act and to rest," and "love's rest is predicated on active faith and hope." More graphically, "faith and hope may be thought of as the two hands of love, giving it an enacted concrete presence."[4] Even acts of judgment—moral, judicial, and political—necessitating coercive responses, such as imprisonment or war, are acts of faith, hope, and love so long as their purpose is to protect and support the communicative associations that compose civil society.

Details matter. They matter for life in general and for the moral life in particular. Minding details is not inherently interesting, much less exciting. It requires focused, unselfed, loving attention, often to little things easily overlooked, day in and day out. The individuals who are best at minding the details have habituated the good of being boring through a steadfast and tenacious love of neighbors—embodied, finite, and needy neighbors. It is love expressed by tending faithfully and hopefully to the mundane details of daily living. It is through the multiplicity of our common callings and ordinary virtues that we freely and gratefully receive and communicate the gift of flourishing.

4. O'Donovan, *Entering into Rest*, 6.

Bibliography

Althusius, Johannes. *Politica*. Edited and translated by Frederick S. Carney. Indianapolis: Liberty Fund, 1995.

Antonaccio, Maria. *A Philosophy to Live By: Engaging Iris Murdoch*. Oxford: Oxford University Press, 2012.

Arendt, Hannah. *The Human Condition*. Chicago: University of Chicago Press, 1998.

———. *The Life of the Mind*. San Diego: Harcourt, 1978.

———. *The Origins of Totalitarianism*. San Diego: Harvest Book, 1968.

———. *The Promise of Politics*. New York: Shocken Books, 2005.

Aquinas, Thomas. *Summa Theologica*. Translated by Fathers of the English Dominican Province. New York: Benziger Bros., 1947.

Aristotle. *Nicomachean Ethics*. Translated by W. D. Ross. The Internet Classics Archive. http://classics.mit.edu/Aristotle/nicomachaen.mb.txt.

———. *Politics: A Treatise on Government*. London: J. M. Dent and Sons, 1912. Kindle Edition.

Auden, W. H. *The Complete Works of W. H. Auden: Prose*. Vol. 2, *1939–1948*, edited by Edward Mendelson. Princeton: Princeton University Press, 2002.

Augustine of Hippo. *The City of God against the Pagans*.

———. *Confessions*.

———. *Of Holy Virginity*.

———. *On Lying*.

———. *On Marriage and Concupiscence*.

———. *On the Good of Marriage*.

———. *On the Holy Trinity*.

———. *On the Morals of the Catholic Church*.

Baillie, D. M. *God Was in Christ: An Essay on Incarnation and Atonement.* New York: Scribner's Sons, 1948.

Banner, Michael. *The Ethics of Everyday Life.* Oxford: Oxford University Press, 2014.

Banville, John. *The Sea.* New York: Knopf, 2005.

Barbery, Muriel. *Gourmet Rhapsody.* New York: Europa Editions, 2009.

Bari, Shahidha. *Dressed: A Philosophy of Clothes.* New York: Basic Books, 2020.

Barth, Karl. *Church Dogmatics.* Translated by Geoffrey Bromiley. Edited by T. F. Torrance. Vols. I–IV, in 13 parts. Edinburgh: T&T Clark, 1956–69.

Baxter, Richard. *A Christian Directory: Part II. Christian Economics, or Family Duties.* Vol. 4 of *The Practical Works of the Rev. Richard Baxter.* London: James Duncan, 1830.

Benne, Robert. *Ordinary Saints: An Introduction to the Christian Life.* Minneapolis: Fortress, 2003.

Bonhoeffer, Dietrich. *Ethics.* London: SCM, 1955.

Borgmann, Albert. *Crossing the Postmodern Divide.* Chicago: University of Chicago Press, 1992.

———. *Power Failure: Christianity in the Culture of Technology.* Grand Rapids: Brazos, 2003.

———. "Reply to My Critics." In *Technology and the Good Life?*, edited by Eric Higgs, Andrew Light, and David Strong, 341–70. Chicago: University of Chicago Press, 2000.

———. *Technology and the Character of Contemporary Life: A Philosophical Inquiry.* Chicago: University of Chicago Press, 1984.

Bowen-Moore, Patricia. *Hannah Arendt's Philosophy of Natality.* London: Macmillan, 1989.

Brockett, L. P. *Our Great Captains: Grant, Sherman, Thomas, Sheridan, and Farragut.* New York: Charles B. Richardson, 1866.

Brown, Peter. *The Body and Society: Men, Women, and Sexual Renunciation in Early Christianity.* New York: Columbia University Press, 1988.

———. *Through the Eye of a Needle: Wealth, the Fall of Rome, and the Making of Christianity in the West, 350–550 AD.* Princeton: Princeton University Press, 2012.

Browning, Don S. *Equality and the Family: A Fundamental, Practical Theology of Children, Mothers, and Fathers in Modern Societies.* Grand Rapids: Eerdmans, 2007.

Browning, Don S., et al. *From Culture Wars to Common Ground: Religion and the American Family Debate.* Louisville: Westminster John Knox, 1997.

Brunner, Emil. *The Divine Imperative: A Study in Christian Ethics.* London: Lutterworth, 1937.

Buckley, F. H. *The Morality of Laughter.* Ann Arbor, MI: University of Michigan Press, 2003.

Carnevali, Barbara. *Social Appearances: A Philosophy of Display and Prestige*. New York: Columbia University Press, 2020.

Carpenter, Humphrey. *The Inklings: C. S. Lewis, J. R. R. Tolkien, Charles Williams, and Their Friends*. Boston: Houghton Mifflin, 1979.

Carr, Nicholas. *The Shallows: What the Internet Is Doing to Our Brains*. New York: Norton, 2010.

Casey, Edward S. *Getting Back into Place: Toward a Renewed Understanding of the Place-World*. 2nd ed. Bloomington, IN: Indiana University Press, 2009.

Charry, Ellen T. *God and the Art of Happiness*. Grand Rapids: Eerdmans, 2010.

Clement of Alexandria. *The Tutor*. In *Complete Works of Clement of Alexandria*. Hastings, UK: Delphi Classics, 2016.

Cochran, Elizabeth Agnew. *Receptive Human Virtues: A New Reading of Jonathan Edwards's Ethics*. University Park, PA: Pennsylvania State University Press, 2011.

DeYoung, Rebecca Konyndyk. *Glittering Vices: A New Look at the Seven Deadly Sins and Their Remedies*. Grand Rapids: Brazos, 2009.

———. *Vainglory: The Forgotten Vice*. Grand Rapids: Eerdmans, 2014.

Dipple, Elizabeth. *Iris Murdoch: Work for the Spirit*. Chicago: University of Chicago Press, 1982.

Dunn, James. "The Household Rules in the New Testament." In *The Family in Theological Perspective*, edited by Stephen C. Barton. Edinburgh: T&T Clark, 1996.

———. *The Theology of Paul the Apostle*. Grand Rapids: Eerdmans, 1998.

Duriez, Colin. *Tolkien and C. S. Lewis: The Gift of Friendship*. Mahwah, NJ: HiddenSpring, 2003.

Edwards, Jonathan. *A Dissertation Concerning the Nature of True Virtue*. rev. ed. Edited by Henry Rogers and Edward Hickman. Kindle Edition, 2011.

———. *A Dissertation on the End for Which God Created the World*.

Ellul, Jacques. *A Critique of the New Commonplaces*. New York: Knopf, 1968.

———. *The Humiliation of the Word*. Grand Rapids: Eerdmans, 1985.

Elshtain, Jean Bethke. *Augustine and the Limits of Politics*. Notre Dame, IN: University of Notre Dame Press, 1995.

———. *Public Man, Private Woman: Women in Social and Political Thought*. Princeton: Princeton University Press, 1981.

Endicott, Marina. *Good to a Fault*. New York: HarperCollins e-books, 2010.

Farrow, Douglas. *Ascension and Ecclesia: On the Significance of the Doctrine of the Ascension for Ecclesiology and Christian Cosmology*. Grand Rapids: Eerdmans, 1999.

Ferguson, Niall. *The Great Degeneration: How Institutions Decay and Economies Die*. New York: Penguin Books, 2013.

Fisher, David. *Morality and War: Can War Be Just in the Twenty-First Century?* Oxford: Oxford University Press, 2011.

Fukuyama, Francis. *Trust: The Social Virtues and the Creation of Prosperity*. New York: Free Press, 1995.

Gessen, Keith. *All the Sad Young Literary Men*. New York: Viking, 2008.

Gordon, David J. *Iris Murdoch's Fables of Unselfing*. Columbia, MO: University of Missouri Press, 1995.

Grant, George. *Lament for a Nation: The Defeat of Canadian Nationalism*. Montreal: McGill-Queen's University Press, 2000.

———. *Philosophy in the Mass Age*. Toronto: University of Toronto Press, 1995.

———. *Time as History*. Toronto: University of Toronto Press, 1995.

Gregory, Eric. *Politics and the Order of Love: An Augustinian Ethic of Democratic Citizenship*. Chicago: University of Chicago Press, 2008.

Griffiths, Paul J. *Lying: An Augustinian Theology of Duplicity*. Grand Rapids: Brazos, 2004.

Gustafson, James M. *Ethics from a Theocentric Perspective*. Vol. 2, *Ethics and Theology*. Chicago: University of Chicago Press, 1984.

Hauerwas, Stanley. *A Community of Character: Toward a Constructive Christian Social Ethic*. London: University of Notre Dame Press, 1981.

Heintzman, Paul. *Leisure and Spirituality: Biblical, Historical, and Contemporary Perspectives*. Grand Rapids: Baker Academic, 2015.

Herdt, Jennifer A. *Putting On Virtue: The Legacy of Splendid Vices*. Chicago: University of Chicago Press, 2008.

Hobbes, Thomas. *Leviathan*. Oxford and New York: Oxford University Press, 1996.

Hogue, David A. *Remembering the Future, Imagining the Past: Story, Ritual, and the Human Brain*. Cleveland: Pilgrim, 2003.

Houston, Mary G. *Ancient Greek, Roman and Byzantine Costume*. Mineola, NY: Dover, 2003.

Huizinga, Johan. *Homo Ludens: A Study of the Play-Element in Culture*. Kettering, OH: Angelico, 2016.

Ishiguro, Kazuo. *The Remains of the Day*. New York: Vintage, 1989.

Jackson, Maggie. *Distracted: The Erosion of Attention and the Coming Dark Age*. Amherst, NY: Prometheus Books, 2008.

James, William. *The Varieties of Religious Experience: A Study in Human Nature*.

John of Salisbury. *Policraticus: Of the Frivolities of Courtiers and the Footprints of Philosophers*. Cambridge: Cambridge University Press, 1990.

Jones, Beth Felker. *Marks of His Wounds: Gender Politics and Bodily Resurrection*. Oxford: Oxford University Press, 2007.

Jones, Idwal. *Chef's Holiday*. New York: Longmans, Green, 1952.

———. *High Bonnet: A Novel of Epicurean Adventures*. New York: Modern Library, 2001.

———. *The Vineyard*. Berkeley: University of California Press, 1997.

Kierkegaard, Søren. *Works of Love*. Princeton: Princeton University Press, 1995.

LaCugna, Catherine Mowry. *God for Us: The Trinity and Christian Life*. New York: HarperCollins, 1991.

Lasch, Christopher. *The Culture of Narcissism: American Life in an Age of Diminishing Expectations*. New York: Norton, 1978.

———. *Haven in a Heartless World: The Family Besieged*. New York: Norton, 1995.

Lewis, C. S. *The Four Loves*. New York: Harcourt, Brace, 1988.

———. *The Great Divorce*. New York: HarperCollins e-books, 2009.

———. *The Problem of Pain*. New York: HarperCollins e-books, 2009.

———. *The Screwtape Letters*. New York: Macmillan, 1961.

———. *Studies in Words*. New York: HarperCollins e-books, 2013.

———. *They Asked for a Paper: Papers and Addresses*. London: Geoffrey Bles, 1962.

———. *The Weight of Glory: And Other Addresses*. HarperCollins e-books, 2019.

Livy. *History of Rome*.

Luther, Martin. *The Freedom of a Christian*. In *Luther's Works*. Vol. 31, *Career of the Reformer I*, edited by Harold J. Grimm and Helmut T. Lehmann. Philadelphia: Fortress, 1957.

———. *The Judgment of Martin Luther on Monastic Vows*. In *Luther's Works*. Vol. 44, *The Christian in Society I*, edited by James Atkinson and Helmut T. Lehmann. Philadelphia: Fortress, 1966.

MacIntyre, Alasdair. *After Virtue: A Study in Moral Theory*. 2nd ed. London: Duckworth, 1985.

Markus, Robert. *The End of Ancient Christianity*. Cambridge: Cambridge University Press, 1990.

Martin, Judith. *Miss Manners: A Citizen's Guide to Civility*. New York: Three River, 1999.

———. *Miss Manners' Guide to Excruciatingly Correct Behavior*. New York: Norton, 2005.

McCarthy, David Matzko. *Sex and Love in the Home: A Theology of the Household*. London: SCM, 2001.

McNamara, Marie Aquinas. *Friendship in Saint Augustine*. Fribourg, Switzerland: University Press, 1958.

Meilaender, Gilbert C. *Faith and Faithfulness: Basic Themes in Christian Ethics*. Notre Dame, IN: University of Notre Dame Press, 1991.

———. *Friendship: A Study in Theological Ethics*. Notre Dame, IN: University of Notre Dame Press, 1985.

———. *The Limits of Love: Some Theological Explorations*. University Park, PA: Pennsylvania State University Press, 1987.

————. *The Theory and Practice of Virtue*. Notre Dame, IN: University of Notre Dame Press, 1984.

Moltmann, Jurgen. *The Crucified God: The Cross of Christ as the Foundation and Criticism of Christian Theology*. New York: Harper & Row, 1974.

————. *The Trinity and the Kingdom: The Doctrine of God*. Minneapolis: Fortress, 1993.

Moore, Max, and Natasha Vita-More, eds. *The Transhumanist Reader: Classical and Contemporary Essays on the Science, Technology, and Philosophy of the Human Future*. Malden, MA: Wiley, 2013.

Morgan, Edmund S. *The Puritan Family: Religion and Domestic Relations in Seventeenth-Century New England*. New York: Harper & Row, 1966.

Murdoch, Iris. "Against Dryness." *Encounter* 16 (1961).

————. "Ethics and the Imagination." *Irish Theological Quarterly* 52, nos. 1–2 (1986): 81–95.

————. *The Fire and the Sun: Why Plato Banished the Artists*. New York: Viking, 1977.

————. *Metaphysics as a Guide to Morals*. London: Penguin Books, 1993.

————. *The Nice and the Good*. New York: Penguin Books, 1978.

————. *The Sea, the Sea*. London: Penguin Books, 1978.

————. *The Sovereignty of Good*. London: Routledge & Kegan Paul, 2001.

Nelson, James B. *Embodiment: An Approach to Sexuality and Christian Theology*. Minneapolis: Augsburg, 1978.

Niebuhr, H. Richard. *Radical Monotheism and Western Culture*. Louisville: Westminster John Knox, 1993.

————. *The Responsible Self: An Essay in Christian Moral Philosophy*. Louisville: Westminster John Knox, 1999.

Nietzsche, Friedrich. *The Gay Science*. New York: Vintage, 1974.

O'Donovan, Oliver. *Common Objects of Love: Moral Reflection and the Shaping of Community*. Grand Rapids: Eerdmans, 2002.

————. *The Desire of the Nations: Rediscovering the Roots of Political Theology*. Cambridge: Cambridge University Press, 1996.

————. *Entering into Rest: Ethics as Theology 3*. Grand Rapids: Eerdmans, 2017.

————. *Resurrection and Moral Order: An Outline for Evangelical Ethics*. Grand Rapids: Eerdmans, 1986.

————. *Self, World, and Time: Ethics as Theology 1*. Grand Rapids: Eerdmans, 2013.

————. *The Ways of Judgment: The Bampton Lectures, 2003*. Grand Rapids: Eerdmans, 2005.

Ohnuki-Tierney, Emiko. *Kamikaze Diaries: Reflections of Japanese Student Soldiers*. Chicago: University of Chicago Press, 2006.

Pannenberg, Wolfhart. *Systematic Theology*. Grand Rapids: Eerdmans, 1991.

Pellegrino, Edmund D., and David C. Thomasma. *A Philosophical Basis of Medical Practice: Toward a Philosophy of the Healing Professions*. New York: Oxford University Press, 1981.

Pieper, Josef. *Faith Hope Love*. San Francisco: Ignatius, 1997.

———. *The Four Cardinal Virtues*. Notre Dame, IN: University of Notre Dame Press, 1966.

———. *Leisure the Basis of Culture*. In *Leisure the Basis of Culture: Including "The Philosophical Act.*" Translated by Alexander Dru. San Francisco: Ignatius, 2009.

Pohl, Christine D. *Making Room: Recovering Hospitality as a Christian Tradition*. Grand Rapids: Eerdmans, 1999.

Porter, Jean. *The Perfection of Desire: Habit, Reason, and Virtue in Aquinas's "Summa theologiae.*" Milwaukee: Marquette University Press, 2018.

———. *The Recovery of Virtue: The Relevance of Aquinas for Christian Ethics*. Louisville: Westminster John Knox, 1990.

Quoist, Michel. *Prayers*. Franklin, WI: Sheed and Ward, 1999.

Ramsey, Paul. "Human Sexuality in the History of Redemption." *Journal of Religious Ethics* 16, no. 1 (Spring 1988): 56–86.

———. *The Patient as Person: Explorations in Medical Ethics*. New Haven: Yale University Press, 1970.

———. *Speak Up for Just War or Pacifism: A Critique of the United Methodist Bishops' Pastoral Letter "In Defense of Creation.*" Eugene, OR: Wipf & Stock, 2016. First published 1988 by Pennsylvania State University Press (University Park, PA).

Raposa, Michael L. *Boredom and the Religious Imagination*. Charlottesville, VA: University Press of Virginia, 1999.

Reichl, Ruth. "Introduction to the Modern Library Food Series." In *High Bonnet: A Novel of Epicurean Adventures*, by Idwal Jones. New York: Modern Library, 2001.

Ricardo, David. *On the Principles of Political Economy and Taxation*. Indianapolis: Liberty Fund, 2004.

Ridley, Matt. *The Rational Optimist: How Prosperity Evolves*. New York: Harper-Collins, 2010.

Robertson, John A. *Children of Choice: Freedom and the New Reproductive Technologies*. Princeton: Princeton University Press, 1994.

Robinson, Marilynne. *Gilead*. New York: Picador, 2004.

———. *Home*. New York: Picador, 2008.

———. *Lila*. New York: Farrar, Strauss & Giroux, 2014.

Royce, Josiah. *The Philosophy of Loyalty*. New York: Macmillan, 1914.

Russell, Bertrand. *Marriage and Morals*. London: George Allen & Unwin, 1929.

Schleiermacher, Friedrich. *The Christian Household: A Sermonic Treatise*. Lewiston, NY: Edwin Mellon, 1991.

Schumpeter, Joseph A. *Capitalism, Socialism and Democracy*. New York: Harper Perennial, 2008.

Scruton, Roger. *The Aesthetics of Architecture*. Princeton: Princeton University Press, 2013.

———. *The Uses of Pessimism: And the Danger of False Hope*. Oxford: Oxford University Press, 2010.

Seabright, Paul. *The Company of Strangers: A Natural History of Economic Life*. Princeton: Princeton University Press, 2004.

Smith, Adam. *An Inquiry into the Nature and Causes of the Wealth of Nations*. Indianapolis: Liberty Fund, 1981.

———. *The Theory of Moral Sentiments*. Indianapolis: Liberty Fund, 1976.

Smith, James K. A. *You Are What You Love: The Spiritual Power of Habit*. Grand Rapids: Brazos, 2016.

Snell, R. J. *Acedia and Its Discontents: Metaphysical Boredom in an Empire of Desire*. Kettering, OH: Angelico, 2015.

Spaemann, Robert. *Persons: The Difference between 'Someone' and 'Something.'* Oxford: Oxford University Press, 2006.

Stegner, Wallace. *Angle of Repose*. New York: Vintage, 1990.

———. *Crossing to Safety*. New York: Penguin Books, 1987.

Stelzer, Cita. *Dinner with Churchill: Policy-Making at the Dinner Table*. New York: Pegasus Books, 2013.

Taylor, Jeremy. *A Discourse of the Nature, Offices, and Measurers of Friendship*. In *The Whole Works of the Right Rev. Jeremy Taylor, D. D*. Vol. 11. London: Longmans, Green, 1839.

Tertullian, *On the Apparel of Women*. In *Fathers of the Third Century: Tertullian, Part Fourth; Minucius Felix; Commodian; Origen, Parts First and Second*. Vol. 4 of *The Ante-Nicene Fathers: Translations of the Writings of the Fathers Down to A.D. 325*, edited by Alexander Roberts and James Donaldson. 10 vols. 1885–1887. Repr., Grand Rapids: Eerdmans, 1979.

Thielicke, Helmut. *Theological Ethics*. Vol. 2, *Politics*. Philadelphia: Fortress, 1969.

Thurman, Howard. *Jesus and the Disinherited*. Richmond, IN: Friends United, 1981.

Tranvik, Mark D. *Martin Luther and the Called Life*. Minneapolis: Fortress, 2016.

Turkle, Sherry. *Alone Together: Why We Expect More from Technology and Less from Each Other*. New York: Basic Books, 2011.

———. *Reclaiming Conversation: The Power of Talk in a Digital Age*. New York: Penguin Books, 2015.

Tyler, Anne. *A Spool of Blue Thread*. New York: Penguin Random House, 2015.

Upson-Saia, Kristi. *Early Christian Dress: Gender, Virtue, and Authority*. New York: Routledge, 2011.

Vanderslice, Kendall. *We Will Feast: Rethinking Dinner, Worship, and the Community of God*. Grand Rapids: Eerdmans, 2019.

Visser, Margaret. *Much Depends On Dinner: Since Eve Ate Apples*. 2nd ed. New York: Grove, 2008.

———. *The Rituals of Dinner: The Origins, Evolution, Eccentricities, and Meaning of Table Manners*. New York: Open Road, n.d.

Voegelin, Eric. *Collected Works*. Vol. 14, *Order and History, Volume 1: Israel and Revelation*. Baton Rouge: Louisiana State University Press, 1989.

Wadell, Paul J. *Becoming Friends: Worship, Justice, and the Practice of Christian Friendship*. Grand Rapids: Brazos, 2002.

———. *Friendship and the Moral Life*. Notre Dame, IN: University of Notre Dame Press, 1989.

Waters, Brent. *Christian Moral Theology in the Emerging Technoculture: From Posthuman Back to Human*. Farnham, UK: Ashgate, 2014.

———. *The Family in Christian Social and Political Thought*. Oxford: Oxford University Press, 2007.

———. *From Human to Posthuman: Christian Theology and Technology in a Postmodern World*. Aldershot, UK: Ashgate, 2006.

———. "The Incarnation and the Christian Moral Life." In *Christology and Ethics*, edited by F. LeRon Shults and Brent Waters, 5–31. Grand Rapids: Eerdmans, 2010.

———. *Just Capitalism: A Christian Ethic of Economic Globalization*. Louisville: Westminster John Knox, 2016.

———. *This Mortal Flesh: Incarnation and Bioethics*. Grand Rapids: Brazos, 2009.

———. "Welcoming Children into Our Homes: A Theological Reflection on Adoption." *Scottish Journal of Theology* 55, no. 4 (2002).

———. "Willful Control and Controlling the Will: Technology and Being Human." *Religions* 8, no. 5 (2017).

Webster, John. *The Culture of Theology*. Grand Rapids: Baker Academic, 2019.

———. *Word and Church: Essays in Church Dogmatics*. Edinburgh: T&T Clark, 2001.

Wheeler, Sondra. *The Minister as Moral Theologian: Ethical Dimensions of Pastoral Leadership*. Grand Rapids: Baker Academic, 2017.

Widdows, Heather. *The Moral Vision of Iris Murdoch*. Aldershot, UK: Ashgate, 2005.

Wilde, Oscar. *The Picture of Dorian Gray*. New York: Dover, 1993.

Wingren, Gustaf. *Luther on Vocation*. Eugene, OR: Wipf & Stock, 2004.

Witte, John, Jr. *From Sacrament to Contract: Marriage, Religion, and Law in the Western Tradition*. Louisville: Westminster John Knox, 2012.

Wong, Bernard K. *Beginning from Man and Woman: Witnessing Christ's Love in the Family*. Carlisle, UK: Langham Monographs, 2017.

Zaleski, Philip, and Carol Zaleski. *The Fellowship: The Literary Lives of the Inklings; J. R. R. Tolkien, C. S. Lewis, Owen Barfield, Charles Williams*. New York: Farrar, Straus & Giroux, 2015.

Scripture Index

Old Testament

Genesis

1:26 34
1:31 8
2:18 12
2:18–24 64
2:24 106
3 5

Exodus

22:21 134

New Testament

Matthew

10:39 29
14:22–33 62n12
15:29–31 62n13
19:5 106
20:1–16 62n11
22:37–40 25
25:14–30 109
25:31–46 137

Mark

10:7 106
12:30–31 30

Luke

10:25–37 62n11, 77
12:27 62n11
15:11–32 62n11

John

1:1–5 7n8
1:14 5
1:46 178
6:1–14 62n13
15:13 193

Romans

8 21n2
8:20 8

1 Corinthians

12:12–31 20
12:21 20
13 15, 25, 27
13:12 27, 204
13:13 247
15 21n2

Galatians

3:28 125
5 21n2
5:6 23

Ephesians

5:22–6:9 124n16

Colossians

3:18–4:1 124n16

1 Timothy

2:8–15 124n16
6:1–2 124n16

Titus

2:1–10 124n16

1 Peter

2:18–3:7 124n16

Revelation

21:1–5 8
21:6 59

Subject Index